Bioarchaeology and Behavior

Bioarchaeological Interpretations of the Human Past:
Local, Regional, and Global Perspectives

UNIVERSITY PRESS OF FLORIDA

Florida A&M University, Tallahassee
Florida Atlantic University, Boca Raton
Florida Gulf Coast University, Ft. Myers
Florida International University, Miami
Florida State University, Tallahassee
New College of Florida, Sarasota
University of Central Florida, Orlando
University of Florida, Gainesville
University of North Florida, Jacksonville
University of South Florida, Tampa
University of West Florida, Pensacola

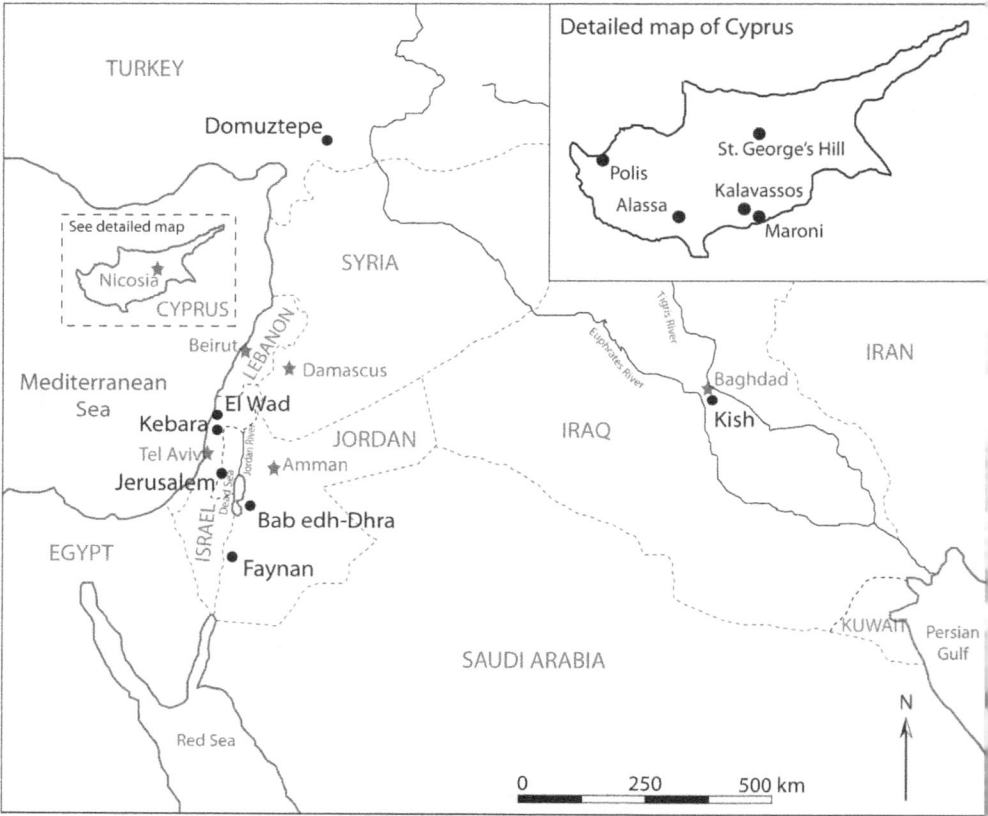

TURKEY

Domuztepe

See detailed map

Nicosia

CYPRUS

SYRIA

Beirut

LEBANON

Damascus

Mediterranean
Sea

El Wad

Kebara

Tel Aviv

Jerusalem

JORDAN

Amman

Bab edh-Dhra

ISRAEL

EGYPT

Faynan

Red Sea

Euphrates River

Tigris River

IRAQ

Baghdad

Kish

IRAN

KUWAIT

Persian
Gulf

SAUDI ARABIA

N

0   250   500 km

Detailed map of Cyprus

St. George's Hill

Polis

Kalavassos

Alassa

Maroni

Bioarchaeology and Behavior

The People of the Ancient Near East

EDITED BY MEGAN A. PERRY

Foreword by Clark Spencer Larsen

University Press of Florida
Gainesville · Tallahassee · Tampa · Boca Raton
Pensacola · Orlando · Miami · Jacksonville · Ft. Myers · Sarasota

This book may be available in an electronic edition.

Frontispiece: Map of the sites reported on in this volume.

23 22 21 20 19 18   6 5 4 3 2 1

First cloth printing, 2012
First paperback printing, 2018

Cataloging-in-publication data is available from the Library of Congress.
ISBN 978-0-8130-4229-9 (cloth)
ISBN 978-0-8130-6478-9 (pbk.)

The University Press of Florida is the scholarly publishing agency for the State University
System of Florida, comprising Florida A&M University, Florida Atlantic University,
Florida Gulf Coast University, Florida International University, Florida State University,
New College of Florida, University of Central Florida, University of Florida, University
of North Florida, University of South Florida, and University of West Florida.

University Press of Florida
15 Northwest 15th Street
Gainesville, FL 32611-2079
http://upress.ufl.edu

Dedicated to one of the pioneers of Near Eastern bioarchaeology,
Donald Ortner (1939–2012)

Contents

List of Figures / ix
List of Tables / xi
Foreword / xiii
Introduction / 1
Megan A. Perry and Jane E. Buikstra

1. On the Tail End of Variation in Late Neolithic Burial Practices: Halaf Feasting and Cannibalism at Domuztepe, Southeastern Anatolia / 8
Suellen C. Gauld, James S. Oliver, Sarah Whitcher Kansa, and Elizabeth Carter

2. An Exploration of Infant Burial Practices at the Site of Kish, Iraq / 35
Christina Torres-Rouff and William J. Pestle

3. The Burial Customs of Early Christian Cyprus: A Bioarchaeological Approach / 60
Sherry C. Fox, Ioanna Moutafi, Eleni Anna Prevedorou, and Despo Pilides

4. A Bioarchaeological Perspective on the Burials and Basilicas of Medieval Polis, Cyprus / 80
Brenda J. Baker and Amy Papalexandrou

5. Condemned to *Metallum*? Illuminating Life at the Byzantine Mining Camp at Phaeno in Jordan / 115
Megan A. Perry, Drew S. Coleman, David L. Dettman, and Abdel Halim al-Shiyab

6. Food for Thought: Isotopic Evidence for Dietary and Weaning Practices in a Byzantine Urban Monastery in Jerusalem / 138
Lesley A. Gregoricka and Susan G. Sheridan

7. Buccal Dental Microwear as an Indicator of Dietary Habits of the Natufian People of El-Wad and El-Kebarah / 165
   Mohammad Alrousan and Alejandro Pérez-Pérez

8. Daily Activity and Lower Limb Modification at Bab edh-Dhra', Jordan, in the Early Bronze Age / 180
   Jaime M. Ullinger, Susan G. Sheridan, and Donald J. Ortner

List of Contributors / 203
Index / 207

Figures

1.1. Location of Domuztepe / 10

1.2. Contour map of Domuztepe showing major areas of excavation / 11

1.3. F1143 skull burial in situ / 17

1.4. F1143 skull burial reconstruction showing blunt force trauma / 17

1.5. Blunt force trauma on right side of cranium 2626.1 / 21

1.6. Internal vault release of cranium 2626.1 / 21

1.7. Butchery damage in the Death Pit human assemblage: percussion scars on proximal femur shaft fragment (2632.2) / 22

1.8. Cut marks on the sciatic notch of innominate (pelvis) fragment (3134.0.5) / 23

1.9. Pot polish on fractured end of femur fragment (2650.0.49) / 24

1.10. Shallow tooth marks accompanied by depressed fractures on 1st metacarpal (2629.9.2) / 25

2.1. Map of Kish / 39

2.2. FM192464 infant skeleton / 45

2.3. Neo-Babylonian infant burial in bowl / 46

4.1. Plan of Polis / 81

4.2. Aerial view of the E.F2 excavation area / 85

4.3. Cist tomb in the E.F2 cemetery / 86

4.4. Aerial view of partially excavated E.G0 basilica / 88

4.5. Burial 34 in the E.G0 narthex / 91

4.6. Burial 34A / 92

4.7. Burial 37 in the E.G0 basilica / 95

4.8. Trauma in an older man from E.G0:g11 Tomb 1 / 106

5.1. Sites located in the vicinity of Khirbet Faynan and Wadi Fidan / 117

5.2. $^{87}Sr/^{86}Sr$ variation in the Levant / 124

5.3. Comparison of $^{87}Sr/^{86}Sr$ values and copper and lead skeletal levels in the individuals from Faynan / 125

6.1. The monastery of St. Stephen's and other important Christian sites within the Old City of Jerusalem / 139

6.2. St. Stephen's Tomb Complex 1 / 140

6.3. Bivariate plot of $\delta^{13}C$ and $\delta^{15}N$ values for the adults and subadults of St. Stephen's / 151

6.4. Age profile of $\delta^{15}N$ for the subadults of St. Stephen's / 151

6.5. Age profile of $\delta^{13}C$ for the subadults of St. Stephen's / 152

7.1. SEM image (0.56 mm^2) of the buccal enamel surface of the upper right premolar (URP4) of one individual from El-Kebarah / 169

7.2. Total striation densities (NT) for the two sites studied / 172

7.3. NH/NV index (X axis) versus total density of scratched (NT) (Y axis) for the two sites studied compared with other samples / 173

8.1. Map of the southern Levant / 181

8.2. Poirer's facet with plaque identified on a right proximal femur (BD 1436.1001) / 188

8.3. Degenerative joint disease (including severe lipping and eburnation) on a right distal femur (BD 1510.14) / 189

8.4. Large squatting facet on a right talus (BD 1502.146) / 190

Tables

1.1. Comparison of mortuary practices in the Mesopotamian Neolithic showing number of burial features / 15

1.2. Age (in years) and sex composition of Death Pit human assemblage / 19

2.1. Context of infant burials at Kish / 44

2.2. Distribution of age at death for the infants of Kish / 45

3.1. Description and demography of tombs at Early Christian sites in Cyprus / 64

5.1. Demographic profile of the Southern Cemetery sample from Khirbet Faynan (Phaeno) / 121

5.2. $^{87}Sr/^{86}Sr$ and $\delta^{18}O$ values and lead and copper levels of archaeological human dental enamel samples at Faynan / 123

5.3. Porotic hyperostosis and dental enamel hypoplasia frequencies from Faynan, Rehovot, and Aila / 126

5.4. Frequency of osteoarthritis (OA) and vertebral osteophytosis (VO) in total sample from Faynan, Rehovot, and Aila / 127

6.1. Stable carbon and nitrogen isotope values of subadults and adults from St. Stephen's monastery / 148

6.2. Means and ranges of stable carbon and nitrogen isotope values of subadults and adults from St. Stephen's monastery / 154

7.1. Summary statistics of the pattern of buccal microwear in the two samples studied / 171

8.1. Number of pubic symphyses in each stage using the Suchey-Brooks method of aging / 185

8.2. Femoral neck alterations in Early Bronze IA and Early Bronze II–III
Bab edh-Dhra' / 192

8.3. Prevalence of degenerative joint disease in the left and right sides
of skeletons from Early Bronze IA and Early Bronze II–III Bab edh-
Dhra' / 193

8.4. Medial and lateral squatting facets in the tibia and talus in Early
Bronze IA and Early Bronze II–III Bab edh-Dhra' / 193

8.5. Kneeling facets on metatarsals 1–5 in Early Bronze IA and Early
Bronze II–III Bab edh-Dhra' / 194

Foreword

The rich archaeological record from the Near East and eastern Mediterranean offers some of the best contexts for understanding the transition from foraging to farming, the appearance and evolution of complex societies, and social and cultural institutions that set the stage for the modern world. Important components of this record are skeletal remains recovered from a variety of contexts. While a graduate student in the late 1930s, J. Lawrence Angel recognized the significance of these remains for developing a more informed understanding of life conditions in the region, especially during the last 10,000 years. He first published on his early investigations in Greece in the late 1930s, and over the next half-century he provided insights into the population history, lifestyles, and quality of life in this diverse and important region. I well recall while I was an undergraduate student interning at the Smithsonian Institution in the early 1970s how Angel told me that this region would one day prove to be a center for understanding human-environment interactions. He gave me a copy of his recently published book about the temporal series of skeletons from Lerna, Greece (Angel 1971) and what these skeletons tell us about the people who lived there. His story didn't focus solely on bones and teeth. Rather, his research emphasized the broad context of culture, environment, and living. As Perry and Buikstra point out in their preface to the chapters of this volume, Angel's research on human remains was for many years largely ignored by prehistorians working in the region. Indeed, it would be years before scholars would begin to appreciate the potential of bioarchaeology for developing a more enriched perspective on the past. Today, however, the communication between anthropological archaeologists, prehistorians, and biological anthropologists has been instrumental in fueling a spate of research programs that rely on contextually informed perspectives of the human past.

A number of these research programs illustrate some of the advances made recently pertaining to older questions, current problems, and hypotheses to be tested. Several of the chapters presented herein provide new and important perspectives on mortuary behavior and ritual, including cannibalism and the significance of numerous juveniles (especially infants) in death assemblages from various settings. By combining many lines of evidence—historical context, behavior, ritual, taphonomy, disease, and demography—we know so much more about these persons as members of once-living populations and not simply as descriptions of collections of skeletons. A new world of scientific exploration has developed with the application of stable isotope chemistry for identifying place and individual movement over the life course. In addition, stable isotope analysis provides a rich record of life history, tracking the record of early nutrition and the transition from infant to adult diet. Viewed in the context of other dietary and activity indicators, bioarchaeologists are contributing to a more informed understanding of foodways and behavior.

This book joins a rich and growing literature on the study of the human condition viewed from the perspective of human remains, the broad context of these remains, and the emerging record of life in the ancient Near East and eastern Mediterranean. We have a considerable way to go, and the path forward will involve increasing collaboration with others interested in the past in this broad and important expanse of the globe. Surely we have a great start in achieving an increased understanding of the ancestors of those who live in the Near East and eastern Mediterranean today.

Clark Spencer Larsen
Series Editor

Reference Cited

Angel, J. Lawrence. 1971. *The People of Lerna: Analysis of a Prehistoric Aegean Population.* Smithsonian Institution Press, Washington, D.C.

Introduction

MEGAN A. PERRY AND JANE E. BUIKSTRA

Bioarchaeology clearly has grown into a well-established method for investigating past populations in many areas of the world. One surprising regional exception is the eastern Mediterranean and Near East. This area has seen extensive archaeological research, including excavations of many graves and other mortuary features. In addition, one of the most influential—and creative—biological anthropologists of the twentieth century, J. Lawrence Angel, spent most of his career investigating ancient peoples of this region. Despite this history, bioarchaeology in this region has lagged far behind other regions.

This volume seeks to carry the mantle of contextual skeletal biology that Angel began. The regional focus of the Near East, Turkey, and Cyprus (as opposed to Egypt) follows Angel's primary focus on the eastern Mediterranean and the Near East. His research provides some of the earliest examples of the population-based, contextualized approach that eventually grew into bioarchaeology. During his career, Angel published seminal articles on ancient population dynamics and health in the eastern Mediterranean, primarily Greece (e.g., Angel 1966, 1967, 1975, 1984) but also early historic populations in the United States (Angel 1976; Angel, Kelley, Parrington, and Pinter 1987; Kelley and Angel 1987). His largest contribution to the field by far involves his contextualized interpretation of these data. Two publications in particular epitomize Angel's influence on modern bioanthropological research: his *People of Lerna* (1971), and his contribution to Polgar's *Population, Ecology, and Social Evolution* (1975). These publications reflect Angel's concern with long-term health and population dynamics in the eastern Mediterranean from the Upper Paleolithic until the twentieth century. He considered the effects of ecological variables such as climate, fluctuations in sea level, and soil chemistry and biological factors such as female longevity and fecundity, capacity for carrying disease, and available "physical and psychological energy" on ancient demography and health (Angel 1975). His uncanny ability to recognize important issues in bioarchaeology before anyone else emerges in these manuscripts. He notes: "Actual disease varies greatly as a limiting factor unless it directly affects fecundity . . . or causes early death: a truly healthy population can carry a big load of minor and chronic disease" (Angel 1975, 168). Physical anthropologists often focus on disease-related mortality, which is not surprising, since they usually work with a sample of the deceased population. Angel's focus on assessing a population's ability to live a fruitful life *with* disease—and warnings not to overinterpret a living population from a dead sample—predates Wood and colleagues' admonitions of the osteological paradox by almost 20 years (Wood, Milner, Harpending, and Weiss 1992).

Eventually researchers in the New *and* Old Worlds recognized Angel's work, although these were mostly bioanthropologists rather than archaeologists. Buikstra's investigation into the frequency of Angel's publications discovered that the top 10 most frequently cited publications from 1976 to 2005 include both articles on the physical anthropology of Greece and studies that are more methodological. In fact, a cross-tabulation of citation frequency with Angel's research region revealed that his articles on the eastern Mediterranean and Greece are the most visible. The relevance of his work in paleopathology, paleodemography, and descriptive osteology also appears to be strong. However, Angel's desire to integrate Classical archaeology and physical anthropology has not infiltrated everyone's consciousness. Buikstra searched in particular for references to his volume on the people of Lerna and his appendices on Troy and Khirokitia in other archaeological publications, thinking they had caught the interest of archaeologists. Most citations of these works, however, are in physical anthropology journals or in books written by physical anthropologists.

Therefore, the plethora of data generated by Angel's research and the varied research questions raised by his speculations means that the eastern Mediterranean and the Near East should have been a center of physical anthropological research, similar to Peru, southern Illinois, the southeastern United States, and the Sudan. Angel's groundwork unfortunately did not stimulate significant momentum in the study of ancient skeletal samples in the eastern Mediterranean and Near East. While mortuary remains have always fascinated archaeologists and art historians interested in the cultures of the Near East and eastern Mediterranean, the human skeletal remains contained in these tombs never garnered much attention. In a recent publication on the archaeology of death in the Near East, for instance, only five out of thirty reports discuss the skeletal remains associated with the burial structures (Campbell and Green 1995). Even fewer provide complete skeletal analysis and interpretation.

One reason for the relative invisibility of skeletal remains may be the academic focus of most archaeologists working in the region (see Perry in press). Bioarchaeology gained prominence in the 1970s in concert with large methodological changes occurring in biological anthropology, such as analyzing data at the level of a population instead of at the individual level and situating these data within their ecological, cultural, and historical contexts. Earlier human osteological studies were primarily descriptive and were rarely integrated with archaeological or historical narratives. Bioarchaeology's link with processual archaeology resulted in an increased emphasis on proper excavation, documentation, and interpretation of human skeletal remains in archaeological research. However, processual archaeology held little interest for scholars immersed in "text-based" archaeologies of the Near East and eastern Mediterranean, such as Biblical or Classical archaeology (see Andrén 1998; Kemp 1984; Meskell 1998). While some "Syro-Palestinian" or Biblical archaeologists attempted to incorporate a processual framework in their research, Classical archaeologists remained somewhat atheoretical (Small 1999, 122). Since processual archaeology never gained serious ground in the Near East, particularly in Classical archaeology, the scientific methods it espoused, such as bioarchaeology, also did not appear.

Further problems for skeletal biologists interested in the region stem from the poor quality of the samples and comparative data available for study. Today most skeletons recovered from earlier excavations remain unstudied, and the location of many samples is unknown. Furthermore, bioanthropological data from samples that actually were studied frequently were—and still are—consigned to the appendices of publications, physically and intellectually removed from historical and archaeological scholarship. Scholars have proposed numerous explanations for the lack of true bioarchaeological research in the region. Judd (2009) suggests that taphonomic factors and burial practices have created poorly preserved samples that often are comprised of comingled skeletal elements that hinder many analyses. Ortner and Frohlich (2008) emphasize the lack of data collection standards that facilitate comparative study and the small sample size of most Near Eastern skeletal samples.

Therefore, it is only recently that bioarchaeologists have turned their attention to skeletal samples from the Near East and eastern Mediterranean. This volume represents a concerted attempt to consolidate papers on new research presented at four conference sessions held over three years (2006–2008) of the annual meeting of the American Schools of Oriental Research, one of the primary professional organizations for Near Eastern and eastern Mediterranean archaeologists. The participants and observers repeatedly remarked on the need to bring together scholars conducting bioarchaeological research in this region and disseminate their research findings to nonspecialists.

This volume continues the goal of these sessions: to bring our biological anthropological interpretations into the realm of archaeology to carry on Angel's work in a well-integrated bioarchaeology of the eastern Mediterranean and Near East (see the frontispiece for a map of sites reported on in this volume). Chapters 1–4 demonstrate the utility of interpreting bioarchaeological data from human skeletons within their mortuary contexts. In Chapter 1, Gauld, Oliver, Kansa, and Carter present a death pit assemblage from Neolithic Domuztepe that demonstrates evidence of unique postmortem rituals, including cannibalism, in Turkey in the sixth millennium BC. In Chapter 2, Torres-Rouff and Pestle discuss the specialized infant burial practices at Kish, Iraq, in the Neo-Babylonian period (1000–539 BC) that indicate the social significance of perinatal death for early Mesopotamian civilizations. Finally, two chapters on burial customs in Late Antique Cyprus focus on the flexibility and variety of internment practices, findings that go against the grain of conventional wisdom. Fox, Moutafi, Prevedorou, and Pilides focus on Early Byzantine (sixth to seventh centuries AD) burials in ecclesiastical contexts in Chapter 3, and Baker and Papalexandrou present Byzantine to Medieval period (sixth to sixteenth centuries AD) burials from the site of Polis Chrysochous in Chapter 4.

The remaining chapters in the volume focus on investigating skeletal remains to clarify migration patterns, population health, and diet through various techniques. In Chapter 5, Perry, Coleman, Dettman, and al-Shiyab rely on strontium and oxygen isotopes in addition to indicators of health and disease to identify possible immigrants and clarify life histories and access to resources at a Byzantine (third to sixth centuries AD) mining camp in southwestern Jordan. Carbon and nitrogen isotope analyses of children recovered from St. Stephen's monastery in Jerusalem in the Byzantine (fifth to seventh centuries AD) provide information on diet and weaning ages in this unique context, as Gregoricka and Sheridan describe in Chapter 6. Alrousan and Pérez-Pérez explore ancient diet and subsistence practices at the sites of El Wad and Kebara in the Natufian period (13,000–10,300 BP) through dental microwear patterns in Chapter 7. Finally, Ullinger, Sheridan, and Ortner illuminate daily activity patterns during increasing sedentism and agricultural intensification at Bab edh-Dhra', Jordan, in the Early Bronze Age (3150–2300 BC) in Chapter 8.

The chapters in this volume are just the tip of an ever-growing iceberg of bioarchaeological research in the region, but they perhaps would make Angel proud. They will add to the increasingly anthropological, interpretive, and scientific approaches to archaeology in the Near East and eastern Mediterranean. Bioarchaeology in particular has been neglected in this region, and this volume will spotlight the potential of this method for investigating the ancient inhabitants of the circum-Mediterranean region. Researchers in other regions also can benefit from the diachronic perspective provided by the studies in this volume, involving various environmental, social, and political-economic contexts. Here we synthesize preliminary results from a number of bioarchaeological investigations in the Near East and eastern Mediterranean.

References Cited

Andrén, A.
1998   *Between Artifacts and Texts: Historical Archaeology in Global Perspective.* Plenum Press, New York.
Angel, J. L.
1966   Porotic Hyperostosis, Anemias, Malarias, and Marshes in the Prehistoric Eastern Mediterranean. *Science* 153:760–763.
1967   Porotic Hyperostosis or Osteoporosis Symmetrica. In *Diseases in Antiquity: A Survey of the Diseases, Injuries and Surgery of Early Populations,* edited by A. T. Sandison and D. Brothwell, pp. 378–389. Charles C. Thomas, Springfield, IL.
1971   *The People of Lerna: Analysis of a Prehistoric Aegean Population.* The Smithsonian Institution Press, Washington, D.C.
1975   Paleoecology, Paleodemography and Health. In *Population, Ecology and Social Evolution,* edited by S. Polgar, pp. 167–190. Aldine, Chicago.
1976   Colonial to Modern Skeletal Change in the U.S.A. *American Journal of Physical Anthropology* 45:723–735.

1984   Health as a Crucial Factor in the Changes from Hunting to Developed Farming in the Eastern Mediterranean. In *Paleopathology at the Origins of Agriculture,* edited by M. N. Cohen and G. J. Armelagos, pp. 51–73. Academic Press, New York.

Angel, J. L., J. O. Kelley, M. Parrington, and S. Pinter
1987   Life Stresses of the Free Black Community as Represented by the First African Baptist Church, Philadelphia, 1823–1841. *American Journal of Physical Anthropology* 74:213–229.

Campbell, S., and A. Green (editors)
1995   *Archaeology of Death in the Ancient Near East.* Oxbow Books, Oxford.

Davies, W. V., and R. Walker (editors)
1993   *Biological Anthropology and the Study of Ancient Egypt.* British Museum Press, London

Judd, M. A.
2009   Bioarchaeology East of the Jordan. In *Studies on Iron Age Moab and Neighbouring Areas in Honour of Michèle Daviau,* edited by P. Bientrowski, pp. 245–273. Peeters Publishers, Leuven.

Kelley, J. O., and J. L. Angel
1987   Life Stresses of Slavery. *American Journal of Physical Anthropology* 74:199–211.

Kemp, B. J.
1984   In the Shadow of the Texts: Archaeology in Egypt. *Archaeological Review from Cambridge* 3:19–28.

Meskell, L.
1998   Introduction: Archaeology Matters. In *Archaeology Under Fire: Nationalism, Politics, and Heritage in the Eastern Mediterranean and the Middle East,* edited by L. Meskell, pp. 1–12. Routledge, London.

Ortner, D. J., and B. Frohlich
2008   Summary of Findings and Conclusions Regarding the EB I People of Bab edh-Dhra'. In *EBI Tombs and Burials of Bab edh-Dhra', Jordan,* edited by D. J. Ortner and B. Frohlich, pp. 297–308. Altamira Press, Lanham, Md.

Perry, M. A.
In press History of Paleopathology in Lebanon, Syria, and Jordan. In *The History of Paleopathology,* edited by J. E. Buikstra and C. Roberts. Oxford University Press, Oxford.

Rose, J. C.
1996   *Bioarchaeology of Ancient Egypt and Nubia: A Bibliography.* British Museum, London.

Small, D. B.
1999   The Tyranny of the Text: Lost Social Strategies in Current Historical Period Archaeology in the Classical Mediterranean. In *Historical Archaeology: Back from the Edge,* edited by P.P.A. Funari, M. Hall, and S. Jones, pp. 122–136. Routledge, London.

Wood J. W., G. R. Milner, H. C. Harpending, and K. M. Weiss
1992   The Osteological Paradox: Problems of Inferring Prehistoric Health from Skeletal Samples. *Current Anthropology* 33:343–370.

Note

For studies in Egypt, where more bioarchaeological research has been done, see Davies and Walker (1993) and Rose (1996).

1

On the Tail End of Variation in Late Neolithic Burial Practices

Halaf Feasting and Cannibalism at Domuztepe, Southeastern Anatolia

SUELLEN C. GAULD, JAMES S. OLIVER, SARAH WHITCHER KANSA,
AND ELIZABETH CARTER

Dating to approximately 6500–5000 BC, the Samarra, Hassuna, Ubaid, and Halaf cultures comprise the Late Neolithic of northern Mesopotamia. In this chapter we discuss how data from the Late Halaf site of Domuztepe both conform with and differ from known Late Neolithic mortuary practices (Akkermans 1989; Campbell 1995). In particular, while the Domuztepe burials are broadly similar to those from other Mesopotamian sites, we briefly summarize our ongoing analysis (Gauld et al. n.d.) of a large pit deposit (Feature 148) that contains the remains of at least 35 humans and a similar number of animals. We suggest that this deposit, less formally known as the Death Pit, documents a ritual communal feast (Kansa and Campbell 2004), where the inclusion of large-scale cannibalism both underscores and expands known variability in Halaf mortuary practices and indicates a degree of cultural dynamism and social complexity not previously evident during this period.

The Halaf tradition is represented in a group of sites distributed in a broad arc across the mountain foothills of northern Mesopotamia, from southeastern Anatolia to western Iran. Distinct markers of its material culture include the presence of both rectangular and round (*tholoi*) structures, decorated polychrome pottery, and stamp seals likely used to mark personal goods (Akkermans and Duistermaat 1996). Throughout most of

Halaf history, villages were small (1 to 3 hectares) with short occupation sequences, low population densities, and architecture generally characterized by small domestic residences and a lack of buildings or spaces that could have served a public function. Subsistence was based primarily on dry farming and animal husbandry augmented by varying degrees of dependence on wild animals and plants (Watson 1982). However, some Halaf sites, particularly Late Halaf period settlements such as Domuztepe, are large, some of them more than 10 hectares. This regional and temporal variability in size, marked by differences in site location, length or season of occupation, and differences in plant and animal exploitation, is reflected in observed variation in Halaf architecture and cultural attributes (Akkermans 1993; Kansa, Kennedy et al. 2009, Tables A1 and A2). Moreover, while Halaf social organization has been described as egalitarian (Akkermans and Schwartz 2003; Joffe 2003; Frangipane 2009), it is likely that the methods used to solve social tensions, particularly those associated with larger population size, also varied within Halaf culture.

Domuztepe

The site of Domuztepe, located between the modern cities of Gaziantep and Kahramanmaraş, Turkey, lies at the northwestern edge of the Halaf cultural tradition (Figure 1.1). Although surveys indicate repeated occupations from the Hellenistic through Middle Islamic periods, recent archaeological investigations (1997–2005) have focused on the site's prehistoric deposits. Material remains from these levels demonstrate clear affinities with the Late Halaf period (Carter, Campbell, and Gauld 2003; Kansa, Gauld et al. 2009). Radiocarbon dates show that these early occupation levels date to between 5800 and 5450 cal BC.

A major distinguishing characteristic of Domuztepe is its size, which at 20 hectares constitutes one of the largest terminal Neolithic sites in the Near East, possibly containing a population that approached 1,500 inhabitants (Carter, Campbell, and Gauld 2003; Kansa, Gauld et al. 2009). Like other large and relatively long-lived Halaf sites, Domuztepe's success is attributable to its location in an area of adequate rainfall and resource productivity. Faunal and botanical remains from the site indicate that its inhabitants relied on a well-established mixed economy dominated by high proportions of the typical suite of Near Eastern domesticates, while

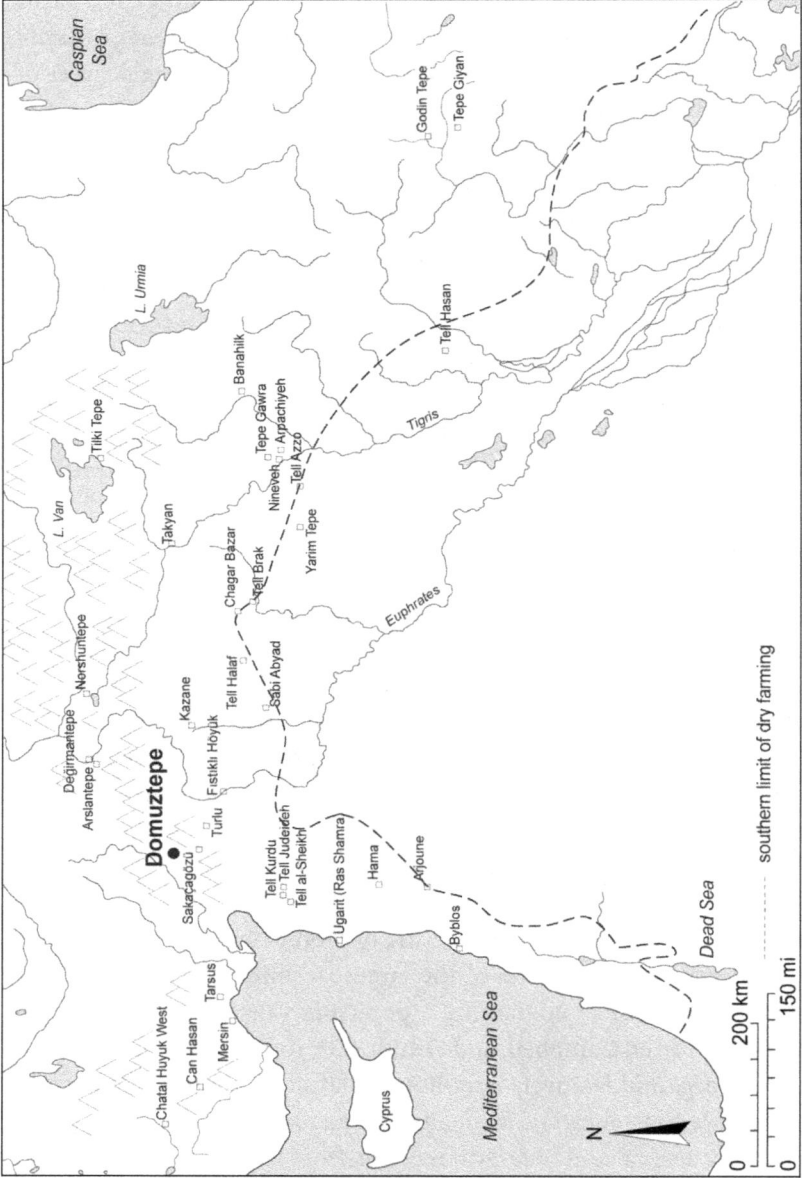

Figure 1.1. Location of Domuztepe in relation to distribution of Halaf Pottery Neolithic sites across northern Mesopotamia. Drawn by J. Dillon, adapted from Carter 2011.

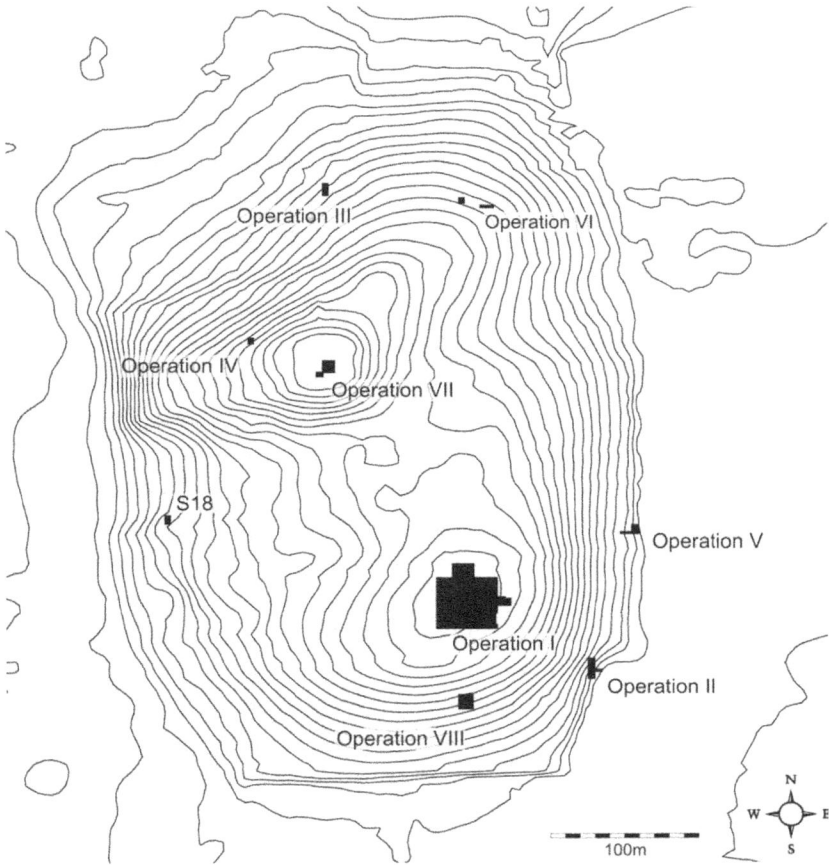

Figure 1.2. Contour map of Domuztepe showing major areas of excavation as of 2005. Drawn by S. Campbell, adapted from Kansa et al. 2009b.

nearby marshy and upland ecological zones likely provided access to a wide variety of non-agricultural resources (Kansa, Kennedy et al. 2009). In addition, ceramics from Domuztepe show strong links with areas to the south along the Levantine coast, while obsidian imported from a variety of sources demonstrates extensive trade networks to the east and west (Carter, Campbell, and Gauld 2003; Kansa, Gauld et al. 2009). These imports suggest that Domuztepe may have garnered some economic benefits from its location on the northwestern boundary of the Halaf cultural world.

Materials

As of 2005, a small but archaeologically interesting sample of burial features has been recovered at Domuztepe. These include six single interments of complete bodies, three single burials containing fractional remains (F1361, F880, and F1143), and F148 (the Death Pit), a large pit deposit measuring 5 meters × 4 meters × 1 meter cut into the southern edge of an artificial terrace that formed an east-west boundary across the northern end of Operation 1 (Figure 1.2). This terrace, which lacks residential architecture and the construction of which predates the pit, appears to be the product of repeated depositions of earth rich in red clay brought into the site and carefully maintained over an extended period, perhaps as long as 300 years (Campbell and Carter 2006).

Excavation of the Death Pit resulted in the recovery of a limited number of cultural materials, including ceramic sherds (mostly pieces of coarse ware with some fragments of fine painted vessels), stone seals, lithic and bone tools, fragments of plaster-lined baskets, numerous beads, one stone pendant (Carter, Campbell, and Gauld 2003; Irving and Heywood 2004; Carter 2011), and approximately 10,000 animal and human bone fragments, whose completeness varies from small numbers of relatively complete elements to large numbers of small fragments, chips, and flakes. Our study samples (Gauld et al. n.d.) are comprised of the 2,554 animal and 3,014 human specimens that preserve enough morphology to be identified to species and skeletal element.

The Death Pit bones show no signs of marked disturbance after deposition. Stratigraphic data (Carter, Campbell, and Gauld 2003; Kansa, Gauld et al. 2009) indicate that the pit's deposits accumulated in a series of closely spaced episodes, perhaps lasting no more than a few days. Deposits in the lower levels and the southern end of the pit are comprised almost exclusively of animal bones, while those in the central and upper levels contain virtually all of the human bones as well as a large proportion of the animal assemblage. In its final phase, the Death Pit was sealed by a thick layer of ash gathered from one or more fires located outside the pit. Postholes indicate that its location was marked, and the absence of architectural remains in overlying strata shows the area was left without structures for several decades.

Taphonomic data (Gauld et al. n.d.) show an absence of sub-aerial weathering damage, a near-absence of carnivore or rodent damage, and an abundance of fresh bone fractures in both animal and human bones, suggesting that death occurred at approximately the same time and that the period between death and deposition was short (Bass 1984; Ubelaker 1997). In the areas containing the human assemblage, the broad distribution of bones belonging to the same individuals and their substantial mixing with animal remains suggests that little attempt was made to preserve the integrity and identity of human (or animal) bodies during deposition. That said, the higher proportion of relatively complete female and sub-adult limb and skull elements in the upper areas of the pit combined with the apparent clustering of some skulls in these areas may indicate deliberate placement of some body parts during deposition (Carter forthcoming) or differential treatment of individuals prior to deposition. Alternatively, it may be unintentional and reflect the sum of unrelated behaviors and natural taphonomic events.

Methods

Humans are known to engage in a wide range of mortuary activities that alter the corpse. For example, flexed burials may require the cutting of tendons, secondary burials often involve dismemberment and defleshing, and corpse desecration can include dismemberment, defleshing, and greenstick fractures. Cremation of corpses may leave bones burned, partially calcined, or completely turned to ash. For a variety of cultural reasons, bodies may be dismembered and in whole or part manipulated, stored, and/or repeatedly disinterred and reburied. Often, however, the bioarchaeological data essential for differentiating these practices and interpreting the behavioral complexity surrounding their use are missing. At Domuztepe we undertook extensive osteological and taphonomic analyses in order to document the complete range of mortuary patterns preserved in the human burials.

To estimate the age and sex in the Domuztepe human assemblage, we used multiple standard methods (e.g., Buikstra and Ubelaker 1994; Steele and Bramblett 1998; White and Folkens 2000) and comparisons with laboratory skeletal materials. Nonmetric traits were scored both for their morphological expression and their position within the seriated assemblage. To facilitate the collection of dental data, all maxillary and mandibular specimens were X-rayed. Because of the small number of assessable attributes in some specimens, we took a conservative approach in our analyses. Adult age classes were kept broad, and estimation of sex was restricted to older adolescents and adults. Determination of the minimum number of individuals (MNI) represented in the Death Pit assemblage was based on an interpolation of the separate MNI calculations for each skeletal element, using age, sex, and anatomical information (White 1992; Lyman 1994).

To sort out the range of predepositional and postdepositional natural and cultural processes surrounding the formation of the Domuztepe burial assemblage, we examined all specimens in the fractional burial and Death Pit samples microscopically using 10X–40X binocular magnification under intense direct light. The location and expression of a variety of surficial modifications and fracture features diagnostic of subaerial exposure, carnivore gnawing, dismemberment, defleshing, hammerstone fracture, and thermal exposure were scored using established diagnostic protocols (Shipman, Foster, and Schoeninger 1984; Blumenshine and Selvagio 1988; Buikstra and Swegle 1989; Oliver 1989; White 1992; Oliver 1993; Lyman 1994; Nilssen 2000). Ambiguous features were excluded from the analysis.

Results and Discussion

Domuztepe Burial Record: Cultural Conformity and Late Neolithic Mortuary Patterns

Mortuary data from the northern Mesopotamian Late Neolithic indicate that although the majority of interments consist of simple single inhumations, on occasion burial remains display evidence of a wide range of symbolically complex activities involving postmortem modification of the corpse (Akkermans 1989; Campbell 1995). For example, isolated skull remains are common burial features in this period. Our literature review (Table 1.1) showed a total of 20 skull burials (some containing multiple individuals) from seven sites, including Tell Arpachiyah (Mallowen and Rose 1935; Hijara 1978; Molleson and Campbell 1995), Tell Hassuna (Lloyd and Safer 1945), Şeyh Höyük (Şenyurek and Tunaken 1951), Yarim Tepe II (Merpert, Munchaev, and Bader 1978; Merpert and Munchaev 1993), Yümük Tepe (Garstang 1953), Köşk Höyük (Bonogofsky 2005), and Domuztepe (this study).

Table 1.1. Comparison of mortuary practices in the Mesopotamian Ceramic Neolithic showing number of burial features (N)

Burial Type	Pre-Halaf Burials[a] N	Halaf Burials[b] N	Post-Halaf Burials[c] N	Domuztepe N
Cemetery Burials	X[d]	24	—	—
Noncemetery Burials				
COMPLETE				
Single interments	142	63	141	6
Multiple interments[e]	4	4	3	—
JAR BURIALS[f]				
Infant	34	—	14	—
Skull single	—	2	—	—
Skull multiple[e]		1		
FRACTIONAL BURIALS[g]				
Skull single	2	6	4	2
Skull multiple[e]		1	2	
Postcranial	—	X[d]	—	—
Mass[h]	—	—	—	1
DISMEMBERED BURIALS				
Single	10	5	1	1
Multiple[e]	2	—	1	—
Infant Jar[f]	2	—	—	—
NONFORMAL BURIALS				
Single	9	8	—	—
Multiple[e]	2	1	—	—
Mass[h]	—	1	—	—
CREMATION BURIALS				
Single	—	8	1	—
Mass[h]	—	1	—	—
TOTAL	207	125	167	10

Notes: a. Based on data from 10 sites (Akkermans and Verhoeven 1995; Al-A'dami 1968; Alpaslan-Roodenberg 2001; Alpaslan-Roodenberg and Maat 1999; Aten 1995; Bader 1993; El-Wailly and Abu Al-Soof 1965; Garstang 1953; Lloyd and Safar 1945; Merpert and Munchaev 1987, 1993a; Merpert, Munchaev, and Bader 1977, 1978; Tekin 2005).

b. Based on data from 17 sites (Akkermans 1989; Akkermans and Verhoeven 1995; AlpaGut 1986; Al-Radi and Seeden 1980; Aten 1996; Garstang 1953; Hijara 1978; Killick and Black 1983, 1985; Mallowan 1936; Mallowan and Rose 1935; Merpert and Munchaev 1969, 1971, 1973, 1984, 1987, 1993a, 1993b; Merpert, Munchaev, and Bader 1976, 1977, 1978, 1981; Molleson and Campbell 1995; Munchaev and Merpert 1971, 1973; Merpert and Munchaev 1984; Parker and Creekmore 2002; Şenyürek and Tunakan 1951; Tobler 1950; von Wickede 1984; von Wickede and Misir 1985; Watson and LeBlanc 1990).

c. Based on data from nine sites (AlpaGut 1986; Alpaslan-Roodenberg 2001; Alpaslan-Roodenberg and Maat 1999; Bonogofsky 2005; Grauer 1994; Hijara 1978; Mallowan and Rose 1935; Merpert and Munchaev 1984; Molleson and Campbell 1995; Özbal and Gerritsen 2004; Tobler 1950).

d. Reported but not published.

e. Defined as containing two to six individuals.

f. Found in or covered by ceramic bowl or plate.

g. Burials containing partial skeletons.

h. Defined here as containing more than six individuals.

At Domuztepe evidence of distinct mortuary treatment is suggested in three burials that show postmortem manipulation of the head. All of these features were recovered from Operation 1 in areas adjacent to and roughly contemporaneous with the Death Pit. Fractional burial F1361 contains the partial cranium of a child 5–6 years old who was interred in an apparently symbolically rich association in a shallow pit alongside a ceramic vase and a pig cranium. Direct evidence of the circumstances surrounding disarticulation of the child's head—that is, whether it represents a perimortem or postmortem activity—is limited by the absence of the mandible, occipital and basicranial elements, where signs of dismemberment trauma would be located. However, preserved portions of the cranium show no evidence of prolonged exposure or deliberate defleshing of the head. In combination, the clean separation of the occipital along its sutures and an absence of defleshing cut marks on the cranium suggest that prior to burial, this head may have been curated long enough for flesh to decay and inferior elements of the skull to fall away.

A second burial (F880) is represented by the skeleton of another child 5–6 years old whose tightly flexed body was interred lying on its side in the ash layer overlaying the Death Pit. Although the remains were otherwise intact and showed no damage other than postdepositional compression fractures of the delicate juvenile skull bones, all cervical vertebrae were missing except for small fragments of C1 and C2. While the loss of these bones may be due to diagenesis or postdepositional disturbance, the evidence is also consistent with postmortem head removal followed by reassociation in approximate anatomical position prior to interment. The fact that the mandible was appropriately articulated indicates the head still retained flesh at burial, suggesting a short disassociation period.

Finally, burial F1143 contains the well-preserved intact skull (i.e. mandible present and articulated) of a (probable) female adolescent aged 15–16 years (Figures 1.3 and 1.4) whose head was placed in a basket for burial. This skull displays evidence of severe blunt force trauma. There is a large area of destruction on the right lateral vault, the edges of which are bordered by percussion marks and depressed fractures and surrounded by radiating and concentric fractures and internal vault bone release, damages that are clearly associated with sudden, violent impact (White 1992; Galloway 1999). Although this trauma may be related to postmortem brain removal, the absence of anvil damage on the well-preserved opposing side and the recovery of many small fragments of bone from the interior of the

Figure 1.3. F1143 skull burial in situ. Photo by S. Campbell.

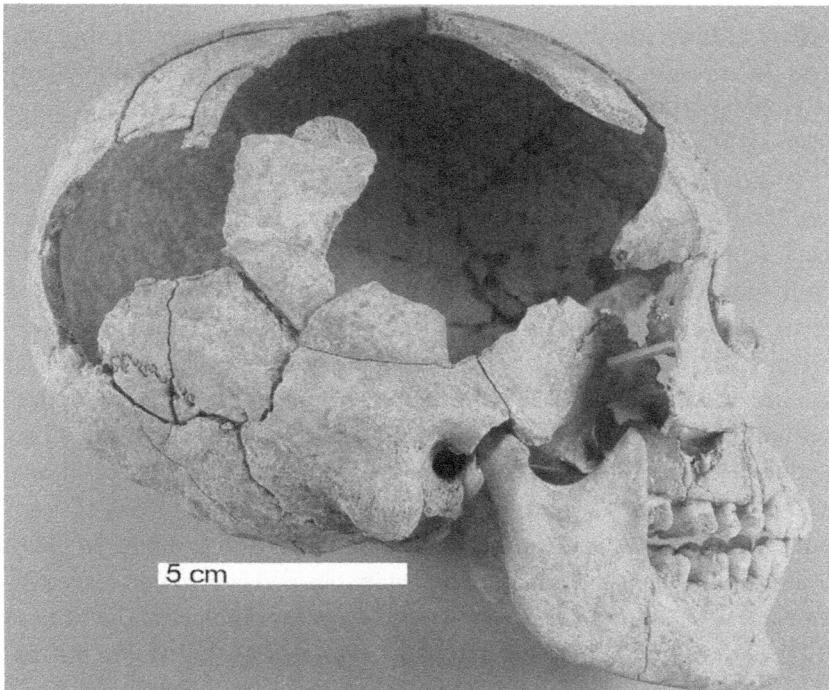

Figure 1.4. F1143 skull burial: post-conjoin reconstruction showing blunt force trauma to right side of skull. Note refit of concentric shaped fragments recovered from interior of cranium; other associated fragments could not be articulated. Photo by S. Gauld.

cranium (some of which are rearticulated in Figure 1.4) suggest that the damage preceded defleshing and that crushed bone was not pulled away from the impact area in order to access the brain. Moreover, evidence of less severe blows clearly unrelated to brain removal are preserved in hammerstone percussion scars that border a fracture line running across the frontal bone. Taken together, the characteristics of these wounds indicate they are unrelated to brain processing. We suggest that it is likely this young woman's death resulted from powerful blows to the head and that her head was separated from her body after death. The location and fate of the rest of the body is unknown.

For the most part, the taphonomic characteristics of complex Near Eastern Neolithic burials have not been investigated, although it is clear from the above presentation that these data provide useful information, even when evidence relating directly to cause of death is obscure. Our analysis of the three Domuztepe burials shows distinct differences in their taphonomic histories. On the one hand, the similar ages of the two sub-adult burials suggests that postmortem head removal, even for a short period of time, may have been part of a commemorative mourning process. In contrast, the head of the female adolescent bears clear evidence of violent perimortem blunt force trauma, suggesting that death resulted from an intentional act.

Although relatively uncommon, mass burials (defined here as burials containing more than six individuals) are also part of the Mesopotamian Late Neolithic burial record. Garstang (1953) very briefly describes a mass cremation (Burial vi) in Level XIX at Yümük Tepe consisting of "good teeth" and unrecognizably burned (completely blackened and calcined) bones (p. 111). At Tepe Gawra, Tobler (1950) recovered the remains of 22 adults (Burials B, C, and D) whose bodies, judging by their "grotesque" positions (p. 49), were thrown into an abandoned well. The bones all lay within 60 cm of fill, suggesting a short-term (if not a single) depositional event. No evidence of perimortem modification to the bones is mentioned in the burial description, and examination of the published photo of Burial B (Plate C.b.) shows complete bones and articulated segments, indicating, as Tobler suggests, that the bodies were intact at deposition. It is worth noting that Tobler and Garstang both concluded that the disrespectful mass depositions at Tepe Gawra and Yümük Tepe were likely related to social violence.

Table 1.2. Age (in years) and sex composition of Death Pit human assemblage

	0–1	1–4	5–9	10–14	15–19	20–29	30–39	40+
Female	—	—	—	—	2	4	2	2
Male	—	—	—	—	—	5	2	1
Indeterminate	2	3	3	5	1	—	2	1
Total	2	3	3	5	3	9	6	4

At Domuztepe, the behavioral context surrounding the Death Pit mass deposition may also reflect social violence. However, while aspects of the mortuary behaviors described at other sites are certainly apparent, the entire suite of damages documented in the Death Pit accumulation are quite dissimilar from those found at Yümük Tepe, Tepe Gawra, or any other Late Neolithic sites to date.

The Death Pit bone assemblage contains multiple taxa, including a minimum of 35 humans (Gauld et al. n.d.) (Table 1.2) and at least 11 cattle, 27 ovicaprids (sheep and goats), 8 pigs, 5 dogs, and a few specimens representing wild taxa (Kansa, Gauld et al. 2009a; Kansa forthcoming). Significantly, both the animal and human assemblages display mortality profiles that inform us about the behaviors surrounding their creation.

The Death Pit livestock, which constitute 98 percent of the animal assemblage, present a distinctive demographic pattern (Kansa forthcoming) that mirrors the structure of a "living herd" (Horwitz and Goring-Morris 2004) rather than the attritional pattern found in "normal" food debris from the rest of the site. For example, where aggregated data from the non–Death Pit cattle and ovicaprid samples display broadly distributed age ranges and relatively even sex ratios, 75 percent of the Death Pit livestock are prime-age adult females, animals whose numbers in living herds would be high because of their value in breeding and dairy production.

The Death Pit human assemblage shows both relatively high mortality among prime-age adults and adolescents and relatively low mortality among individuals under the age of 10 and over the age of 40 (Table 1.2). This pattern contrasts with the typical attritional mortality pattern describing preindustrial agricultural populations, including the Near Eastern Late Neolithic (published age data are scarce, but see Alpaslan-Roodenberg and Maat 1999 and Alpaslan-Roodenberg 2000 for Halaf burials from Menteşe Höyük; and Eshed et al. 2001 for the Pre-Pottery Neolithic C Levant site of Atlit Yam), where mortality is characterized by initially high death rates among young children followed by a sharp decline lasting from adolescence through prime adulthood (presumably because individuals have survived childhood malnutrition, disease, and trauma), culminating in rising mortality with the onset of senescence (Acsádi and Neméskeri 1970; Paine 2000).

Mortality patterns such as the ones describing the Death Pit livestock and humans are indicative of "catastrophic" (single-occurrence) death events because their composition approximates the demographic profile of the living population. That is, if the typical attritional mortality pattern shows a low death rate among young adults, the living population will contain a high proportion of these individuals, which would be reflected in the mortality profile of a single-event death assemblage.

Determination of cause of death, which is difficult in the best archaeological circumstances, presents an even greater challenge when bones are highly fragmented. Crania in the Death Pit livestock sample display heavy processing and are represented mostly by gnathic remains and horn cores (Kansa forthcoming). In contrast, although their completeness varies greatly, the skulls of the Death Pit dogs and humans are among the best-preserved elements. Like the F1143 skull burial described above, the crania in both of these groups show abundant evidence of perimortem impact damage (depressed and crushing fractures with incipient flakes, percussion scars, concentric and radiating fractures, and internal vault release) (White 1992; Galloway 1999). Our analysis (Gauld et al. n.d.) shows that 26 of the 31 human crania display severely destructive blunt force trauma to the lateral vault (n = 23) and/or evidence of less acute impact trauma on the frontal and facial areas of the skull (n = 14) (Figures 1.5 and 1.6). Again, the relationship between these damages and cause of death cannot be determined with certainty, but their abundance and well-patterned distribution, combined with the presence of similar wounds on dogs, animals who have a close working relationship with humans (Kansa, Gauld et al. 2009a), indicates that individuals in the Death Pit assemblage were likely killed by powerful blows to the head in an act of sacrifice. That said, our comparison of damage patterns by sex and age shows that the crania of males sustained much higher levels of trauma and destruction than the crania of females and subadults, indicating that males were also the target of great postmortem violence, perhaps including brain processing.

As expected, the Death Pit livestock display cut mark, impact, and thermal damage consistent with butchery, carcass processing and food

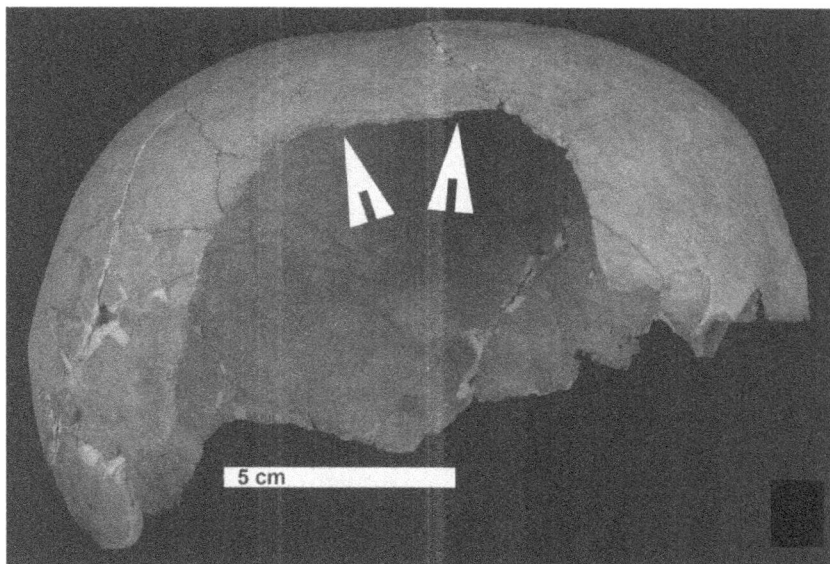

Figure 1.5. Blunt force trauma in the Death Pit human assemblage: lateral fracture zone on right side of cranium 2626.1. Blunt force trauma is indicated by depressed fractures with incipient concentric flakes along the superior parietal fracture edge. Photo by S. Gauld.

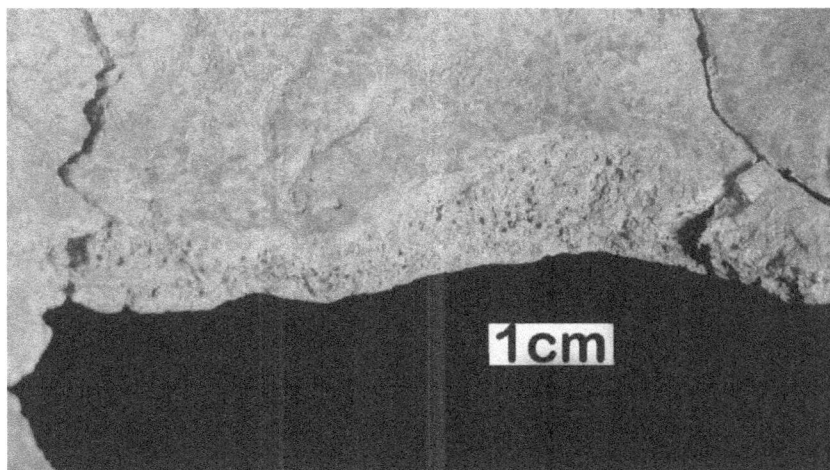

Figure 1.6. Blunt force trauma in the Death Pit human assemblage: internal vault release of cranium 2626.1. Although additional skull fragments representing portions of the mandible and cranial base were recovered, the sex of this specimen could not be determined. Photo by S. Gauld.

Figure 1.7. Butchery damage in the Death Pit human assemblage: percussion scars on proximal femur shaft fragment (2632.2). Photo by S. Gauld and J. Oliver.

preparation. What was surprising, however, was the fact that the Death Pit humans also preserve abundant evidence of deliberate postmortem culinary processing. Moreover, this damage, both in its frequencies and locational patterns, is similar to the patterns found in other cannibalism assemblages (e.g., White 1992).

Fourteen percent of the assemblage displays well-patterned cut marks that document systematic butchery (Lyman 1994; Nilssen 2000). Cuts on the crania, mandibles, and cervical vertebrae are in locations consistent with scalping, disarticulation, and defleshing of the cranium and mandible. On the postcranial skeleton, cut mark locations demonstrate dismemberment of all body segments and thorough defleshing of large muscle masses from the trunk, buttocks, and limbs. Hammerstone impact damages in the form of percussion marks and other fracture features such as concentric and radiating fractures, flake scars, notches, and opposing anvil damage (Blumenshine and Selvagio 1988; Oliver 1989; Oliver 1993) are present on 20 percent of the postcranial sample (Figures 1.7 and 1.8). However, their distribution is markedly focused on elements that are rich in grease (pelvis and vertebrae) and marrow (femur, tibia, and humerus), as are extremely high frequencies of extensive fragmentation (Kansa, Gauld et al. 2009; Gauld et al. n.d.).

Cooking is indicated by evidence of low temperature thermal exposure on 48 percent of the human remains, visible as a mottled discoloration and localized burning of bone surface areas not protected by deep tissue (Shipman, Foster, and Schoeninger 1984; Buikstra and Swegle 1989) and by the presence of pot polish, which is incurred as bones are stirred in clay pots (White 1992), on 13 percent of long bone fragments. Evidence of consumption is documented by small shallow tooth marks and depressed fractures that co-occur on a variety of elements, particularly the delicate metacarpals and metatarsals (Figures 1.9 and 1.10). This pattern of damage, which is distinct from the tooth damages created by nonhuman carnivores, is preserved in several well-accepted hominin cannibalism

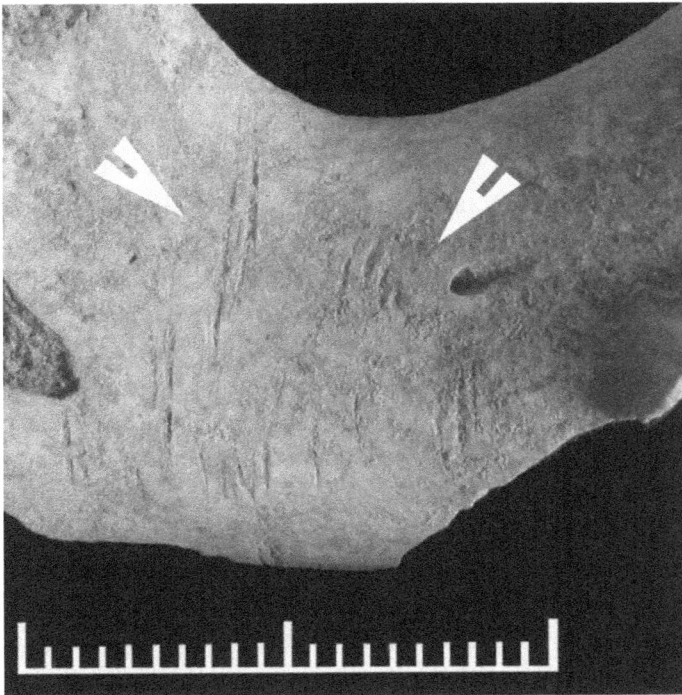

Figure 1.8. Cut marks on the sciatic notch of innominate (pelvis) fragment (3134.0.5). Photo by S. Gauld and J. Oliver.

Figure 1.9. Evidence of cooking and consumption in the Death Pit assemblage: pot polish on fractured end of femur fragment (2650.0.49). Photo by S. Gauld and J. Oliver.

assemblages (e.g., White 1992; Andrews and Fernández-Jalvo 2003; Cáceres, Lozano, and Saladie 2007), and its relationship to human chewing has now been demonstrated experimentally (Fernández-Jalvo and Andrews 2011).

While aspects of other mortuary behaviors are present in the Death Pit bones, the suite of documented characteristics is distinctive. Evidence of short-term deposition combined with intensive carcass processing that is highly focused on meat and marrow retrieval clearly rule out mortuary practices such as cutting tendons to facilitate flexed burials or storage in containers, cleaning the corpse for secondary burial, and/or random mutilation of the corpse to destroy evidence of its existence. Cooking rather than cremation is indicated by the presence of low-temperature thermal exposure and pot polish. Finally, the presence of small shallow tooth marks combined with an absence of carnivore or rodent damage suggests that humans, not animals, acted as primary agents in the Death Pit accumulation. In sum, when the *entire* complex of damages and behaviors documented in the Death Pit assemblage is considered, not only do the

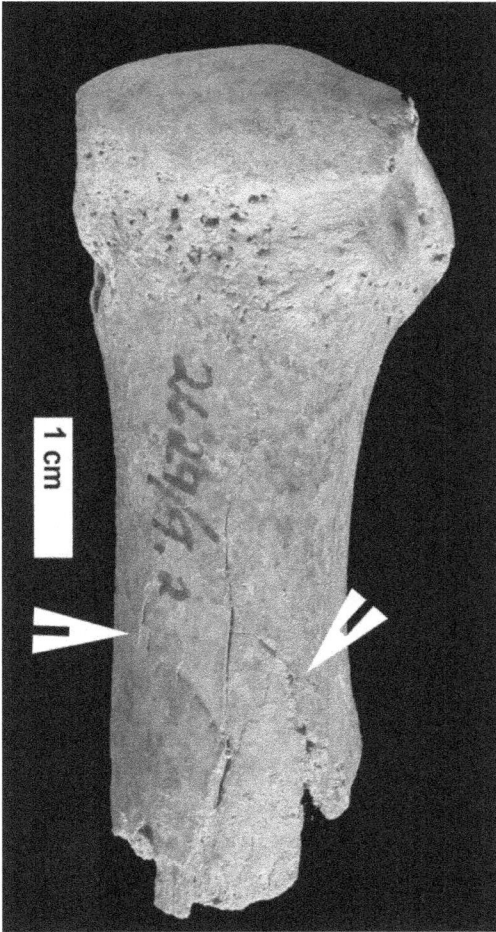

Figure 1.10. Evidence of cooking and consumption in the Death Pit assemblage: shallow tooth marks accompanied by depressed fractures on 1st metacarpal (2629.9.2). Photo by S. Gauld and J. Oliver.

data meet all the criteria required to infer cannibalism in the archaeological record (e.g., Villa and Mahieu 1991; White 1992; Turner and Turner 1999), they also cannot be explained by reference to other previously described Late Neolithic mortuary patterns.

Halaf Feasting and the Death Pit

Certainly a large communal feast involving cannibalism on the scale documented in the Death Pit human assemblage would have had great significance for members of the Domuztepe community. The event's importance is clearly expressed in the ritual overtones that surround its performance (Kansa and Campbell 2004; Kansa, Gauld et al. 2009; Carter forthcoming). These include (but are not limited to): a) the purposeful construction of the pit; b) the pit's location adjacent to a terrace that may have served as an important boundary and/or community space; c) the age and sex data of animals that document single-event mortality of valuable prime-age females for the feast; d) the deliberate sacrifice of humans and dogs, whose skulls display evidence of blunt force trauma; and e) the differential treatment of some individuals, including more intensive processing of male crania and the (perhaps) deliberate arrangement of skulls in the pit. While the ritual significance of the Death Pit event seems obvious, deciphering the specific motivations and intentions that inspired its execution is difficult. Nonetheless, it is possible to delineate certain conditions that may shed light on the reasons for its performance and, perhaps, how participants viewed this event.

Clearly the large size and shared short-term depositional context of the animal and human assemblages indicate that cannibalism at Domuztepe was not related to nutritional need (e.g., Hardesty 1997) or to the compassionate consumption of individuals as an aspect of funerary mourning (e.g., Conklin 2001). Rather, the strong indications of intentional violence, thorough consumption processing, and the unceremonious mixing of animal and humans during deposition makes the Death Pit data commensurate with a well-documented link between cannibalism and agonistic behavior (Kantner 1999), where activities are driven by a need to take revenge on or humiliate enemies or where social intimidation is used to achieve civil and/or religious control (e.g., Sahlins 1983; Harris 1985; Petrinovitch 2000).

One hypothesis is that the Death Pit feast may represent an example of a predatory violation ritual (Bloch 1982), in which a group of humans were both denied a proper burial necessary for their continued spiritual existence and incorporated or used by the living for social reproduction. As such, it may represent a type of empowerment feast (Dietler 2001), in this case one in which the forcible destruction of one group was used to eliminate a threat or to punish a transgression while simultaneously establishing or enhancing the power of another. The ability of one segment of the population to sanction the execution and consumption of so many people would assert their leadership position in a most visible, memorable, and unequivocal act. Participation in the feasting activities would not only authenticate this leadership but also bind neighbors and kin groups together in a remarkable expression of community solidarity and shared identity.

Moreover, ethnographic and archaeological evidence demonstrate that the practice of agonistic cannibalism is often expressed within a complex framework of religious symbolism (see Petrinovitch 2000 for examples). Thus, the death and consumption of victims, which may be designed to deny them a spiritual existence, may also be manifested as a highly ritualized sacrifice intended to honor, appease, or gain the favor of god(s).

Regardless of the complex (and likely culturally unique) interplay of motivations that describe its objectives, the Domuztepe Death Pit feast provides insight into the way one large terminal Neolithic community may have attempted to solve the problems and tensions associated with an increasingly complex social landscape. Larger population size, location on the boundary of the Halaf cultural tradition, and increasing intercommunity and/or intracommunity economic and social distinctions may have on occasion disrupted the solidarity of a traditional egalitarian community structure, enabling or even requiring the exercise of religious or political authority. At Domuztepe these persons may have been civil and/or religious leaders endowed with the political skills and special knowledge of the symbolic requirements necessary to unite the community and transform consensus into action.

Conclusions

In this study we used osteological and taphonomic methods to examine the mortuary activities surrounding a small but interesting set of Halaf burials at the Late Neolithic site of Domuztepe. Our goal was to use bioarchaeological data to enhance our understanding of these activities and to test a variety of hypotheses about the behavioral motivations surrounding their enactment. Data from two juvenile burials suggest that in some instances, head removal at Domuztepe may represent a shared component of a generalized and varied lexicon of ritual mourning activities. However, data from an adolescent skull burial indicates that head removal may also (on occasion) be associated with violence.

Finally, although the debate over its existence has been contentious and often culture bound, recent research, based on a combination of ethnographic, archaeological and biological evidence, demonstrates that human cannibalism has a long history that spans time, continents, cultures, and even hominin species (e.g., Villa et al. 1986; Conklin 2001; White 1992; Defleur et al. 1999; Degusta 1999; Fernández-Jalvo et al. 1999; Turner and Turner 1999; Andrews and Fernández-Jalvo 2003; Mead et al. 2003; Cáceres, Lozano, and Saladie 2007). Our data show that the Death Pit animal and human remains are best explained as the end product of a large communal ritual feast that involved the consumption of a great many valuable animals and at least 35 people. We suggest the Death Pit data also conform to a model of agonistic cannibalism, where ritualized sacrifice and feasting may serve as a visible and symbolic affirmation of both established hierarchy and community integration. Most significantly, our study broadens the explanatory framework for viewing Late Neolithic burial practices by providing the first evidence of cannibalism in the ancient Near East.

References Cited

Acsádi, G. Y., and J. Neméskeri
1970   *History of Human Life Span and Mortality.* Akademiai Kiado, Budapest.
Akkermans, P. M. M. G.
1989   Halaf Mortuary Practices: A Survey. In *To the Euphrates and Beyond,* edited by O. M. C. Haex, H. H. Curvers, and P. M. M. G. Akkermans, pp. 75–88. A. A. Balkema, Brookfield.
1993   *Villages in the Steppe: Later Neolithic Settlement and Subsistence in the Balikh Valley, Northern Syria.* International Monographs in Prehistory, Ann Arbor, Mich.
Akkermans, P. M. M. G., and K. Duistermaat
1996   Of Storage and Nomads: The Sealings from Late Neolithic Sabi Abyad, Syria. *Paléorient* 22(2):17–44.
Akkermans, P. M. M. G., and G. M. Schwartz
2003   *The Archaeology of Syria.* Cambridge University Press, Cambridge.
Akkermans, P. M. M. G., and M. Verhoeven
1995   An Image of Complexity: the Burnt Village at Late Neolithic Sabi Abyad, Syria. *American Journal of Archaeology* 99(1):5–32.
Al-A'dami, K. A.
1968   Excavations at Tell es-Sawwan. *Sumer* 24:57–60.
Alpağut, B.
1986   The Human Skeletal Remains from Kurban Höyük (Urfa Province). *Anatolica* 13:149–163.
Alpaslan-Roodenberg, S.
2001   Newly Found Human Remains from Menteşe in the Yenişehir Plain: The Season of 2000. *Anatolica* 27:1–14.

Alpaslan-Roodenberg, S., and G. J. R. Maat
1999   Human Skeletons from Menteşe Höyük Near Yenişehir. *Anatolica* 25:37–51.
Al-Radi, S., and H. Seeden
1980   The AUB Rescue Excavations at Shams ed-Din, Tannira. *Berytus* 28:88–126.
Andrews, P., and Y. Fernández-Jalvo
2003   Cannibalism in Britain: Taphonomy of the Creswellian (Pleistocene) Faunal and Human Remains from Gough's Cave (Somerset, England). *Bulletin of the Natural History Museum: Geology* 58:59–81.
Aten, N.
1996   Note on the Human Skeletal Remains. In *Tell Sabi Abyad: The Late Neolithic Settlement,* vol. 1, edited by P. M. M. G. Akkermans, pp. 114–118. Historisch-Archaelogisch Instituut Te Istanbul, Leiden.
Bader, N. D.
1993   Summary of the Earliest Agriculturalists of Northern Mesopotamia (1989). In *Early Stages in the Evolution of Mesopotamian Civilization: Soviet Excavations in Northern Iraq,* edited by N. Yoffee and J. J. Clark, pp. 63–71. University of Arizona, Tucson.
Bass, W. M.
1984   Time Interval Since Death, a Difficult Decision. In *Human Identification, Case Studies in Forensic Anthropology,* edited by T. A. Rathbun and J. E. Buikstra, pp. 136–147. Charles C. Thomas, Springfield, Ill.
Bloch, M.
1982   Death, Women and Power. In *Death and the Regeneration of Life,* edited by M. Bloch and J. Parry, pp. 211–230. Cambridge University Press, Cambridge.
Blumenschine, R. J., and M. M. Selvagio
1988   Percussion Marks on Bone Surfaces as a New Diagnostic of Hominid Behaviour. *Nature* 333:763–765.
Bonogofsky, M.
2005   A Bioarchaeological Study of Plastered Skulls from Anatolia: New Discoveries and Interpretations. *International Journal of Osteoarchaeology* 15:124–135.
Buikstra, J. E., and M. Swegle
1989   Bone Modification Due to Burning: Experimental Evidence. In *Bone Modification,* edited by R. Bonnichsen and M. Sorg, pp. 247–258. Center for the Study of the First Americans, University of Maine at Orono, Orono.
Buikstra, J. E., and D. H. Ubelaker
1994   *Standards for Data Collection from Human Skeletal Remains.* Arkansas Archaeological Survey Research Series 44. Arkansas Archaeological Survey, Fayetteville, Ark.
Cáceres, I., M. Lozano, and P. Saladie
2007   Evidence of Bronze Age Cannibalism in El Mirador Cave (Sierra de Atapuerca, Burgos, Spain). *American Journal of Physical Anthropology* 133:899–917.
Campbell, S.
1995   Death for the Living in North Mesopotamia. In *Archaeology of Death in the Ancient Near East,* edited by S. Campbell and A. Green, pp. 33–38. Oxbow Monograph no. 51. Oxbow Books Ltd., Oxford.

Campbell, S., and E. Carter
2006   Excavations at Domuztepe, 2005. *Kazi Sonuşlari Toplantisi* 28:269–277.
Carter, E.
2011   The Glyptic of the Middle-Late Halaf Period at Domuztepe, Turkey (ca 5755–5450 BC). *Paléorient* 36(1):159–177.
Forthcoming   On Human and Animal Sacrifice in the Late Neolithic at Domuztepe. In *Sacrifice and Archaeology: Perspectives from the Ancient Near East and Beyond*, edited by A. Porter and G. Schwartz, Eisenbrauns Press, Winona Lake, Ind.
Carter, E., S. Campbell, and S. Gauld
2003   Elusive Complexity: New Data from Late Halaf Domuztepe in South Central Turkey. *Paléorient* 29(2):117–134.
Conklin, B. A.
2001   *Consuming Grief: Compassionate Cannibalism in an Amazonian Society*. University of Texas Press, Austin.
Defleur, A., T. White, P. Velensi, L. Slimak, and E. Crégut-Bonnoure
1999   Neanderthal Cannibalism at Moula-Guercy, Ardèche, France. *Science* 286:128–131.
DeGusta, D.
1999   Fijian Cannibalism: Osteological Evidence from Navatu. *American Journal of Physical Anthropology* 110:215–241.
Dietler, M.
2001   Theorizing the Feast: Rituals of Consumption, Commensal Politics, and Power in African Context. In *Feasts: Archaeological and Ethnographic Perspectives on Food, Politics, and Power*, edited by M. Dietler and B. M. Hayden, pp. 65–114. Smithsonian Institution Press, Washington, D.C.
El-Wailly, F., and B. Abu Al-Soof
1965   The Excavations at Tell es-Sawwan: First Preliminary Report. *Sumer* 21:17–32.
Eshed, V., A. Gopher, T. B. Gage, and I. Hershkovitz
2004   Has the Transition to Agriculture Reshaped the Demographic Structure of Prehistoric Populations? New Evidence from the Levant. *American Journal of Physical Anthropology* 124:315–329.
Fernández-Jalvo, Y., and P. Andrews
2011   When Humans Chew Bones. *Journal of Human Evolution* 60(1):117–123.
Fernández-Jalvo, Y., J. Diez, I. Cáceres, and J. Rosell
1999   Human Cannibalism in the Early Pleistocene of Europe (*Gran Dolina, Sierra de Atapuerca*, Burgos, Spain). *Journal of Human Evolution* 37:591–622.
Frangipane, M.
2009   Different Types of Egalitarian Societies and the Development of Inequality in Early Mesopotamia. *World Archaeology* 39(2):151–176.
Galloway, A. (editor)
1999   *Broken Bones: Anthropological Analysis of Blunt Force Trauma*. Charles C. Thomas, Springfield, Ill.

Garstang, S.
1953 *Prehistoric Mersin, Yümük Tepe in Southern Turkey: the Neilson Expedition.* Clarendon Press, Oxford.
Gauld, S. C., J. S. Oliver, S. W. Kansa, E. Carter, and S. Campbell
N.d. Late Neolithic Cannibalism at Domuztepe, Mesopotamia. Unpublished paper.
Grauer, A.
1989 Paleopathological Analysis of Four Late Chalcolithic Burials from Hacinebi Tepe. *Anatolica* 20:173–176.
Hardesty, D. L. (editor)
1997 *The Archaeology of the Donner Party.* University of Nevada Press, Reno.
Harris, M.
1985 *Good to Eat.* Simon and Schuster, New York.
Hijara, I.
1978 Three New Graves at Arpachiyah. *World Archaeology* 10(2):125–128.
Horwitz, L. K., and N. Goring-Morris
2004 Animals and Ritual During the Levantine PPNB: A Case Study from the Site of Kfar HaHoresh, Israel. *Anthropozoologica* 39(1):165–178.
Irving, A., and C. Heywood
2004 The Ceramics in the Death Pit at Domuztepe: Conservation and Analysis. *Anatolian Archaeology* 10:6.
Joffe, A. H.
2003 Slouching toward Beersheva: Chalcolithic Mortuary Practices in Local and Regional Context. In *The Near East in The Southwest, Essays in Honor of William G. Dever,* edited by B. Alpert-Nakhai, pp. 45–67. Annual of the American Schools of Oriental Research 58. American Schools of Oriental Research, Chicago.
Kansa, S. Whitcher
Forthcoming Non-Human Remains from the "Death Pit." In *Prehistoric Domuztepe,* vol. 1, edited by S. Campbell and E. Carter. Cotsen Institute of Archaeology, Monumenta Archaeologica, University of California, Los Angeles.
Kansa, S. Whitcher, and S. Campbell
2004 Feasting with the Dead? A Ritual Bone Deposit at Domuztepe, South Eastern Turkey (c. 5500 cal BC). In *Behaviour Behind Bones,* edited by S. J. O'Day, and W. Van Neer, pp. 2–13. Oxbow Books, Oxford.
Kansa, S. Whitcher, S. Gauld, S. Campbell, and E. Carter
2009 Whose Bones Are Those? Preliminary Comparative Analysis of Fragmented Human and Animal Bones in the "Death Pit" at Domuztepe, a Late Neolithic Settlement in Southeastern Turkey. *Anthropozoologica* 44(1):159–172.
Kansa, S. Whitcher, A. Kennedy, S. Campbell, and E. Carter
2009b Resource Exploitation at Late Neolithic Domuztepe: Faunal and Botanical Evidence. *Current Anthropology* 50(6):897–914.
Kantner, J.
1999 Survival Cannibalism or Sociopolitical Intimidation? Explaining Perimortem Mutilation in the American Southwest. *Human Nature* 10(1):1–50.

Killick, R., and J. Black
1985   Excavations in Iraq 1983–84. *Iraq* 47:215–239.
Killick, R., and M. Roaf
1983   Excavations in Iraq, 1981–82. *Iraq* 45:206.
Lloyd, S., and F. Safer
1945   Tell Hassuna. *Journal of Near Eastern Studies* 4(4):255–289.
Lyman, R. L.
1994   *Vertebrate Taphonomy.* Cambridge Manuals in Archaeology. Cambridge University Press, Cambridge.
Mallowan, M. E. L.
1936   The Excavations at Tell Chagar Bazar and an Archaeological Survey of the Habur Region, 1934–35. *Iraq* 3:1–87.
Mallowan, M. E. L., and J. C. Rose
1935   Excavations at Tell Arpachiyah. *Iraq* 2:1–178.
Mead, S., M. P. H. Stumpf, J. Whitfield, J. A. Beck, M. Poulter, T. Campbell, J. Uphill, D. Goldstein, M. Alpers, E. M. C. Fischer, and J. Collinge
2003   Balancing Selection at the Prion Protein Gene Consistent with Prehistoric Kuru Like Epidemics. *Science* 300:640–643.
Merpert, N. I., and R. M. Munchaev
1969   The Investigation of the Soviet Archaeological Expedition in Iraq in the Spring 1969. *Sumer* 25:125–131.
1971   Excavations at Yarim Tepe, Second Preliminary Report. *Sumer* 27:9–22.
1973   Early Agricultural Settlements in the Sinjar Plain, Northern Iraq. *Iraq* 35:93–113.
1984   Soviet Expedition's Research at Yarim Tepe III Settlement in Northwestern Iraq, 1978–1979. *Sumer* 43:54–68.
1987   The Earliest Levels at Yarim Tepe I and Yarim Tepe II in Northern Iraq. *Iraq* 49:1–36.
1993a   Yarim Tepe I. In *Early Stages in the Evolution of Mesopotamian Civilization: Soviet Excavations in Northern Iraq,* edited by N. Yoffee and J. J. Clark, pp. 73–114. University of Arizona, Tucson.
1993b   Burial Practices of the Halaf Culture. In *Early Stages in the Evolution of Mesopotamian Civilization: Soviet Excavations in Northern Iraq,* edited by N. Yoffee and J. J. Clark, pp. 207–224. University of Arizona, Tucson.
Merpert, N. I., R. M. Munchaev, and N. Bader
1976   The Investigations of the Soviet Expedition to Iraq 1973. *Sumer* 32:25–61.
1977   The Investigations of the Soviet Expedition to Iraq 1974. *Sumer* 33:65–104.
1978   Soviet Investigations in the Sinjar Plain 1975. *Sumer* 34:27–71.
1981   Investigations of the Soviet Expedition in Northern Iraq, 1976. *Sumer* 37:22–54.
Molleson, T., and S. Campbell
1995   Deformed Skulls at Tell Arpichiyah: The Social Context. In *Archaeology of Death in the Ancient Near East,* edited by S. Campbell and A. Green, 45–55. Oxbow Monographs no. 51. Oxbow Books Ltd., Oxford.

Munchaev, R. M., and N. I. Merpert
1971   The Archaeological Research in the Sinjar Valley 1971. *Sumer* 27:23–32.
1973   Excavations at Yarim Tepe 1972, Fourth Preliminary Report. *Sumer* 29:3–16.

Nilssen, P. J.
2000   An Actualistic Butchery Study in South Africa and Its Implications for Re-
        constructing Hominid Strategies of Carcass Acquisition and Butchery in the
        Upper Pleistocene and Plio-Pleistocene. Unpublished Ph.D. dissertation, Uni-
        versity of Cape Town.

Oliver, J. S.
1989   Analogues and Site Context: Bone Damages from Shield Trap Cave (24CB91),
        Carbon County, Montana, U.S.A. In *Bone Modification,* edited by R. Bon-
        nichsen and M. Sorg, pp. 73–98. Center for the Study of the First Americans,
        Orono, Me.
1993   Carcass Processing by the Hadza: Bone Breakage from Butchery to Consump-
        tion. In *From Bones to Behavior: Ethnoarchaeological and Experimental Con-
        tributions to the Interpretation of Faunal Remains,* edited by J. Hudson, pp.
        200–227. Occasional Paper No. 21. Southern Illinois University, Center for
        Archaeological Investigations, Carbondale.

Özbal, R., and F. Gerritsen
2004   Tell Kurdu Excavations 2001. *Anatolica* 30:69–107.

Paine, R. R.
2000   If a Population Crashes in Prehistory, and There is No Paleodemographer
        There to Hear It, Does It Make a Sound? *American Journal of Physical Anthro-
        pology* 112:181–190.

Parker, B., and A. Creekmore
2002   The Upper Tigris Archaeological Research Project: A Final Report from the
        1999 Field Season. *Anatolian Studies* 52:19–74.

Petrinovitch, L.
2000   *The Cannibal Within.* Aldine de Gruyter Press, New York.

Sahlins, M.
1983   Raw Women, Cooked Men and Other "Great Things" of the Fiji Islands. In
        The Ethnography of Cannibalism, edited by P. Brown and D. Tuzin, pp. 72–93.
        Society for Psychological Anthropology, Washington, D.C.

Şenyürek, M., and S. Tunaken
1951   The Skeletons from Şeyh Höyük. *Belleten* 60:431–445.

Shipman, P., G. Foster, and M. Schoeninger
1984   Burnt Bones and Teeth: An Experimental Study of Color, Morphology, Crystal
        Structure and Shrinkage. *Journal of Archaeological Science* 11:307–325.

Steele, D. G., and C. A. Bramblett
1998   *The Anatomy and Biology of the Human Skeleton.* Texas A&M University Press,
        College Station.

Tekin, H.
2005   Hakemi Use: A New Discovery Regarding the Northern Distribution of Has-
        sunan/Samarran Pottery in the Near East. *Antiquity* 79(303):1–9.

Tobler, A.
1950   *Excavations at Tepe Gawra.* Vol. 2. University of Pennsylvania Museum of Archaeology and Anthropology, Philadelphia.

Turner, C. G., and J. A. Turner
1999   *Man Corn: Cannibalism and Violence in the Prehistoric American Southwest.* University of Utah Press, Salt Lake City.

Ubelaker, D. H.
1997   Taphonomic Applications in Forensic Anthropology. *In Forensic Taphonomy: The Postmortem Fate of Human Remains,* edited by W. D. Haglund and M. H. Sorg, pp. 77–90. C. R. C. Press, New York.

Villa, P., C. Bouville, J. Courtin, D. Helmer, E. Mahieu, P. Shipman, G. Belluomini, and M. Branca
1986   Cannibalism in the Neolithic. *Science* 233:431–437.

Villa, P., and E. Mahieu
1991   Breakage Patterns of Human Long Bones. *Journal of Human Evolution* 21:27–48

von Wickede, A.
1984   Çavi Tarlasi 1983. *Kazi Sonuçlari Toplantisi* 6:191–196.

von Wickede, A., and A. Misir
1985   Çavi Tarlasi 1984 Kazi Kampanyasi. *Kazi Sonuçlari Toplantisi* 7:103–109.

Watson, P. J.
1982   The Halafian Culture: A Review and Synthesis. In *The Hilly Flanks and Beyond: Essays on the Prehistory of Southwestern Asia,* edited by T. Cuyler Young, P. E. L. Smith, and P. Mortensen, pp. 231–249. Studies in Ancient Oriental Civilization, no. 36. Oriental Institute of University of Chicago, Chicago.

Watson, P. J., and S. A. LeBlanc
1990   *Girikihaciyan: A Halafian Site in Southeastern Turkey.* Cotsen Institute of Archaeology Monograph 33. Cotsen Institute of Archaeology Press, University of California, Los Angeles.

White, T. D.
1992   *Prehistoric Cannibalism at Mancos 5MTUMR-2346.* Princeton University Press, Princeton, N.J.

White, T. D., and P. A. Folkens
2000   *Human Osteology.* 2nd ed. Academic Press, San Diego.

2

An Exploration of Infant Burial Practices at the Site of Kish, Iraq

CHRISTINA TORRES-ROUFF AND WILLIAM J. PESTLE

In the third millennium BC, the city of Kish, located on the Euphrates floodplain in modern Iraq, was the dominant regional polity in Mesopotamia. From 1923 to 1933, the Joint Oxford–Field Museum Expedition to Kish undertook substantial archaeological excavation inside and outside the ancient boundaries of the city. Skeletal remains from over 750 individuals, representing nearly every era of the site's occupation, were recovered. These remains, along with the material culture from Kish, have recently been systematically reanalyzed.

Osteological analysis of this collection of largely incomplete and poorly preserved individuals revealed the unexpected presence of a number of well-preserved neonate skeletons, suggesting a distinct class of funerary treatment for infants who died near full term. Integration of the osteological data with long-separated burial records and field notes revealed further aspects of the mortuary ritual afforded to infants at Kish. At least five infants were buried in a cache associated with a Neo-Babylonian (1000–539 BC) period temple, while two others were recovered from opulent Early Dynastic (third century BC) graves, suggesting the possibility of a special category of burial practice reserved for infants of this age group. Here, we explore the social significance of infant death at Kish.

The death of a child can be a profoundly disruptive familial and societal moment. Reactions to such a death can vary between groups but may manifest in distinct mortuary practices that reflect the ways a particular society understands and values children and childhood. Archaeologists generally work within a framework that engages the lifeways of adults (Kamp 2001) and rarely examine the unique social identity of children.

Age-specific study of mortuary practices can illuminate the social and cultural meaning of different phases of the life course and the creation of distinct social personae. Burial practices for infants, including children interred in domestic spaces, those buried in the same manner as adults, and even sectors specifically reserved for children, may in fact reflect significantly different views of the role and place of children in a given society. Here we explore a small group of infant burials from the Mesopotamian site of Kish in an effort to glimpse the patterns surrounding infant death at the site. These children often were buried in a way that separated them from the adults and juveniles buried at the site. We argue that these distinct mortuary practices may suggest a particular social significance for infant death at Kish.

Archaeology and the Life Course: A Bioarchaeology of Children

Even though they have less impact on their surroundings than adults, children form an important (in fact, essential) part of society, and they leave important traces for archaeologists to explore. The absence of children in the archaeological record has been explained as a result of the ephemeral nature of childhood, sociocultural constructions of childhood, differential preservation of the remains of adults and children, and, most critically, a pervasive disciplinary bias toward adult life (Kamp 2001; Walker, Johnson, and Lambert 1988). In Kamp's (2001, 24) groundbreaking article calling for an archaeology of childhood, she writes, "Archaeologists have not attempted to systematically reconstruct a detailed picture of childhood in any single prehistoric culture or to relate their studies to the broader literature." Following gender scholars, archaeologists have begun to consider the culturally constructed categories used to classify life stages (Lewis 2007, 3; Perry 2005, 89). Considering children from these perspectives can provide us with a more complete and nuanced view of the role of children in a particular society.

The examination of childhood as one stage in an emic, culturally constructed understanding of the human life course has allowed scholars to focus on such diverse elements as gender roles (e.g., the engendering of children) and material culture (e.g., studies of ancient toys). Rather than focusing on the material culture that was used by or belonged to children in life, most archaeologists have focused instead on the mortuary rituals afforded children in death because they can often be tied directly to a particular infant (e.g., Baxter 2005; Borič and Stefanovič 2004; Finlay 2000). As Robb (2007, 287) notes, funerary rites "furnish a locus for legitimation of a social order, or for struggle and contestation of one." Thus, the study of infant burial gives archaeologists the chance to explore specifics surrounding the treatment and perception of childhood.

While we do not attempt to speak to the broad range of issues concerning childhood, we employ some of the ideas put forward by scholars working in this area (e.g., Baxter 2005; Kamp 2001; Lewis 2007; Perry 2005; Sofaer Derevenski 2000; Wileman 2005) about the practices surrounding infant death. In Romania and Serbia, Borič and Stefanovič (2004, 543) explored the "social and symbolic importance of newborn[s]" through analysis of infant burial style, concluding that they carried social weight equal to that of "big-men of the community." Finlay (2000, 408), analyzing infant burial in Irish contexts, found that "the liminal character of those outside of traditional rites of passage is reflected in burial practices and that this tends to reinforce their marginal status." Others have focused on how during certain periods in the ancient Near East, infants and young children were buried in domestic spaces while adults were interred in cemeteries in abandoned parts of settlements, perhaps suggesting that infants were not fully incorporated into the social hierarchy and reinforcing differences within the community (Harris 2000, 15–16; Pollock 1999, 205–206). Such examples show how more nuanced understandings of the lives and workings of past societies can result from research that combines mortuary studies and the archaeology of childhood. Applying these ideas to a broader program of mortuary analysis should reveal different aspects of life at Kish than would an analysis focused solely on adults.

Research Problem

Researchers have historically neglected the hundreds of burials from Kish, in great part as a result of poor preservation and contextual problems. In particular, the infant burials were treated in a sensational way upon their discovery (Field 1930) and were then set aside. Ultimately, this served to deny their potential for providing insight into lives and practices at the site. Here we explore two possibilities concerning infant burial at Kish: 1) the likelihood that infant deaths had differential social significance that is reflected in their graves; and 2) the hypothesis of infanticide put forth by earlier scholars as an explanation for a cluster of Neo-Babylonian period perinatal graves (ibid.). We investigate changes in burial practice by age that may indicate the boundary of a socially important stage for individuals who died between birth and the first year of life. Unfortunately, the limitations of the sample mean that the present work poses as many (if not more) questions about these topics than it is capable of answering.

Site Description

The archaeological site of Kish (Figure 2.1; 32°30' N, 44°35' E) is located on the floodplain of the Euphrates River in modern Iraq, 12 kilometers east of ancient Babylon and approximately 80 kilometers south of Baghdad. The site is made up of more than 40 mounds scattered over an area 24 kilometers square that is divided by the ancient course of the Euphrates. The eastern complex (known in ancient times as Hursagkalamma) is dominated by the Ingharra mounds, while the ziggurat of Uhaimir towers over the western remains of the city.

In the context of the highly fractious political environment of the early third millennium BC (the Early Dynastic period), Kish emerged as an influential city-state in the region (and perhaps the most influential). Kish eventually wielded control over not just its immediate environs but over the whole of the lands of Sumer and Akkad (Charvát 2001; Maisels 1993). Sculptures, public buildings, and archaic tablets attest to the existence of a developed administrative center by the last quarter of the fourth millennium BC (Moorey 1978). Kish's regulatory power waned during the Akkadian period (2334–2154 BC), but its cachet as the first major regional seat of power lingered for centuries and is demonstrated by the fact that foreign leaders who aspired to regional power conquered Kish so they could add the title "King of Kish" to their list of names. This honorific added legitimacy to their claim of power (Gibson 1972a). Despite this powerful association with the concept of kingship, Kish's fortunes waxed and waned through the following millennia, and it never again regained the position of power it had occupied in the Early Dynastic period. In the Neo-Babylonian period (1000–539 BC), which we consider in more detail below, the eastern portion of Kish experienced a renaissance and became a sizeable city that featured a major temple complex on Ingharra/Hursagkalamma (Gibson 1972b, 116).

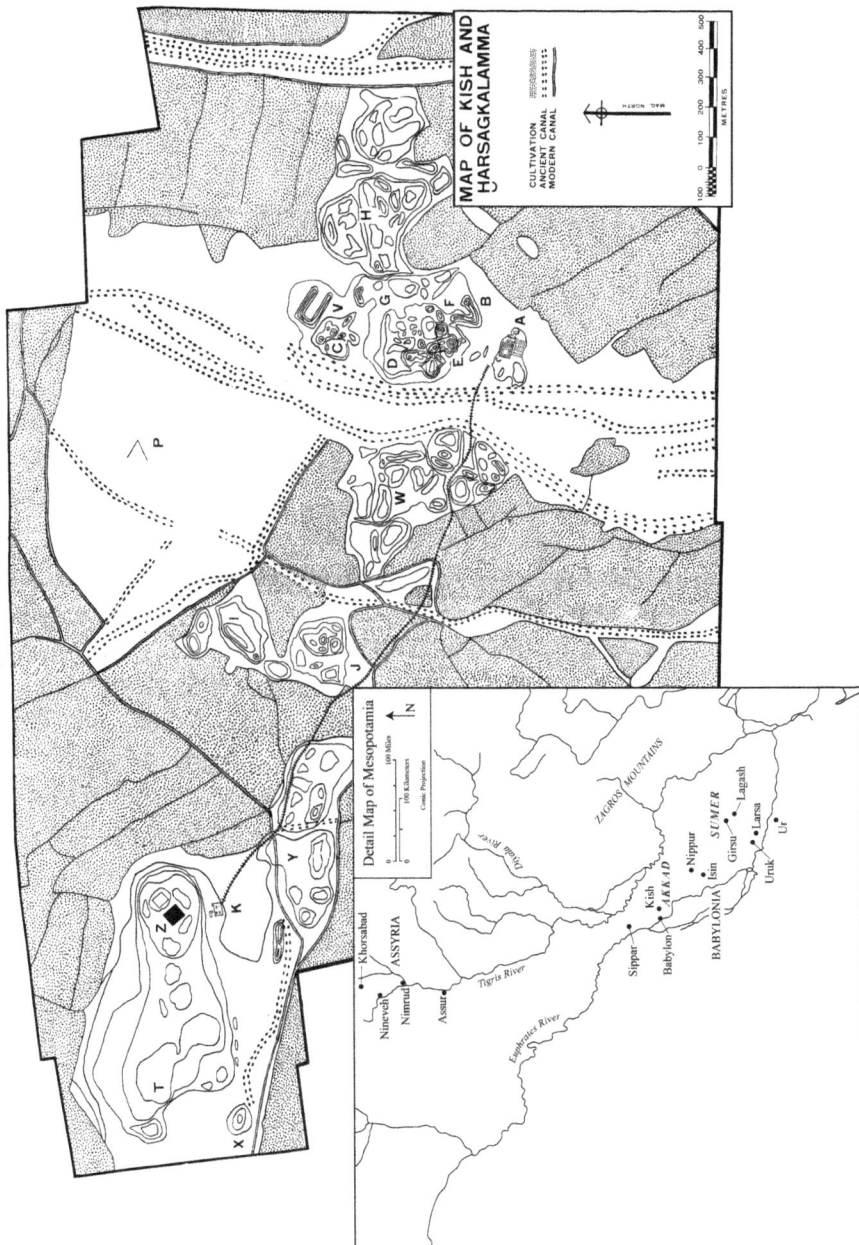

Figure 2.1. Map of Kish site; inset, map of Mesopotamia. Site map courtesy Field Museum; inset map courtesy Jill Seagard, Field Museum.

The Joint Oxford–Field Museum Expedition to Kish

In March 1923, Ernest Mackay, protégé of famed archaeologist Sir Flinders Petrie and later the excavator of Mohenjo-Daro, began the first season of excavations of the Joint Oxford–Field Museum Expedition to Kish. Excavations continued during the next ten years (1923–1933) under the absentee direction of Stephen Langdon (University of Oxford) and the field generalship of Mackay and (from 1926 on) Louis Charles Watelin. These enormous excavations employed hundreds of local men and boys who were overseen by just a handful of "Europeans." This labor force worked at a breakneck pace to remove soil to depths of 15 or more meters in trenches that measured tens of meters on a side. The excavators discovered massive ziggurats and palaces of the Early Dynastic period (2900–2334 BC), a substantial temple of the Neo-Babylonian period (1000–539 BC), and several clusters of burials dating from the Early Dynastic periods through the Achaemenid period (539–331 BC).

At the end of each season, following guidelines established in 1923, the retained objects were divided; the Iraq Museum received half of the artifacts and all one-of-a-kind pieces, and the two excavating institutions divided the remainder (Pestle et al. 2006). Oxford retained inscribed objects while the Field Museum received archaeological, skeletal, and scientific materials. Excavation records were similarly dispersed. While this was standard procedure for the time, note keeping for this project was subpar, as were many other elements of the excavation. Seton Lloyd (1969, 48) described Kish as "badly excavated . . . badly recorded, and the records . . . correspondingly badly published." The end result was a single coherent assemblage that was arbitrarily split into three with little record of the relationships among the scattered elements.

Past and Current Analyses of the Kish Skeletal Materials

A few American and British physical anthropologists and anatomists analyzed the Kish skeletal material at the time of its excavation, and a handful of studies have focused on portions of the remains in the decades since then (Buxton 1924; Buxton and Rice 1931; Carbonell 1958, 1960, 1966; Field 1932; Neiburger 2000; Neiburger et al. 1998; Penniman 1934; Rathbun 1975). Unfortunately, these previous attempts have been hamstrung by the poor quality of the excavation, a lack of good chronological control for the burials, and the division of the excavated materials among institutions. Together, these issues have effectively precluded a full consideration of the Kish skeletal material, an omission that we have sought to remedy through our recent reanalysis.

Rather than focusing on matters of race and type, the present work is rooted in the discipline of bioarchaeology. As formulated by Buikstra (1977) and employed by contemporary scholars, bioarchaeology encompasses more than simply description and data collection of human remains. It is a contextualized and problem-oriented approach that integrates physical anthropology directly with archaeology (Buikstra 1977; Buikstra and Beck 2006; Larsen 1997). A bioarchaeological study of the remains of children holds special promise for understanding the processes by which the social order of the city would have been reproduced.

The bioarchaeological analysis presented here is just one small part of a much larger reassessment of these materials known broadly as the Kish Project. The generally poor quality of the excavation and the early deaths of the directors resulted in only interim reports and small studies about the site. Since 2003, an international team of scholars has made substantial progress in reconciling the scattered records and collections of this expedition and has worked to produce a long-delayed site report for the Joint Oxford–Field Museum Expedition at Kish. The ongoing work of the Kish Project and the online database of excavated materials can be found at http://archive.fieldmuseum.org/kish/. A published site report is forthcoming that will provide a synthesis of the work done at the site in the 1920s and 1930s.

Materials and Methods

As part of the larger Kish Project, the authors undertook a complete bioarchaeological reanalysis of all the human skeletal remains from Kish. Skeletal remains from 757 individuals representing nearly every era of the site's occupation are now in the care of the Field Museum of Natural History in Chicago (n = 692) and the Natural History Museum in London (n = 65). This collection may be the largest sample of human remains from Mesopotamia currently available for study. Given the poor preservation of skeletal material from this area, the historical lack of quality physical anthropological/bioarchaeological studies on Mesopotamian remains, the ongoing political difficulties of the region, and, most notably, the importance of the site of Kish, the existence of such a large sample of remains is extremely exciting.

Reanalysis of the skeletal remains followed, in broad terms, the protocols in *Standards for Data Collection from Human Remains* (Buikstra and Ubelaker 1994) and other established methods for studying skeletal remains (e.g., Buzon et al. 2005). We collected a wide array of information, including demographic data, metric and nonmetric traits, and pathological information on all available individuals. As bioarchaeology relies heavily on historical and archaeological context, a principal task was reconstructing contextual data for any and all remains. Through examination of published sources, unpublished field notes, photographs, and correspondence, we amassed previously unavailable data on the temporal and spatial attributes of the burials and invaluable information on mortuary practices and grave furnishings.

The work at hand focuses on a small subset of the full corpus of remains from Kish: the comparatively well preserved remains of some 27 infants and young children. As was the case with all Kish remains, these were examined using established bioarchaeological protocols (e.g., Buikstra and Ubelaker 1994; Buzon et al. 2005). In the case of these 27 remains, age estimation was performed by measuring eleven skeletal elements (pars petrosa, pars basilaris, mandibular body, clavicle, humerus, distal humeral breadth, radius, ulna, femur, distal femoral breadth, and tibia) for the individuals in question and comparing those measurements with compiled metric data from infant/child skeletal populations of known age (Fazekas and Kósa 1978; Jeanty 1983; Scheuer, Musgrave, and Evans 1980). The age determinations made from individual elements and different reference populations were then reconciled and each individual was assigned to one of the following age categories: fetal (less than 37 fetal weeks), perinatal (38–42 fetal weeks), or a specific range of time after birth (six months to one year). No attempt was made to determine sex for these individuals because most scholars, with some notable exceptions (e.g., Schutkowski 1993; Weaver 1980), maintain that sexually discriminatory features are not present in the skeleton before puberty. All remains were also examined and scored for evidence of pathology (including linear enamel hypoplasia, cribra orbitalia, porotic hyperostosis, dental caries, and arthopathies) and trauma, following Larsen (1997).

The demographic data for these remains in concert with reconstructed temporal and cultural contexts has provided some intriguing insights into ancient mortuary practice and the meaning of infancy and childhood at Kish. This latter aspect of our study was greatly aided by the epigraphic and historical work of researchers who have reconstructed the rich vocabulary of terms that attest to and describe the various age-grades and stages of pregnancy, birth (both successful and not), and infancy in the societies of the ancient Near East (Harris 2000; Stol and Wiggermann 2000). For example, beyond simple classifications of individuals as young (*tur.meš*) and old (*gal.meš*) or adult (*guruš*) and child (*guruš.tur.tur*), epigraphic data attest to numerous emic subdivisions of infancy and early childhood, including fetus (*ša libbiša*), newborn (*ina mêšu*), baby (*šerru*), nursing baby (*tur.gaba* or *lakû*), and weaned child (*pirsu*), to say nothing of the special terms reserved for stillbirths or other adverse pregnancy outcomes (*kūbu* or *nigìn*) discussed below (Harris 2000, 6–10).

The 27 burials discussed here are from different periods of the site's occupation, and a portion cannot be assigned to a chronostratigraphic period. Because of this, one would not expect that the burials necessarily reflect homogeneous cultural or mortuary practices, and it is quite possible that the mortuary treatment of infants may reflect the social significance of certain period-specific age stages or may have been motivated by different beliefs at different times. However, several noteworthy cultural phenomena may be gleaned from subsets of these remains. In the following sections, we present bioarchaeological data on all of the infants from Kish before focusing our attention on a detailed analysis of a cluster of burials from the Neo-Babylonian period.

Results

The demographic profile of the 27 Kish infants, as judged by the metric indices of Fazekas and Kósa (1978), Jeanty (1983), and Scheuer and colleagues (1980), is presented in Table 2.1. Infants were classified as fetal, perinatal, 0–3 months, 3–6 months, and 6–12 months. While not identical, these age-grades closely parallel the emic age categories of fetus (*ša libbiša*), newborn (*ina mêšu*), and baby (*šerru*) or nursing baby (*tur.gaba* or *lakû*). No children over 12 months were included in this analysis. The most notable aspect of the distribution of age at death is the large number (n = 16) of the infants who were between 38 and 42 weeks postconception at death (Table 2.2). These are best understood as neonates/perinates: infants who died at or around full term or birth. We saw no skeletal evidence

Table 2.1. Context of infant burials at Kish

Catalog	Burial	Age	Mound	Trench	Period	Goods	Vessel
192351-B	Z303	Perinatal	Ingharra	Z-3	EDIII		No
192433-A	Y362	6 mos.–1 yr.	Ingharra	Y	EDI/EDIII	Pots, stone vessels, lamps, shells	No
192452		Perinatal				Fish vertebrae	
192464		Perinatal	Ingharra	Y			
192513	B398	Perinatal	Ingharra	B-3	UrIII/OB		Yes
192516	B401	Perinatal	Ingharra	B-3	NB		Yes
192521	B402	Perinatal	Ingharra	B-3	NB	Fish bones	Yes
192567	RR214	Perinatal	Ingharra	N/S Railway	UrIII/OB		No
192572	Z219	Fetal	Ingharra	Z-a	AKK		No
192585-B	Z258	6 mos.–1 yr.	Ingharra	Z-a	UrIII/OB		
192591	Z271	Perinatal	Ingharra	Z-2	EDIII		No
192593	Z270	6 mos.–1 yr.	Ingharra	Z-2	EDIII		
192594	Z275	6 mos.–1 yr.	Ingharra	Z-2	EDIII		
192612-A	Z317	ca. 3 mos.	Ingharra	Z-2	EDIII/AKK	Rich objects including ivory, beads, etc.	No
192615-B	Z334	6 mos.–1 yr.	Ingharra	Z-1	UrIII/OB		
192632	B403	Perinatal	Ingharra	B-3	NB		Yes
192633	B404	Perinatal	Ingharra	B-3	NB		Yes
192639	C504	Perinatal	Ingharra	C-4			No
192650	619	3–9 mos.					
192713		Perinatal	Ingharra	Y			
192726-A	Y636	3–6 mos.	Ingharra	Y		Stone bead	
192726-B	Y636	3–6 mos.	Ingharra	Y		Stone bead	
192727-B		Perinatal	Ingharra	Y			
192789-B		6 mos.–1 yr.	W		Achaemenid		
231793		Perinatal					Yes
236460		Perinatal			NB	Faunal tooth	Yes
FB1		Perinatal					

Table 2.2. Distribution of age at death for the infants of Kish

Age	Number of Individuals
Fetal (to 37 weeks)	1
Perinatal (38–42 wks)	16
0–3 Months	1
3–6 Months	3
6–12 Months	6

of trauma or other pathology in the infant remains. Given the likely high mortality rates at ancient Kish, this detail is not surprising.

It should be noted that the preservation of the neonatal/perinatal remains (those between 38 and 42 weeks of age) is remarkable. High soil salinity and frequent inundation contribute to the poor preservation of Mesopotamian skeletal collections in general and specifically at Kish. In contrast to the poor quality of representation and preservation in the juvenile and adult skeletons, many infant remains were remarkably complete and free of taphonomic alteration (figure 2.2).

Of the 22 infant remains that could be reconciled with some archaeological context based on archival data, 21 are from the Tell Ingharra/Hursagkalamma complex in the eastern section of Kish (areas marked D, E, and F in figure 2.1).[1] The majority were likely solitary intramural burials interred in domestic settings beneath house floors, as was the Mesopotamian norm for both adults and children (Baker 1998; Harris 2000, 15; Postgate 1980). Nevertheless, our data suggest that some of these children, specifically those who died at or around the time of birth, were

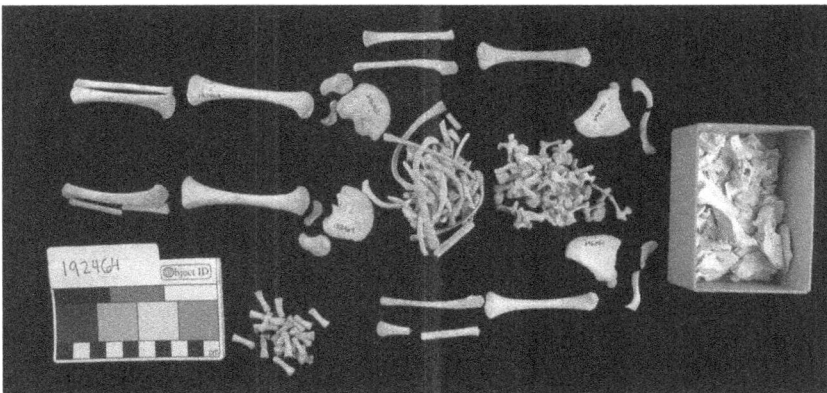

Figure 2.2. FM192464 showing remarkable completeness and preservation of infant skeleton. Photo by William J. Pestle.

Figure 2.3. Archival photograph of Neo-Babylonian infant burial in bowl. Image courtesy Field Museum, ID# CSA58505.

given specialized burial practices and may have been buried in dedicated precincts. Most significantly, excavators noted that five of the infants we present here, all perinatal, were found in a cluster of jar burials (Field 1946, 117–118) that have been dated by stratigraphy and artifacts to the Neo-Babylonian period (1000–539 BC).

It appears that as many as seven of the 27 children considered here were buried in vessels, ranging in type from Early Dynastic period bevel-rimmed bowls (possibly a museum pastiche) to vertical-sided jars of the Neo-Babylonian period (figure 2.3). Although not a universal practice, infant jar burials are common in Mesopotamia (Akkermans and Schwartz 2003; Baker 1998; Lloyd, Safar, and Braidwood 1945; Speiser 1937; Stein 2001, 273). At Kish, burial in quotidian vessels (jars or bowls) appears to be a form of specialized burial treatment reserved for children, although a few of the Neo-Babylonian or Achaemenid period adult burials from Mound W were found in large storage jars (Moorey 1978, 49–53). We feel that this practice, as opposed to the plain, earthen graves more commonly attested to at the site (Mackay 1925, 1929; Watelin and Langdon 1934), may have contributed to the quality of preservation of these otherwise fragile remains.

The majority of the Kish infant graves lacked material goods. Only seven of the 27 infants were buried with grave goods and, of these, only three were solitary burials (table 2.1). The three graves of solitary infants (FM192521, FM192452, and FM23646) included only faunal remains (canine teeth and fish vertebrae). Provisioning with food for the afterlife is common in Mesopotamian adult graves (Potts 1997, 223–224). Of the four remaining children interred with goods, two infants aged 3–6 months old who were buried together had a stone bead (FM192726-A and FM192726-B), and two others were in opulent graves of the Early Dynastic period (2900–2330BC) that also included adults (FM192433-A and FM192612-A). These graves contained ivory beads, bronze cosmetic containers, and stone vessels of nonlocal origin. However, it is possible that the adults were the intended recipients of this wealth. Four other infants (FM192351-B, FM192585-B, FM192727-B, and FM192789-B) were also buried with adults, but their graves contained no artifacts. The combined interment of adults and infants raises the provocative question of whether the children in vessels were part of the burial assemblage, or even grave goods, of the adults with whom they were buried. Nevertheless, at Kish the incorporation of infants into shared mortuary spaces with adults indicates a different form of societal assimilation than that of groups who spatially segregated the infants they buried. Spatial segregation also took place at Kish in other periods of occupation.

Thus, in the assemblage of infant remains recovered from Kish we find multiple temporally distinct mortuary treatments for infants, including burial in both domestic and public spaces; the provisioning of graves with food and rich artifacts; and the combined burial of adults and small children. In the following section we elaborate on one subset of these mortuary traditions, the clustered jar burials of the Neo-Babylonian period. We discuss the possible origins of this cluster and attempt to discern what it might tell us about the nature and meaning of infancy and childhood among the Neo-Babylonian period inhabitants of Kish.

Interpreting Infant Burial at Kish: The Neo-Babylonian Period

One of the more intriguing findings in the present study concerns the cluster of Neo-Babylonian period (1000–539 BC) perinate jar burials found in Trench B-3 on Ingharra (Figure 2.1, area E; Figure 2.3). Baker (1998) documents substantial variability in the Neo-Babylonian period treatment of the dead, including adult and child burials outside cemetery contexts and children in vessels, as we see at Kish. Nevertheless, the Neo-Babylonian period cluster at Kish is distinct from other contemporary adult and child burials at the site in its aggregation of similarly aged, similarly treated remains in close proximity to a functioning temple complex.

As the excavators noted, this cluster was comprised of at least five burials (burials B400–B404) found in the center of the trench at a depth of 7 meters above the plain level (Field 1946, 117–118). We were able to analyze the remains of four of these five individuals (FM192516, FM192521, FM192632, FM192633). There are no remains curated at the Field Museum or the Natural History Museum for the fifth individual. To this number we are tempted to add the remains of FM231793, a Neo-Babylonian period vessel that contains the remains of a perinate, and those from burial B398 (FM192513), a perinate who, despite being vertically separated by as much as two meters from the rest of the cluster, was in the same approximate horizontal area of the trench and seems to have received a similar mortuary treatment. Regardless of exact number, the cluster of jar burials appears to have been placed immediately adjacent to and at approximately the same depth as the footings of a large Neo-Babylonian period temple complex. While the excavations did not reveal a dedicatory brick or peg from the time of the temple's original construction (Watelin 1930, 13–14), an inscribed brick dating to a reconstruction undertaken by Merodachbaladan associates the temple with Ninlil, the local title for the mother goddess Ishtar.

ana $^{d.}$Nin-lil belti rabî-ti belti ṣir-ti ummi rim-ni-ti a-ši-bat é-kur na'itti (?) ša ki-rib Hur-sag-[kalam-ma . . .]

[For Nin-lil, great queen, farfamed queen, merciful mother, who sits in Ekur, the *revered*, who in Hursagkalamma . . .] (Langdon 1930, 17–18; emphasis in the original)

Insofar as the poor quality of the excavation allows, it appears that the burials and the temple were closely associated, intentionally so (Field 1930). The existence of this cluster in proximity to the temple raises obvious questions of causality and intent (how and why did these infants come to be buried alongside the temple's walls?) and broader questions about how this mortuary treatment might relate to Neo-Babylonian period understandings of birth and infancy.

There are (at least) three possible explanations for the nature and cause of the cluster. First, it could be the result of public child sacrifice, as Henry Field (1930, 1) proposed when he theorized that the remains were of female children who "may have been sacrificed to propitiate the gods in whose honor the buildings were erected." Second, the cluster could be the result of infanticide, after which other members of this society would have deposited the victims close to the temple for religious reasons. Finally, the cluster could be evidence of the existence of a precinct for children's graves on Ingharra, where the youngest members of society, having fallen victim to complications during birth or a natural death shortly thereafter, could be afforded protection by the temple and its deity or deities. While we believe the latter two explanations have more supporting evidence, we briefly examine all three possibilities. Regardless of which interpretation one takes, it is clear that this cluster is distinct from Neo-Babylonian period mortuary practices seen elsewhere at the site and in the region more broadly (Baker 1998; Moorey 1978).

Although child sacrifice is related to the practice of infanticide, it differs in that it is typically performed in public with religious motivations and carries different social meanings than "domestic" infanticide (Scott 2001, 12). While this is attested to in religious and historical texts for some Semitic-speaking people of the Near East in the first millennium BC (Rundin 2004), we are not aware of any archaeological, epigraphic, or historical documentation of this practice by Babylonian period peoples of the mid-first millennium BC. Therefore it would seem that the hypothesis that this collection provides evidence of child sacrifice could be rejected out of hand.[2]

Infanticide, the intentional killing of undesired or supernumerary children at birth, is a more likely explanation for the Neo-Babylonian period cluster of jar burials than child sacrifice. Infanticide is attested to in anthropological and historical literature in societies the world over and in ancient Mesopotamia and is understood principally as a means of controlling family size or sexual composition (Langer 1974; Lewis 2007; Williamson 1978). Mesopotamian lexical idioms for exposed children and foundlings are well known. They include he/she "who was found in a well," "who was taken in from the street," and "who was snatched from the dog's mouth" (Harris 2000, 15). The appropriateness of infanticide is mediated by culture; in some cultures, as is the case in prehistoric England, the status of "personhood" (and thus protection against the termination of life) was not granted for some time after birth (Mays 2000). Also, as Harris (2000, 15) argues, the practice of infanticide in ancient Mesopotamia, as in many societies, existed side by side with solicitous care of children and was often a last resort for ill or deformed children or in cases of extreme poverty. This provides a framework for considering changing roles over an individual's life course. Mays (2000) has posited that in the archaeological record, infanticide might explain a suite of observed phenomena, including 1) clusters of infant burials outside traditional local cemetery settings; 2) infant burials below the foundations of important structures; 3) imbalanced sex ratios among infant skeletal remains; and 4) demographic profiles that show a spike of deaths within the perinatal age range.

Quite often, however, a definitive determination of infanticide in a particular archaeological context is difficult to reach because of confounding factors. First, detailed contextual data is required to demonstrate clustering or special depositional patterns, and this information is often lacking from early archaeological investigations. Second, sex assessment in infant remains is most reliably performed through aDNA analysis, which is destructive and costly (e.g., Faerman et al. 1998; Mays and Faerman 2001). Third, some authors have taken issue with the accuracy and biases of the methods used to reconstruct age among perinatal skeletons (Lewis 2007, 94). Finally, even if a strong demographic anomaly is detected, it can be quite difficult, particularly in the case of preindustrial societies, to differentiate between intentional infanticide and the increase in mortality resulting from natural deaths at birth, which is a particularly dangerous and tenuous event in a child's life (ibid., 81–84).

Based on several of the criteria outlined in Mays (2000), the Neo-Babylonian period cluster of perinate jar burials could be considered to have resulted from a practice of selective infanticide. Specifically, we note that the clustered internments (Mays's first criterion) were buried largely apart from contemporary adult burials,[3] positioned against the walls of a Neo-Babylonian period temple (Mays's second criterion) and consisted of individuals who were all perinatal (Mays's fourth criterion). These are in line with expectations for infanticide. Unlike Henry Field (1930, 1), we are unable to determine infant sex, evidence that might further strengthen an argument for selective infanticide (Mays's third criterion). The existence of an all-female cluster would coincide with arguments that the practice of infanticide/infant exposure in ancient Mesopotamia, which is known from epigraphic evidence to have been widespread if not frequent (Harris 2000, 15; Stol and Wiggermann 2000, 214), was more common for female children (Nemet-Nejat 1998, 130).

The final possible explanation for the Neo-Babylonian period cluster is that these infants may have died of natural causes at or around the time of birth and were subsequently buried close to the temple because of their liminal status at death and because of the association of their life stage at death with the temple's deities. From writings of the Neo-Babylonian period, we know of the special social and religious significance of a child who was miscarried, was stillborn, or died during delivery (variously termed a *kūbu* or *nigìn*) (Harris 2000, 9; Stol and Wiggermann 2000, 29–31). The *kūbu* in particular was a semi-supernatural being associated with chthonic deities that had special shrines in temples and were capable of both benevolent and malevolent interaction with the living (Harris 2000, 9; Stol and Wiggermann 2000, 29–31). Similarly, *nigìn* (probably a term for the miscarried fetus) had special chapels or chambers in temples of Inanna/Ishtar[4] (*nigìngar*) (Stol and Wiggermann 2000, 29). Jacobsen (1987, 475n1) interprets *nigìngar* as "a temple which served as a cemetery for stillborn or premature babies and as a depository for stillbirths."

The association of the *nigìngar* cemeteries with temples of the goddess Inanna/Ishtar is of particular relevance here. On the basis of epigraphic data, some of which is discussed above, Langdon identified the larger half of the temple on Ingharra with Ninlil or Ishtar of Hursagkalamma (Langdon 1930, 18). While the attributes and qualities of Inanna-Ishtar are complex and multifaceted and scholars question the notion that she served as an archetypal "mother goddess," she nonetheless had many powerful associations with love, fertility, sex, birth, and child rearing (Harris 1991; Stol and Wiggermann 2000, 29). It is against the walls of her temple that the perinate cluster we focus on was buried. Given this association, it seems to us that the cluster of perinate jar burials was the result of natural deaths around the time of birth and subsequent burial in a sacred precinct reserved for children who had met such a fate (for an interesting parallel, see Gregoricka and Sheridan, this volume). If, as we suggest, these infant burials were intentionally placed in association with the temple, this could help answer Roger Moorey's concern (1978, 92) that a functioning Neo-Babylonian period temple would not be a likely place for a concentration of burials.

Moving beyond child sacrifice and other sensationalist explanations for the Neo-Babylonian period infant burial cluster, approaching these remains through a contextualized bioarchaeology has allowed us to identify this cluster as anomalous in terms of age structure, mortuary treatment, and burial location and to carefully explore potential causes for its existence. It is particularly noteworthy that this type of analysis is possible only when the data from the body can be integrated with information about burial location and the mortuary context more broadly as well as with archaeological information.

Conclusion

As previously mentioned, it is likely that the information we have concerning the mortuary treatment of infants at Kish is an amalgam of Mesopotamian practices representing the range of periods the burials occupy as well as the changing role of children in this society. Nonetheless, bioarchaeological analysis of the infant remains from Kish has revealed clear social significance attached to infant death for the Neo-Babylonian period population and provides glimpses into the lived experience of adults and children at Kish. Our analysis gives a sense of differential treatment over the life course. This is manifest not only in the spectacular Neo-Babylonian period case presented here but also in the practice of burial in vessels and the manner in which children accompany adults in the mortuary context.

The varied mortuary patterns in the assemblage of infant remains from Kish show conflicting indications of the meaning and position of infants in Mesopotamian society. On the one hand, distinct practices such as jar burial and burial in dedicated spaces such as near temples may speak to the dissociation of infants from the general rules and order of society writ large. Infants may not have been full people and thus did not receive the treatment that a full person might merit. Other practices, including intramural burials and the provisioning of food for the afterlife, speak to a greater degree of sociocultural integration, as both of these treatments follow the mortuary practices typical of adults in Mesopotamian societies. That some children were afforded rich grave goods typically associated with high-status individuals suggests that children were incorporated into adult systems of class and power. However, the burial of small children with adults can also be read as indicating equivalency between age-grades or perhaps as the objectification of children as material with which to furnish the grave of an adult. In general, then, this mortuary data provides a somewhat muddled picture of the meaning of infancy in Mesopotamian societies. In large part, this may be the result of different patterns in different periods that, when combined, make for a noisy picture.

If, as we suggest, the Neo-Babylonian period cluster is made up of perinates who died naturally and were buried against a temple wall for protection, we can use this information to explore the meaning of childhood during this period at Kish. First, the fact that the mortuary treatment of jar burial at the temple foundation appears to have been restricted to perinatal deaths strengthens the case for the existence of a restricted emic age-grade reserved for newly born children in Neo-Babylonian period society (similar, perhaps, to the modern Western grade of newborn as opposed to a more general category of baby). Second, since this special canon of mortuary practices (in terms of both method and placement of burial) appears to have been reserved for children who had met such a fate (at least in the evidence in our sample), we can infer that such events were frequent enough to require a special set of practices. Third, that children who died at the doorstep of life required divine protection or supervision (depending on whether the spirits of these children were seen as malevolent or benevolent) can be interpreted as evidence of a realization that while such children were physically weak, they had spirits powerful enough to affect the health and well-being of individuals or whole communities (Stol and Wiggermann 2000, 31). Can this, then, be seen as evidence, albeit evidence cloaked in ritual terms, of a realization of the adult potential even in a small child? If so, this would seem to contradict suggestions that the lives (and deaths) of infants had little or no impact on their society (Harris 2000, 15).

As this small bioarchaeological analysis suggests, by marrying disparate lines of evidence the broader Kish osteological project will attempt to make a lasting summary statement about diachronic changes in demography, identity, status, health, disease, and mortuary practice in this early Mesopotamian city. Human skeletal remains, long neglected as a research focus in Mesopotamian archaeology, have the potential to contribute to discussions of the pressing questions of scholars working in the region.

Hopefully, this brief treatment of the infant burials at Kish helps illustrate this promise.

Acknowledgments

This project was generously supported by NEH Grant PI-500014-04, The Field Museum of Natural History, Colorado College, and the Associated Colleges of the Midwest. Our thanks go to Megan Perry for her work on this volume and the original invitation to participate in her symposium at the annual meeting of the American Schools of Oriental Research. We would also like to extend our sincere gratitude to Nina Cummings, Blair Daverman, Jill Seagard, and Karen Wilson for their help during the research and writing of this chapter and to Ted Rathbun for his pioneering work with the collection.

Notes

1. The sole outlier was excavated from Mound W, an individual aged between 6 and 12 months (FM192789-B) dating to the Neo-Babylonian or Achaemenid periods.

2. That the specter of child sacrifice would be raised by a member of the Kish Expedition should come as no surprise: this was, after all, the same project that purported to have found de facto remnants of the biblical flood and never failed to shy away from the sensational in a quest for greater media coverage.

3. Only four other burials were noted from the entirety of the B-3 trench, which was several hundred cubic meters in volume, and even these were fairly distant, as far as can be determined from the excavation records.

4. Ninlil is the local name for Ishtar (Akkadian) or Innana (Sumerian) (Langdon 1930, 18).

References Cited

Akkermans, P. M. M. G., and G. M. Schwartz
2003   *The Archaeology of Syria.* Cambridge University Press, New York.
Baker, H.
1998   Neo-Babylonian Burials Revisited. In *The Archaeology of Death in the Ancient Near East,* edited by S. Campbell and A. Green, pp. 209–220. Oxbow Monograph in Archaeology no. 51. Oxbow, Oxford.
Baxter, J. E. (editor)
2005   *Children in Action: Perspectives on the Archaeology of Childhood.* Archaeological Papers of the American Anthropological Association no. 15. University of

California Press for the American Anthropological Association, Berkeley, Calif.

Borič, D., and S. Stefanovič
2004   Birth and Death: Infant Burials from Vlasac and Lepenski Vir. *Antiquity* 78(301):526–546.

Buikstra, J. E.
1977   Biocultural Dimensions of Archaeological Study. In *Biocultural Adaptation in Prehistoric America,* edited by R. Blakely, pp. 67–84. University of Georgia Press, Athens.

Buikstra, J. E., and L. A. Beck (editors)
2006   *Bioarchaeology: The Contextual Analysis of Human Remains.* Elsevier, New York.

Buikstra, J. E., and D. H. Ubelaker
1994   *Standards for Data Collection from Human Skeletal Remains.* Arkansas Archeological Survey, Fayetteville, Ark.

Buxton, L. H. D.
1924   On the Human Remains Excavated at Kish. In *Excavations at Kish,* edited by S. Langdon. Vol. 1. Paul Geuthner, Paris.

Buxton, L. H. D., and D. T. Rice
1931   Report on the Human Remains Found at Kish. *Journal of the Royal Anthropological Institute of Great Britain and Ireland* 61:57–119.

Buzon, M. R., J. T. Eng, P. M. Lambert, and P. L. Walker
2005   Bioarchaeological Methods. In *Handbook of Archaeological Methods,* edited by M. H. and C. Chippendale, pp. 871–918. Altamira Press, Lanham, Md.

Carbonell, V. M.
1958   The Dentition of the Kish Population, 3000 B.C. Unpublished MA thesis, University of Chicago.
1960   The Tubercle of Carabelli in the Kish Dentition, Mesopotamia, 3000 B.C. *Journal of Dental Research* 39(1):124–128.
1966   The Paleodental Pathology of Ancient Mesopotamians. *Journal of Dental Research* 45:413.

Charvát, P.
2001   *Mesopotamia Before History.* Routledge, New York.

Faerman, M., G. K. Bar-Gal, D. Filon, C. L. Greenblatt, L. Stager, A. Oppenheim, and P. Smith
1998   Determining the Sex of Infanticide Victims from the Late Roman Era through Ancient DNA Analysis. *Journal of Archaeological Science* 25(9):861–865.

Fazekas, I. G., and F. Kósa
1978   *Forensic Fetal Osteology.* Akadémiai Kiadó, Budapest.

Field, H.
1930   Child Sacrifice at Kish. *Field Museum News* 10:1.
1932   Human Remains from Jemdet Nasr, Mesopotamia. *Journal of the Royal Asiatic Society of Great Britain and Ireland* 1:967–970.

1946   Human Remains from Kish, Iraq. Document on file at the Field Museum of Natural History, Chicago.

Finlay, N.

2000   Outside of Life: Traditions of Infant Burial in Ireland from Cillin to Cist. *World Archaeology* 31:407–422.

Gibson, M.

1972a   *The City and Area of Kish*. Field Research Projects, Coconut Grove, Fla.

1972b   The Archaeological Uses of Cuneiform Documents: Patterns of Occupation at the City of Kish. *Iraq* 34(2):113–123.

Harris, R.

1991   Inanna-Ishtar as Paradox and a Coincidence of Opposites. *History of Religions* 30(3):261–278.

2000   *Gender and Aging in Mesopotamia: The Gilgamesh Epic and Other Ancient Literature*. University of Oklahoma Press, Norman.

Jacobsen, T.

1987   *The Harps That Once . . . Sumerian Poetry in Translation*. Yale University Press, New Haven, Conn.

Jeanty, P.

1983   Fetal Limb Biometry. *Radiology* 147(2):601–602.

Kamp, K. A.

2001   Where Have All the Children Gone? The Archaeology of Childhood. *Journal of Archaeological Method and Theory* 8(1):1–34.

Langdon, S.

1930   Inscribed Brick of Merodachbaladan. In *Excavations at Kish,* edited by L. C. Watelin and S. Langdon, pp. 17–20. Vol. 3. Paul Geuthner, Paris.

Langer, W. L.

1974   Infanticide: A Historical Survey. *History of Childhood Quarterly* 1:353–367.

Larsen, C. S.

1997   *Bioarchaeology: Interpreting Behavior from the Human Skeleton*. Cambridge University Press, Cambridge.

Lewis, M. E.

2007   *The Bioarchaeology of Children: Perspectives from Biological and Forensic Anthropology*. Cambridge Studies in Biological and Evolutionary Anthropology. Cambridge University Press, Cambridge.

Lloyd, S.

1969   Back to Ingharra: Some Further Thoughts on the Excavations at East Kish. *Iraq* 31(1):40–48.

Lloyd, S., F. Safar, and R. J. Braidwood

1945   Tell Hassuna Excavations by the Iraqi Government Directorate General of Antiquities in 1943 and 1944. *Journal of Near Eastern Studies* 4(4):255–289.

Mackay, E.

1925   *Report on the Excavation of the "A" Cemetery at Kish, Mesopotamia*. Field Museum of Natural History Anthropology Memoirs 1(1). Field Museum of Natural History, Chicago.

1929   *A Sumerian Palace and the "A" Cemetery at Kish, Mesopotamia*. Field Museum of Natural History Anthropology Memoirs 1(2). Field Museum of Natural History, Chicago.

Maisels, C. K.

1993   *The Emergence of Civilization: From Hunting and Gathering to Agriculture, Cities, and the State in the Near East*. Routledge, London.

Mays, S.

2000   The Archaeology and History of Infanticide, and Its Occurrence in Earlier British Populations. In *Children and Material Culture*, edited by J. S. Derevenski, pp. 180–190. Routledge, Florence.

Mays, S., and M. Faerman

2001   Sex Identification in Some Putative Infanticide Victims from Roman Britain Using Ancient DNA. *Journal of Archaeological Science* 28(5):555–559.

Moorey, P. R. S.

1978   *Kish Excavations, 1923–1933: With a Microfiche Catalogue of the Objects in Oxford Excavated by the Oxford-Field Museum, Chicago, Expedition to Kish in Iraq, 1923–1933*. Clarendon Press, Oxford.

Neiburger, E. J.

2000   Dentistry in Ancient Mesopotamia. *Journal of the Massachusetts Dental Society* 49(2):16–19.

Neiburger, E. J., M. Cohen, J. Lieberman, and M. Lieberman

1998   The Dentition of Abraham's People. Why Abraham Left Mesopotamia. *The New York State Dental Journal* 64(9):25–29.

Nemet-Nejat, K. R.

1998   *Daily Life in Ancient Mesopotamia*. Greenwood, Westport, Conn.

Penniman, T. K.

1934   A Note on the Inhabitants of Kish before the Great Flood. In *Excavations at Kish*, edited by L. C. Watelin. Vol. 4. Paul Geuthner, Paris.

Perry, M. A.

2005   Redefining Childhood through Bioarchaeology: Towards an Archaeological and Biological Understanding of Children in Antiquity. In *Children in Action: Perspectives on the Archaeology of Childhood*, edited by J. E. Baxter, pp. 89–111. Vol. 15. Archaeological Papers of the American Anthropological Association, Washington, D.C.

Pestle, W. J., K. Wilson, S. Nash, and S. Coleman

2006   Reconciling the Past: A Catalogue of Scattered Collections. In *Archäologie und Computer, Kulturelles Erbe und Neue Technologien (Cultural Heritage and New Technologies)*, pp. 1–11. Stadtarchäologie Wien, Vienna.

Pollock, S.

1999   *Ancient Mesopotamia*. Cambridge University Press, New York.

Postgate, J. N.

1980   Excavations at Abu Salabikh, 1978–79. *Iraq* 42(2):87–104.

Potts, D.
1997   *Mesopotamian Civilization: The Material Foundations.* Cornell University
         Press, Ithaca, N.Y.
Rathbun, T.
1975   *A Study of the Physical Characteristics of the Ancient Inhabitants of Kish, Iraq.*
         Field Research Projects, Coconut Grove, Fla.
Robb, J.
2007   Burial Treatment as Transformation of Bodily Ideology. In *Performing Death:
         Social Analyses of Funerary Traditions in the Ancient Near East and Mediterra-
         nean,* edited by N. Laneri, pp. 287–297. The Oriental Institute of the University
         of Chicago, Chicago.
Rundin, J. S.
2004   Pozo Moro, Child Sacrifice, and the Greek Legendary Tradition. *Journal of
         Biblical Literature* 123(3):425–447.
Scheuer, J. L., J. H. Musgrave, and S. P. Evans
1980   The Estimation of Late Fetal and Perinatal Age from Limb Bone Length by
         Linear and Logarithmic Regression. *Annals of Human Biology* 7(3):257–265.
Schutkowski, H.
1993   Sex Determination of Infant and Juvenile Skeletons: I. Morphognostic Fea-
         tures. *American Journal of Physical Anthropology* 90:199–205.
Scott, E.
2001   Killing the Female? Archaeological Narratives of Infanticide. In *Gender and
         the Archaeology of Death,* edited by B. Arnold and N. L. Wicker, pp. 3–22.
         Altamira, Walnut Creek, Calif.
Sofaer Derevenski, J. (editor)
2000   *Children and Material Culture.* Routledge, London.
Speiser, E. A.
1937   Three Reports on the Joint Assyrian Expedition. *Bulletin of the American
         Schools of Oriental Research* 66:1–19.
Stein, G. J.
2001   Indigenous Social Complexity at Hacinebi (Turkey) and the Organization of
         Uruk Colonial Contact. In *Uruk Mesopotamia and Its Neighbors: Cross Cul-
         tural Interactions in the Era of State Formation,* edited by M. S. Rothman, pp.
         265–306. School of American Research, Santa Fe, N.M.
Stol, M., and F. A. M. Wiggermann
2000   *Birth in Babylonia and the Bible: Its Mediterranean Setting.* Brill, Groningen.
Walker, P. L., J. Johnson, and P. M. Lambert
1988   Age and Sex Biases in the Preservation of Human Skeletal Remains. *American
         Journal of Physical Anthropology* 76:183–188.
Watelin, L. C.
1930   The Great Temple of Kish (Hursagkalamma). In *Excavations at Kish,* edited by
         L. C. Watelin and S. Langdon, pp. 1–15. Vol. 3. Paul Geuthner, Paris.
Watelin, L. C., and S. Langdon
1934   *Excavations at Kish IV.* Paul Geuthner, Paris.

Weaver, D.

1980   Sex Differences in the Ilia of a Known Sex and Age Sample of Fetal and Infant
        Skeletons. *American Journal of Physical Anthropology* 52:191–195.

Wileman, J.

2005   *Hide and Seek: The Archaeology of Childhood*. Tempus Publishing, Gloucester-
        shire.

Williamson, L.

1978   Infanticide: An Anthropological Analysis. In *Infanticide and the Value of Life*,
        edited by M. Kohl, pp. 61–75. Prometheus, Buffalo, N.Y.

3

The Burial Customs
of Early Christian Cyprus

A Bioarchaeological Approach

SHERRY C. FOX, IOANNA MOUTAFI, ELENI ANNA PREVEDOROU,
AND DESPO PILIDES

The purpose of this paper is to dispel some common misconceptions about the burial customs of the Early Christian period in Cyprus through the use of bioarchaeological analysis. Such beliefs would include that all burials from this period have a west-east orientation, that there are no apse burials in churches, and that infants are not buried within the church. Additionally, although there is general uniformity in burials, there are subtle differences too. There is evidence of secondary burial and individuals are buried singly or multiply in simple pits, cist graves, tile graves, a broken pithos, tombs, sarcophagi, and a disused kiln and there is a mass burial in a cistern. Although grave goods are minimal, iron nails occasionally found in burial contexts attest to the presence of wooden coffins. Bodies are buried in a supine position and with arms folded across the pelvis, abdomen or possibly the chest. These results are based upon the analyses of the human skeletal remains at four ecclesiastical sites from five rural churches/basilicas near the south coast (Alassa-Ayia Mavri, Kalavasos-Kopetra, and Maroni-Petrera), and one urban and inland church with multiple phases (the Hill of Agios Georgios in Nicosia). The combined sample from the south coast is 53 individuals whereas the Early Christian phase of the inland sample contains 27 individuals for a total sample of 80 individuals. At least one of the sites is thought to have been a monastery. Cyprus enjoyed prosperity in the sixth and seventh centuries AD, as demonstrated by dense populations, but settlement patterns changed following the Arab incursions during the mid-seventh century.

The study of burial customs has long played a role in the better understanding of the social, ideological, and life conditions of ancient societies. Approaches to this study have been greatly enriched over the last few decades by the advances of both processual and postprocessual archaeology. Current research in mortuary analyses has demonstrated the significance of thoroughly grasping the specific practices of different burial customs, as the best approach to the complicated meanings that are embedded therein, and the complex relationships between these practices, social structure and human agency (e.g., Parker Pearson 1999). In this framework, the specific characteristics of burials (i.e. type, depth, orientation of the grave, body arrangement of the deceased, number of interments, number and types of grave goods, indications of secondary activities, etc.) need to be explored contextually in order to understand people's choices in mortuary behavior. Despite the general acceptance of such approaches within prehistoric archaeology, this is not often the case in the study of funerary practices from historic periods. Perhaps an overdependence upon written sources as the only adequate evidence for "truth" still results in neglect for broader, multidisciplinary approaches as Morris (1987) has emphasized. As Green (1977, 46) stated over thirty years ago, "Few if any Christian cemeteries have been studied as entities, as major sources for the study of both the early Church and the population of the Roman Empire."

Bioarchaeology is a key component in the contextual analysis of burial customs. The integration of material and skeletal evidence, viewed within their theoretical and historical context, can offer a more holistic picture of burial practices (see seminal works, e.g., Larsen 1997; Buikstra and Beck 2006; and Gowland and Knüsel 2006). Particularly in the Mediterranean, the divide remains wide between scientific research and the archaeology of historic periods. Nevertheless, important bioarchaeological studies have been conducted recently for Byzantine Greece, significantly enhancing our understanding of Christian burial customs (e.g., Bourbou 2004; Tritsaroli 2006). In Cyprus, the first osteological analyses of Early Christian remains have already appeared, although they have been usually relegated to appendices of site reports (Fox 1996; Fox 2003; and Fox 2002). These studies, along with Baker and Papalexandrou (this volume) are allowing a broader understanding of life and death conditions of society and burial habits of the period. The present paper is an initial effort to bridge this gap and aims to reveal the potential of contextual bioarchaeological analyses of Early Christian burial customs in Cyprus. The result is that some common misconceptions about the burial customs from this period—such as all burials are positioned in a west-east orientation; that there are no burials within church apses; and that burials of infants are not allowed within the church—can be dispelled. Although there is general conformity to a burial pattern subtle differences exist as well. Furthermore, secondary burial was practiced as were single and multiple interment burials within a variety of final resting places—including pits, cist graves, tile graves, tombs, sarcophagi, a disused kiln, and there is even a mass burial in a cistern.

There is abundant ceramic evidence representing this time period from around Cyprus, and the excavations of a number of churches have been published (see below), yet relatively little has been published about either domestic architecture or the cemeteries from the Early Christian period. In essence, where people lived and where they were buried has been given little attention. "The Christians, in death as in life, were exclusive, setting aside special plots for their use, and dictating the use of particular burial rites" (Green 1977, 46). A number of basilicas have been excavated on the island, such as at Ayios Philon (du Plat-Taylor 1980; du Plat-Taylor and Megaw 1981), Salamis (Megaw 1974), Kourion (Megaw 2007), and Peyia (under the direction of A. Papageorghiou). Additionally, those with associated human skeletal remains that have been studied include Alassa-Ayia Mavri (Flourentzos 1996; Fox 1996), Kalavasos-Kopetra (Rautman 2003; Fox 2003), Maroni-Petrera (Manning 2002; Fox 2002) and the Hill of Agios Georgios in Nicosia excavated by D. Pilides. There is a current excavation of a basilica of the same period at Geroskipou-Ayioi Pente directed by D. Michaelides with associated human remains as well along with another recent excavation of a basilica in the Paphos District (see Baker and Papalexandrou, this volume). The Early Christian period is also known in Cyprus as the Late Roman period, and in Greece, it is more commonly referred to as the Early Byzantine period. For the purposes of this article, the term Early Christian period will denote the fifth to mid-seventh centuries AD, given that the burials and their associated human remains under study are from church or basilica contexts.

Materials and Methods

In this study, bioarchaeological data have been collected from four sites with associated human skeletal remains. Three basilica or church sites are located within sight of the island's south coast: Alassa-Ayia Mavri (AAM) is approximately 12 km inland, Kalavasos-Kopetra (KK) is about 3 km inland, and Maroni-Petrera (MP) is located approximately only 2 km inland. In Nicosia, the Hill of Agios Georgios (HAG) is the sole site under study that is truly an inland site. Although the last site is situated only about 18 km from the north coast, the Kyrenia mountain range separates it from the coast. All of the sites under study are positioned on rises and adjacent to rivers. Two of the sites are located within the current Larnaka District, including KK and MP. KK is located to the east of the Vasilikos River. MP is located to the east of the Ayios Minas River, and AAM is located at the confluence of the Kouris and Potamos tou Limnati Rivers in the Limassol District. One of the sites, KK, is thought to have been a monastic complex and actually supported three basilicas. The HAG is situated east of the Pedieos River in the Nicosia District. The site may have housed a monastery at a later date. Aside from the seat of local ritual authority, and civic pride and power, the Early Christian basilica represented the local identity and ideology to those in the vicinity as well (Manning 2002).

Demographic data for the south coast sites, including the minimum number of individuals, the estimation of age at death, and the determination of biological sex, has been collected using accepted morphological methods (Bass 1971; Stewart 1979; and Krogman 1962) and following the guidelines espoused by the Paleopathology Association (Rose et al. 1991). Application of the *Standards for Data Collection from Human Skeletal Remains* has been employed for the human skeletal remains from the HAG (Buikstra and Ubelaker 1994). Table 3.1 provides a summary of results. A minimum number of 21 individuals was recovered from KK, 6 from MP and 27 from AAM, while the minimum number from the HAG was 37 individuals. Both males and females were represented among the remains from each site and the ages at death range from late fetal to old age.

In addition to the minimum number of individuals and their ages and sexes, this paper will examine each site in greater detail and will provide evidence for the archaeology of the people of Early Christian Cyprus including grave locations, body orientations, types of graves, and any associated artifacts. Cremation burial was not practiced on the island at this

Table 3.1. Description and demography of tombs at Early Christian sites in Cyprus

Site	Tomb	Tomb Type	Tomb Location	Tomb Position	Orientation	N	Sex	Age	Position of Hands
Kalavasos-Kopetra	KK1	Gypsum tomb	Crypt	Above ground	N-S	4	4 Males	4 adults	?
	KK2	Gypsum tomb	Crypt	Above ground	W-E	3	2 Males	2 adults; juvenile	Pelvis
	KK3	Gypsum tomb	Aisle	Above ground	W-E	2	2 Males	2 old adults	Pelvis
	KK4	Cist	narthex	Below ground	N-S	1	Male	old adult	?
	KKSarc.	Sarcophagus	Apse?	Above ground (?)	?	2	2 Males	2 adults	Pelvis
	KKCist.	Cistern	Cistern	Below ground (?)	?	9	Male	2 adults; 7 juveniles	?
Maroni-Petrera	MP1	Gypsum Cist	Apse	Below ground	W-E	1	?	Young adult	?
	MP2/3	Gypsum Cist	Aisle	Below ground	W-E	5	?	5 infants	?
Alassa-Ayia Mavri	AAM1	Cist	North	Below ground	?	2	?	Infant; adolescent (17.5 yrs.)	?
	AAM2	Cist	North	Below ground	?	1	Female	Young adult (20–24 yrs.)	?
	AAM3	Cist	North	Below ground	?	1	?	Infant (0–6 mos.)	?
	AAM4	Cist	N ossarium	Below ground	?	3	?	2 infants; young adult	?
	AAM5	Cist	NE	Below ground	W-E	1	?	Child (7–9 yrs.)	?
	AAM6	Cist	N ossarium	Below ground	?	1	Female	Young adult (23–28 yrs.)	?
	AAM7	Cist	?	Below ground	?	1	?	Neonate	?
	AAM8	Pithos	East	Below ground	W-E	1	?	Neonate	?
	AAM9	Cist	East	Below ground	W-E	1	?	Child (6–7 yrs.)	?
	AAM10	Cist	East	Below ground	W-E	2	?	Fetus; infant	?
	AAM11	Cist	N ossarium	Below ground	?	1	?	Adult?	?
	AAM12	Cist	NE	Below ground	W-E	2	?	Infant; child (2–3 yrs.)	?
	AAM15	Cist	?	Below ground	?	1	Male?	Young adult	?
	AAM16	Tomb	N ossarium	Below ground	W-E	1	Female?	Adult (24–32 yrs.)	?
	AAM17	Cist	NE	Below ground	W-E	1	Male	Adult (24–32 yrs.)	?
	AAM18	Cist	NE	Below ground	W-E	2	Female;	?*	?

AAM20	Cist	East	Below ground	W-E	3	Female	Child; Adolescent; Adult	?
Hill of Agios Georgios								
HAG14	Pit	East	Below ground	W-E	1	?	Young adult (20–25 yrs.)	?
HAG21	Pit	East	Below ground	W-E	1	?	Adult	?
HAG23	Pit	East	Below ground	W-E	1	Female	Adult (25–35 yrs.)	?
HAG74	Pit	North	Below ground	W-E	1	Female	Adult (25–35 yrs.)	Chest
HAG90	Pit	East	Below ground	W-E	1	Male	Adult (35–45 yrs.)	Pelvis
HAG100	Pit	East	Below ground	W-E	1	?	Infant (3–6 mos.)	?
HAG120	Pit	East	Below ground	W-E	1	?	Adult	?
HAG124	Pit	East	Below ground	W-E	2	Male; Female	?*	?
HAG126	Pit	East	Below ground	W-E	1	?	Adult	?
HAG127	Pit	South	Below ground	W-E	1	Female?	Adult	?
HAG128	Built	South	Below ground	W-E	1	Male	Old adult (50+ yrs.)	pelvis
HAG130	Pit	East	Below ground	W-E	1	?	Middle adult (~45 yrs.)	?
HAG131	Pit	East	Below ground	W-E	2	Female; Male	Old adult (50+ yrs.); adult	?
HAG133	Kiln	East	Below ground	W-E	1	Female?	Adult	Chest
HAG137	Gypsum Cist	South	Below ground	W-E	1	Male?	Middle adult (45–50 yrs.)	Pelvis
HAG139	Pit	East	Below ground	W-E	1	?	Old adult	?
HAG150	Pit	East	Below ground	W-E	1	?	Child (6.5 yrs.)	Pelvis
HAG152	Pit	East	Below ground	W-E	1	?	Child (8 yrs.)	?
HAG154	Tile	East	Below ground	W-E	1	?	Infant (9 mos.)	?
HAG159	Pit	North	Below ground	W-E	1	?	Adult	?
HAG168	Pit	East	Below ground	W-E	1	?	Adult	?
HAG178	Pit	North	Below ground	W-E	1	?	Adult	?
HAG181	Pit	North	Below ground	W-E	1	?	Old adult	Abdomen
HAG185	Pit	North	Below ground	W-E	1	Male	Old adult (55 yrs.)	Abdomen

time. For the most part, individuals were interred in graves, the majority of which were located below ground. Despite general uniformity in human behavior related to funerary customs during the Early Christian period, a greater understanding of variation in burial customs will be appreciated during this period on the island. It has been successfully argued by Rautman (2003) among others that the Roman Empire continued until the mid-seventh century on the island. The south coast sites were mostly abandoned by the mid-seventh century, but the inland site of the Hill of Agios Georgios survived the tumultuous times and continued into the later medieval period with multiple phases of church buildings.

Kalavasos-Kopetra

Kalavasos-Kopetra was a probable monastic site that is composed of three basilicas including the locality known as Kalavasos-Sirmata (also known as Area I) that contains a basilica constructed of gypsum slabs (Rautman 2003, 66–67). The site was abandoned by the eighth century (Manning 2002). Preliminary results of the study of the human remains from KK were published (Fox 2003), including a section on the burial customs observed at the site. All of the burials are inhumations. Although some artifacts were recovered within the tombs, no grave goods were found in association with any of the burials from KK. This is common among Christian burials for this period (Green 1977).

Articulated human skeletal remains were also observed within a feature at the site. This feature, a cistern, is located just north of the Sirmata basilica. In addition, prior to excavations, a sarcophagus was found while a farmer was plowing the area. The sarcophagus may have been originally located in or near the southern apse of this basilica. Within the sarcophagus were found the human skeletal remains of two adult males adjacent to one another, similar in that both were in extended and supine positions, each with hands folded across the pelvises. Both of the skeletons were missing their lower extremities as a result of damage sustained to the sarcophagus from earthmoving equipment. The human remains from this feature have not been fully studied since they have not been completely excavated and are still within the sarcophagus.

A crypt associated with this basilica was discovered at the bottom of a staircase directly west of the narthex. The crypt houses two tombs. Tomb 1 is located on the east wall of the crypt and is larger and earlier than Tomb

2 (Rautman 2003). Initially, Tomb 1 was thought to have been an ossuary (Fox 2003). The archaeologist who excavated the tomb, Susan Langdon, subdivided the structure into quadrants. The following year Fox studied the material from the tomb, and recognized that only upper body bones were found within the boxes of bones from the northern quadrants and lower body bones from the southern quadrants (ibid.). Photographs taken during the excavation confirmed that there were articulated remains within this tomb.

Four adult males from Tomb 1 were presumably primary burials that have been reconstructed to lie in north-south orientations. The bodies had been interred in supine and extended positions with their heads positioned at the northern end of the tomb. There were some postdepositional diagenetic and taphonomic effects as well as commingling of some skeletal elements, undoubtedly due to the seasonal flooding of the tomb over time. Additionally, placement of later burials within the tomb would have caused further disturbance to the earlier burials.

Within the later constructed Tomb 2, positioned adjacent to Tomb 1, three individuals were recovered from primary interments, including two adult males and a juvenile of approximately 9–11 years of age at death (Fox 2003). Both tombs displayed evidence for having been opened, for viewing or placement of new remains, based upon the presence of different plasters affixed to the lids (Rautman 2003). The bottom slabs of both tombs were intentionally perforated as well. Gypsum plaster was also found within Tomb 2 and excavating the remains was extremely difficult at times as the lower bones were essentially encased in plaster (Fox 2003). Furthermore, the tomb lid had partially collapsed. Green (1977) suggests that gypsum plaster burials or lime-packed inhumations are significant for the identification of Christian burials. Green states, "Not all plaster burials occur in Christian contexts and they are not the sole feature distinguishing these cemeteries from others, but they are distinctive features which may pinpoint possible sites. . . . Plaster burial is an exotic custom transmitted across the Empire by the spread of an exotic religion and is a rite of significance only to the followers of that faith" (1977, 52). Furthermore, he has identified these types of burials in North Africa, Britain and Germany. Cyprus can be added to the list (see also Baker and Papelaxandrou in this volume for evidence of the use of lime in burials from Cyprus). Unfortunately, plaster burials are not always identified in the field.

Additionally, iron nails were found within Tomb 2, suggesting the original presence of wooden coffins. The bodies had been interred in the usual west-east orientations (Rahtz 1977) with the heads to the west and the bodies were recovered in extended and supine positions. Again, the hands had been folded across the pelvises. A portion of the tomb cover had collapsed onto the northernmost male. The juvenile had been interred last (and was therefore most superficial) and was the poorest preserved of the three.

Within a bottle-shaped cistern in a courtyard directly to the north of this basilica were found nine individuals, including two adult males, an adolescent—possibly female—three children (5–10 years of age at death), one neonate, and the remains of two late-term fetuses. This material was among the best preserved from the site due to the more stable microenvironment provided by the structure of the cistern, however the context of the material from this feature remains enigmatic. A mid-seventh century date for this deposit is supported by ceramic evidence (Rautman 2003, 71). The human skeletal remains from this mass burial were articulated as previously stated (Fox 2003). The bodies had not been carefully deposited within the cistern as the articulated remains were found in haphazard positions suggestive of tossing the corpses into the receptacle. This assemblage does not represent secondary burials of cleaned-out tombs, but likely a single catastrophic episode, such as possible victims of an Arab incursion, or of a mass disaster, including a plague or earthquake (see Baker and Papalexandrou this volume for a similar example from this time period). Fox (2003, 275) has stated the following, "An alternate explanation might be an epidemic such as the plague under Justinian, which is said to have lasted 52 years. According to Procopius at the peak of the epidemic 'more than 10,000 people died each day, and it became impossible to bury all of the bodies,' with half the inhabitants of the Byzantine Empire dying by 565 (Patrick 1967, 246); but since viral epidemics rarely leave any detectable evidence on bones, interpretation of the physical evidence remains speculative." Future analysis of this material is required and it is hoped that results of ancient DNA analysis for plague pathogens may shed light on the events that led to this catastrophe.

What is known is that deposition of bodies within a cistern is not at all consistent with normal burial practice during this time period. A rich faunal assemblage was found above the human remains, including many birds, snakes and rodents, in addition to a fox and at least one large equine (Rautman 2003). Although many of these animals, including scavengers, could have accidentally found their way into the cistern and become trapped, the equine body was more likely to have been deposited by humans. The completion of the stratigraphic study of the cistern and the fauna recovered from it could help to clarify this issue. In any case, both fouling of the water supply and abandonment of the site suggest a catastrophic event. No gross signs of trauma were found on the human skeletal remains, but they require additional examination in a laboratory setting.

The South Church in Area II lies approximately 200 meters west of the hill (Area I). The bema (a raised stone speaker's platform) and late chapel have a floor mosaic and there is a tomb (Tomb 3) along the east side of the north wall in the south aisle (Rautman 2003). Within Tomb 3 are the human skeletal remains of two adult males (Fox 2003). The tomb is oriented in a west-east direction with the heads to the west. Once again, the skeletons are in supine and extended positions. The position of the hands is more difficult to discern among the last interred (more superficial) of the males due to some postmortem disturbance, but it appears that a similar pattern is observed among the other individuals found within the tombs or the sarcophagus at the site with the hands folded in the abdomen or pelvic region. Fox (2003, 275) states, "This body position and orientation reflect common practice in Cyprus today."

Area V contains the North Church with a floor of opus sectile construction. A grave was excavated in an area before the central narthex or entrance door to the church in a shallow recess with a north-south orientation with the head to the north (Rautman 2003). It contains the only single burial recovered from the site and the skeleton from this cist grave is the poorest preserved of all of the human remains from KK. This individual was an older adult of indeterminate sex and could have dated to the original construction of the basilica (Fox 2003; Rautman 2003).

In conclusion, a minimum of 21 individuals were recovered associated with each of the three basilicas at KK. Although the exact location of the limestone sarcophagus will never be known, it was recovered near the south apse of the largest of the three basilicas at KK in the locality known as Sirmata. All of the four tombs were found within a basilica or within a crypt attached to a basilica. Two tombs (Tomb 1 and Tomb 4) containing a combined five individuals were oriented in a north-south direction with heads to the north and two tombs (Tombs 2 and 3) containing a combined five individuals were oriented in a west-east direction with heads to the west. All of the four tombs were built tombs that were constructed of gypsum slabs with the exception of Tomb 4, which resembled a cist grave that was located in a recess before the central narthex door. It is possible that the basilica was dedicated to this individual.

All of the individuals associated with the basilicas at KK may have been important personages affiliated with the nearby monastery. Every basilica in the complex contained at least a single interment burial within or beneath its structure. In addition, minimally nine individuals were recovered from another feature, a cistern in a courtyard adjacent to the largest basilica. This mass burial is indicative of some sort of catastrophe reflected by the unusual deposit. With the exception of the human skeletal remains from the cistern, all of those interred at KK were in supine and extended positions with their hands folded across their abdomens or pelvises. Orientation is usually west-east, with the exception of two tombs oriented in a north-south manner, with the heads positioned to the north.

All of the adults for whom sex could be determined (n = 13) from KK were male and 9 were found in tombs that were within the basilicas or within a crypt. The lack of females is not surprising, since KK is purportedly a monastic site (Rautman 2003). Although subadults, including a possible female, were recovered from the cistern, only one subadult was recovered from a tomb associated with the ecclesiastical structures, a 9–11 year old juvenile from Tomb 2. Infants in particular were not recovered from other contexts at the site with the exception of the cistern. The average age at death of the adults (all males) recovered from the tombs was 40 years (n=5). Finally, artifacts found in the tombs included iron nails, and gypsum plaster may be associated with the inhumation burials of Tomb 2. No grave goods or associated artifacts were found with any of the interred individuals from KK.

Maroni-Petrera

The church at Maroni-Petrera has multiple phases; the plan during its final phase conforms to the basilica type (Manning 2002). This is the smallest of the church complexes presently under study. It likely covered less than a single hectare in area, but, according to Manning (2002), it was the dominant focal point for the lower Maroni Valley. It has been suggested that the site was closely linked economically as well with KK, which is only 5 km from MP along with the coastal site of Petrini. The site of MP was founded in the mid-fifth century and was abandoned two centuries later in the mid-seventh century (ibid.).

Very little extant remains of the church/basilica complex are preserved to any appreciable height (approximately only 20 cm in places due to, among other factors, agricultural plowing). Like the basilicas from the adjacent river valley at KK, the church at MP is constructed of gypsum slabs.

A minimum of six individuals was recovered from two cist graves located within the central aisle of the church (Fox 2002). Burial 1 was a single burial recovered from the apse. The pitched gypsum and limestone slabs formed a cist grave that was oriented west-east with the head to the west. The inhumed individual was a young adult of indeterminate sex (ibid.). This individual was recovered in a likely extended and perhaps supine position. The human skeletal remains from Burial 1 were not well preserved and the individual was incomplete although most bones were represented (ibid.).

Burial 2/3 was positioned in the central aisle of the church in a presumably west-east orientation and, like Burial 1, the cist walls were comprised of pieces of gypsum (Manning 2002). Although no teeth were recovered from Burial 1, Burial 2/3 is represented mostly by dentition. A minimum of five infants were recovered ranging in age from a fetus of approximately 8 lunar months to four infants ranging in age at death from 6 to 18 months (Fox 2002). Preservation was fair, at best, and nothing much could be stated about the head orientations or body positions of this special deposit of fetal/infant remains. Due to poor preservation, it cannot be determined with any certainty whether these were primary or secondary burials.

In conclusion, Burial 2/3 represents the greatest number of individuals recovered from any tomb in this study. The special grave for babies in the central apse of a church is, to date, unique for Cyprus in the Early Christian period. There were no grave goods associated with the burials from either of the cist graves.

Alassa-Ayia Mavri

Material from 20 graves from the excavations at AAM have been studied (Fox 1996). However, two of these are believed by the excavator to be intrusive burials dating perhaps to the medieval period (Tombs 13 and 14; see Flourentzos 1996). Early Christian graves from the site were found extramurally or outside the walls of the basilica. With the exception of a pithos burial (Tomb 8) and the martyrion or *martyrium* (Tomb 16) and the remains from an ossuary (Tombs 4, 6, 11 and 16), simple cist graves marked with limestone slabs predominate at the site. Twenty-eight percent of the tombs were located east of the basilica (Tombs 8, 9, 10, 19 and 20); thirty-nine percent were situated to the north of the basilica (Tombs 1, 2, 3, 4, 6, 11, and 16); and twenty-two percent of the graves from the site are northeast of the basilica (Tombs 5, 12, 17 and 18). The location of tombs 7 and 15 are unspecified in the drawing of the final site report by Flourentzos (1996).

In conclusion, 18 graves are associated with the basilica at AAM (Fox 1996). Only one of the tombs, Tomb 11, is possibly oriented in a north-south direction, but this could be part of an ossuary (see below). At least 10 of the graves (Tombs 5, 8, 9, 10, 12, 16, 17, 18, 19, and 20) appear to have been positioned in a roughly west-east orientation. One of these graves (Tomb 8) was actually formed by part of a pithos. The excavator, P. Flourentzos, suggests that tombs designated 4, 6, 11 and 16 were shallow graves in the northern aisle that were part of an *ossuarium* or ossuary representing secondary burials. He also suggests that one of the tombs, Tomb 16, was a *martyrium*, or the tomb housing a Christian martyr (Flourentzos 1996). This tomb was constructed of limestone and resembled a sarcophagus. Associated artifacts were found among some of the burials, including a bronze earring from Tomb 1, a silver earring from Tomb 4, and six glass bracelets found in situ on the arms of a 7–9 year old child from Tomb 5. A ceramic grave marker was associated with Tomb 7.

Minimally 27 individuals were represented among the 18 graves (Fox 1996). There were 1–3 individuals represented per tomb. Tombs 2, 3, 5–9, 11, 15–17 represented single inhumation burials. A minimum of two individuals was found in Tombs 1, 10, 12, 18 and 19 and three individuals within Tombs 4 and 20. Sex was determined for six females and three males. Ages ranged from a late fetus (about 9 1/2 lunar months) from Tomb 10 to an adult female from Tomb 19 with an age estimated to have been approximately 32–52 years at the time of death (ibid). For those who could be aged, adult females had an average age at death of 28 years (n = 6). Aside from an adolescent male, who was estimated to have been 13–15 years of age at the time of his death, there was only one other male for whom an age estimate could be provided, a 24–32 year old. The average age at death for all individuals from the site is about 13.8 years.

The Hill of Agios Georgios

The Hill of Agios Georgios is the only inland and urban site under study and is situated adjacent to the Pedieos River in the Nicosia district. At the northern part of the excavation, a complex of ecclesiastical buildings was revealed, consisting of at least four successive phases of a church/basilica dating from the seventh century to the sixteenth century. Like KK, HAG may have become a monastery during one of its later phases, but there is no evidence of a monastic complex during Early Christian times (cf. Hadjisavvas 2000, 685–688). The total number of confirmed graves associated with the earliest phase of the basilica at the HAG is 27. All burials were thought to have been below ground, and none of them were located within the church. Simple pit graves predominate (n = 20, 74 percent of the total). The remaining tomb types include a built tomb of gypsum slabs (for an old adult male), a cist grave, a tile grave and another grave impinging on an older kiln. All of the graves are oriented in a west-east direction with heads of the deceased placed to the west. Hands were positioned across the chest, abdomen and pelvis. There are 11 single interments, five double interments, and two triple interments. Sixteen burials were recovered from the east of the church, five from the north and three from the south. There does not seem to be a pattern represented by the age or sex of individuals with the location of the grave in relation to the church.

Artifacts were found in some burial environments including iron nails in four graves (HAG 124, 128, 131 and 133) as well as glass and metal fragments of objects. A cross was engraved on a stone to mark the burial of two individuals (HAG 100, an infant of 3–6 months at the time of death; and HAG 154, another infant of approximately 9 months of age at death). Grave goods including a copper ring (HAG 131) and a silver earring (HAG 133) were recovered, the latter of which was from a possible adult female.

The sexes of those interred at the HAG during the Early Christian Period include 6 males and 6 females, among those for whom sex could be attributed. Ages ranged from 3 months to 55 years. The average age at death for females was approximately 37 years and for males it was 48 years. For all individuals from the site, the average age at death was 33.5 years.

Discussion and Conclusions

In this study, 80 individuals from 50 tombs have been studied. The majority of burials from these sites are below ground level, and only at KK are 8 percent of the tombs visible above ground level. Tomb types in Cyprus appear to be more varied than in Greece. Bourbou (2002) reports four types of tombs, including simple pits possibly covered by ceramic or stone slabs, roofed tile graves (common), cist graves (common), built tombs with corbelled roofs, along with occasional rock-cut tombs. Indeed, in this study, the two most common types of tombs are cist graves and pit graves, accounting for nearly 30 percent and 40 percent, respectively, of all encountered grave types. In addition to these types of burials, a sarcophagus burial exists at KK, along with a sarcophagus-like burial at AAM 15. Tile burials are not as common on the island as Bourbou has found in Greece, with only one tile burial from HAG 154 represented in this study. There is also a burial in a fragment of pithos from AAM 8, a built tomb of gypsum slabs from HAG 128, and a crypt associated with a basilica at KK housing two tombs. It appears that gypsum was the material of choice for the built tombs for the period. Furthermore, no rock-cut tombs have been identified, to date, from Early Christian contexts in Cyprus.

Finally, the exceptional case of a cistern contained the largest number of individuals recovered from any single context to date in Early Christian Cyprus. The deposit of remains in the cistern represents evidence for a yet unknown mass disaster. The clarification of the cistern's state of functioning at the time (whether it was out of use or not) might illuminate this burial choice. In any case, it seems that this feature provided an easy option for quick burials of a number of individuals

In terms of grave location, the various patterns can be explored as they appear within the interior and the exterior of the churches. According to Bourbou (2002, 30–51) the phenomenon of burial within churches appeared much earlier in the east during the Byzantine Empire and progressively spread to the west. Bourbou (2002, 38, paraphrased by co-author Moutafi) states specifically that "by the fifth c. onward, there was a tendency toward burial outside the church. . . . It was considered more humble to put sarcophagi in the narthex and in the area around the church. . . . This is to avoid confusion between the burials and the ritual (since the narthex is considered of lesser importance for the ritual and the other area is out of the main church). . . . This phenomenon led to limitations on the available space, provoking expansion of churches and additional buildings around them, and the creation of ossuaries or multiple burials within the same tomb." Approximately 14 percent (n = 7) of the total number of tombs in this study contained burials within or under the churches (from the monastic site of KK and its neighboring MP). An apse burial was found at MP, while the disturbed sarcophagus found in the area of the southern apse at KK could have been originally situated inside the apse as well. Two tombs were also found in the aisles of the church or basilica (KK Tomb 3 and MP Burial 2/3). Finally, a cist grave was found under the narthex of one of the basilicas at KK.

Of the extramural tombs from non-monastic contexts, the following tomb locations are noted: 21 burials were located to the east of the basilica; 11 north; 3 south; and 4 to the northeast. Burials to the east are represented twice as often as all others combined. No burials are recorded outside the entrance of basilicas (to the west) from this study; however, burials located to the west do exist from later periods at the HAG and other sites.

In terms of orientation, Sirmata at KK was the only site to certainly possess tombs (n = 2) with north-south orientations. Heads were found positioned to the north in 4 percent of the combined total of 50 tombs. All other primary burials were probably west-east burials. One tomb from AAM (Tomb 11) may have had a north-south orientation but this shallow burial could have been part of an ossuary. According to Bourbou (2002), only monastic cemeteries are the product of specific organization and planning, while the others (in the context of churches) are the product of the spontaneous demands of believers to be buried in sanctified grounds; therefore, usually the burials in these cemeteries do not hold to a specific orientation or plan. This seems to hold true for the Cyprus cases here, both in terms of the general spatial disorder and the exceptions in the orientation: excavation data suggest that the unusual (N-S) choices are the result of practical concerns due to the particular topography (e.g., of the narthex) and lack of space.

Hand position was also noted and hands were found in undisturbed burials folded across the pelvis (n = 7), abdomen (n = 2), or chest (n = 2) among individuals from the cemeteries of KK and the HAG. Unfortunately, arm position was not always recorded at the time of excavation, although photographs can be quite useful in recording hand positions. At least for the case of the HAG excavations, to date, recorded arm position has been provided.

Artifacts such as iron nails were recovered in 5 tombs from the sites of KK (Tomb 2) and the HAG (Tomb 124, 128, 131 and 133) or 10 percent of all tombs included in the study. Nails may indicate the presence of wooden coffins for the dead. Plaster was also recovered from at least one tomb (Tomb 2) from KK and one from the HAG (Tomb 128) (see above for the presence of plaster around inhumation burials as a possible indicator of Christian cemeteries, Green 1977). Crosses engraved on stones were recovered in association with the burials from the HAG 100, 130 and 154 (approximately 6 percent of all graves) to mark graves. Other less common findings include a jar fragment to mark a grave and metal artifacts and glass fragments within the grave itself.

Artifacts were associated with individuals[1] from two sites, both AAM and HAG, and they include a copper ring (HAG 131), two silver earrings (AAM 4 and HAG 133), a bronze earring (AAM 1), and six glass bracelets found on the arms of a 7–9 year old child from Tomb 5 at AAM. The percentage of associated artifacts within all of the graves from the study is about 10 percent.

The practice of secondary burial is an interesting aspect of early Christian burial customs. In this study there was no clear evidence of secondary deposition in the form of proper "ossuaries." The only exception consists of the ossuary of AAM; however, this is a complex context, including both primary and perhaps secondary deposits. There is clear evidence for both successive and multiple interments. Although multiple interment burials are recovered from all of the sites, MP boasts the single largest number of individuals per tomb at 5 in the unique grave for infants. At least four individuals are represented from Tomb 1 at KK and three from two tombs (4 and 20) at AAM. Most of the graves at the HAG are single inhumation burials although there are two double burials. The average number of individuals per tomb is 1.6 from the entire site. Finally, the possibility of complex secondary rituals, that might include a practice of repetitive grave opening in order to view the remains, has been suggested (Rautman 2003 for two KK tombs) but cannot be confirmed.

Among the human skeletal remains, there are at least 21 males and 13 females represented in total. Not including the males from the site of KK, a monastic site comprised almost exclusively of males, the burials of 9 males and 13 females are represented. Therefore, it seems that selective factors in burial inclusion based on sex were only applied within the monastic context (and even there not exclusively). Ages at death of the deceased range from late fetal to old adult individuals of at least 55 years. The combined average age at death for this study is 20 years. Individuals from the HAG apparently lived longer than those at the other sites, but more adult remains were represented there.

In summary, a number of myths (or at least widely accepted pre-conceived ideas) on Early Christian burial customs have been dispelled from this study of four church/basilica sites in Cyprus. There is evidence for apse burials, as well as other types of burial within the church interior. Infants can be buried not only in surrounding grounds, but even within the church. Artifacts (whether considered grave goods or not) have been found at times associated with human skeletal remains. Finally, the tomb types, grave orientation, and body positions indicate a more varied situation than previously thought during this tumultuous time for the island, with choices reflecting both ritual beliefs and practical concerns.

Note

1. The authors believe that special caution is needed with relation to the use of the term "grave goods" in cases where this refers to personal ornaments, parts of clothing, etc.; therefore, the more neutral term "associated artifacts" is used here.

References Cited

Bass, W.
1971   *Human Osteology*. Missouri Archaeological Society, Columbia.
Bourbou, C.
2002   Bioarchaeological Approach to the Populations of Elutherna (Crete) and Messene (Peloponnese) During the Proto-byzantine (6th–7th centuries AD) Era. Ph.D. dissertation, University of Crete.
2004   *The People of Early Byzantine Eleutherna and Messene (6th–7th centuries A.D.): A Bioarchaeological Approach*. University of Crete, Athens.
Buikstra, J. E., and L. A. Beck (editors)
2006   *Bioarchaeology. The Contextual Analysis of Human Remains*. Academic Press, New York.
Buikstra, J. E., and D. H. Ubelaker
1994   *Standards for Data Collection from Human Skeletal Remains*. Archeological Survey Research Series no. 44. Arkansas Archeological Survey, Fayetteville, Ark.

du Plat-Taylor, J.

1980   Excavations at Ayios Philon, The Ancient Carpasia. Part I: The Classical to Roman periods. *Report of the Department of Antiquities, Cyprus,* 152–116, pls. xxv–xxix.

du Plat-Taylor, J., and A. H. S. Megaw

1981   Excavations at Ayios Philon, The Ancient Carpasia. Part II: The Early Christian Buildings. *Report of the Department of Antiquities, Cyprus,* 209–250, pls. xxvii–xliv.

Flourentzos, P.

1996   *Excavations in the Kouris Valley II. The Basilica of Alassa.* Department of Antiquities, Cyprus, Nicosia.

Fox, S. C.

1996   The Human Skeletal Remains from Alassa-*Ayia Mavri*, Cyprus. In *Excavations in the Kouris River Valley II,* edited by P. Flourentzos, pp. 39–64. Department of Antiquities, Nicosia.

2002   Human Skeletal Remains. In *The Late Roman Church at Maroni Petrera,* edited by S. W. Manning, pp. 38–40. A. G. Leventis Foundation, Oxford.

2003   The Human Skeletal Remains: A Preliminary Report. In *A Cypriot Village of Late Antiquity: Kalavasos-Kopetra in the Vasilikos Valley,* edited by M. Rautman, pp. 274–277. Journal of Roman Archaeology, Portsmouth, R.I.

Gowland, R., and C. Knüsel

2006   *The Social Archaeology of Funerary Remains.* Oxbow Books, Oxford.

Green, C.

1977   The Significance of Plaster Burials for the Recognition of Christian Cemeteries. In *Burial in the Roman World,* edited by R. Reece, pp. 46–45. Council for British Archaeology Research Report no. 22. London: The Council for British Archaeology.

Hadjisavvas, S.

2000   Chronique des fouilles et decouvertes archaeologiques a Chypre en 1999. *Bulletin de Correspondence Hellénique* 124:665–699.

Harper, N. K., and S. C. Fox

2008   Recent Research in Cypriot Bioarchaeology. *Bioarchaeology of the Near East* 2:1–38.

Krogman, W. M.

1962   *The Human Skeleton in Forensic Medicine.* Charles C. Thomas, Springfield, Ill.

Larsen, C. S.

1997   *Bioarchaeology: Interpreting Behavior from the Human Skeleton.* Cambridge University Press, Cambridge.

Manning, S. W.

2002   *The Late Roman Church at Maroni Petrera.* A. G. Leventis Foundation, Nicosia.

Megaw, A. H. S.

1974   Byzantine Architecture and Decoration in Cyprus: Metropolitan or Provincial? *Dumbarton Oaks Papers* 28:57–88.

2007   *Kourion: Excavations in the Episcopal Precinct.* Dumbarton Oaks Studies no. 38. Dumbarton Oaks, Washington, D. C.

Morris, I.

1987   *Burial and Ancient Society.* Cambridge University Press, Cambridge.

Parker Pearson, M.

1999   *The Archaeology of Death and Burial.* Texas A&M University Press, College Station.

Patrick, R.

1967   Disease in Antiquity: Ancient Greece and Rome. In *Disease in Antiquity,* edited by D. Brothwell and A. T. Sandison, pp. 238–246. Charles C. Thomas, Springfield, Ill.

Rahtz, P.

1977   Late Roman Cemeteries and Beyond. In *Burial in the Roman World,* edited by R. Reece, pp. 53–64. Council for British Archaeology Research Report no. 22. Council for British Archaeology, London.

Rautman, M.

2003   *A Cypriot Village of Late Antiquity: Kalavasos-Kopetra in the Vasilikos Valley. Journal of Roman Archaeology* Supplementary Series 52.

Stewart, T. D.

1979   *Essentials of Forensic Anthropology.* Charles C. Thomas, Springfield, Ill.

Tritsaroli, P.

2006   Pratiques Funéraires en Grèce Centrale à la période Byzantine: Analyse à partir des données archéologiques et Biologiques. Ph.D. dissertation, Departement de Prehistoire, Institut de Paléontologie Humaine, Muséum National d'Histoire Naturelle.

4

A Bioarchaeological Perspective on the Burials and Basilicas of Medieval Polis, Cyprus

BRENDA J. BAKER AND AMY PAPALEXANDROU

Introduction

The modern town of Polis is located on the northwest coast of the Republic of Cyprus, approximately 21 miles (36 km) north of Paphos. Located on the coast along the Chrysochou Bay to the east of the rugged Akamas peninsula, Polis sits on a bluff above the Chrysochou River and the Mediterranean Sea (Figure 4.1). In 1983, Princeton University's archaeological research commenced in several different areas of Polis under the direction of William A. P. Childs (Childs 1988). Excavations have revealed substantial occupation from the late Archaic (sixth century BC) through the Venetian period (AD 1489–1570).

The Classical settlement, known as Marion, became the seat of one of the kingdoms of Cyprus by the fifth century BC, deriving its wealth from nearby copper mines (Childs 1988). After Marion was destroyed in 312 BC, the city of Arsinoë was established by Ptolemy II Philadelphos around 270 BC in honor of his wife (Childs 1988, 2008; Purcell 1968, 97). By the early fifth century AD, Arsinoë was the seat of a bishopric and had workshops, wells, water lines and drainage channels, and a network of streets (Childs 1988; Papalexandrou 2012). At least two churches built in the late fifth or early sixth century served the town's population in both life and death. Each was a basilica, a type of church structure in the form of a longitudinal hall.

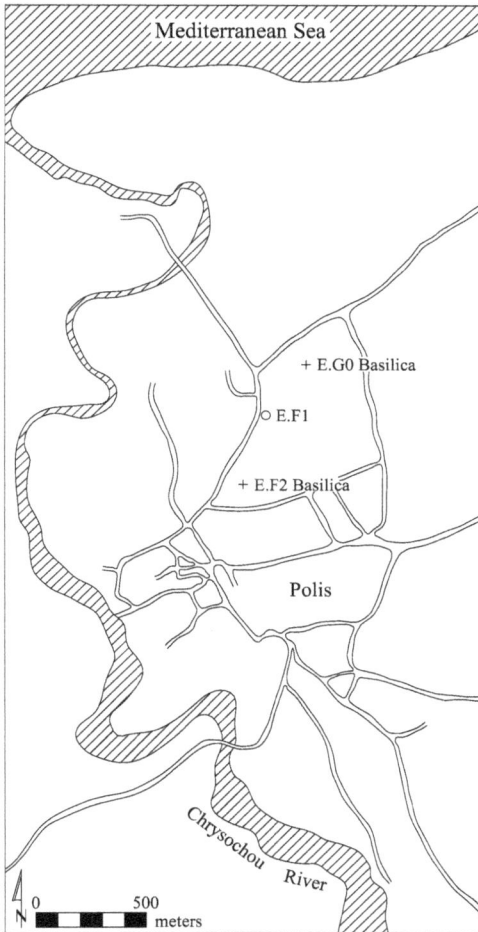

Figure 4.1. Plan of Polis. The three westernmost Princeton excavation areas include those of the two basilicas in E.G0 and E.F2. Remnant walls of the ancient city parallel the modern north-south road to the east of the E.G0 basilica.

Although many Early Christian churches are known in Cyprus, the absence of recorded cemeteries led one scholar to ask where the Early Christian population was buried and to assume that they reused older tombs (Bakirtzis 1999, 40). This notion is now being reassessed thanks to recent discoveries on the island (Fox et al. this volume; Prokopiou 1995), although formal cemeteries dating to the Late Antique and Byzantine periods remain a rarity among the island's excavated churches. The large number of burials associated with the two Polis basilicas is, therefore, especially significant and demonstrates the importance of excavating church contexts fully.

At Polis, analysis of the bulk of the human skeletal remains within and around the southernmost of the two basilicas was conducted by Stacey Buck (1993). Her study assessed demography and health in this skeletal sample. More recent bioarchaeological work on human remains began in 2005. Although many skeletons appear to be complete and in good condition upon exposure, soil characteristics and roots have caused brittleness and cracking that preclude lifting most bones intact. Prior to 2005, burials were excavated by field personnel who lacked osteological expertise, so assessment of sex and age is hampered by the fragmented nature of most skeletal elements encountered in the laboratory. Buck (1993, 49) used standard morphological features of the pelvis and skull to assess sex in adults (see Buikstra and Ubelaker 1994), accompanied by metric analysis of extant elements where standard features were unobservable. Age estimation for children was based on skeletal and dental development. In adults, poor preservation led Buck (1993, 47–48) to rely largely on dental wear to place individuals in broad phases of young adult, middle adult, or old adult. Where possible, age estimates were accompanied by pubic symphysis, auricular surface, or sternal rib end techniques to provide somewhat narrower age ranges. Since 2005, sex and age have been documented by the senior author during burial excavation, using standard criteria (Buikstra and Ubelaker 1994). Examination in situ typically yields more secure sex determinations and narrower age ranges than are possible from laboratory analysis alone. Additionally, individuals in Buck's (1993) study will be reevaluated as work proceeds. The results of the full analysis of human remains from both basilicas will be published in a future volume of Princeton's planned series on the Polis project.

Ongoing bioarchaeological research at Polis will investigate three principal questions. First, how do individuals buried in and around the two basilicas compare in terms of their treatment (location, type of grave, positioning, grave inclusions, and ritual symbolism) and identity (age, sex, social status, etc.) and how does change manifest through time? Second, why were tombs containing multiple burials constructed as part of one basilica and who was interred in them? Finally, what was everyday life like for the medieval inhabitants of Polis? The preliminary results of this investigation and future directions of bioarchaeological research at Polis form the basis of this chapter. Our focus is how the broad contributions of such study add to our understanding of mortuary practices and lifestyles in Late Antique and medieval Cyprus.

The Basilicas and Burial Contexts

Burials are clustered in and around two basilicas situated within and adjacent to a small-scale urban context (Najberg, Nicklies, and Papalexandrou 2002; Papalexandrou 2012). Although both basilicas were constructed in the fifth or early sixth century and are situated only about 200 meters apart (Figure 4.1), aspects of their original purpose and use histories differ. The southernmost basilica and the cemetery surrounding it (the excavation area designated E.F2) were likely used only until the eleventh century given the lack of ceramic evidence from later periods within or immediately around it. The northern basilica (in the E.G0 excavation area) was abandoned sometime after the mid-seventh century but was rebuilt after the ninth century. This building and the space around it eventually accommodated burials from the thirteenth to sixteenth centuries, during the Latin occupation of the island by the Lusignans and later the Venetians. Grave goods have helped date the span of use for each basilica, though intrusion of graves into their floors and reuse of some graves have complicated the stratigraphy. A precise chronology is difficult to establish but will be clarified through ongoing study of the ceramic evidence.

This section focuses on comparison of mortuary evidence from both basilicas. This evidence indicates various ways of accommodating the dead. Grave location, construction, and the type and variety of grave goods permit us to understand different types of interments, with temporal change accounting for some of the observed variation. Proximity to the sanctuary and its consecrated altar, especially in death, was of vital importance. Although legislation by both imperial and canon law prohibited burial of the laity within churches, it was nevertheless common for privileged or influential members of a community to receive this honor (Constas 2006; Ivison 1996). Burial emplacement has, in fact, been regarded as a clearer indication of privilege than grave goods in the fourth to eighth centuries (Sapin 1999, 39).

The E.F2 Basilica

The basilica in the E.F2 area, which measures 23 meters long by 12.5 meters wide, was fully excavated from 1986 to 1990 (Childs 1988, 127–28; Papalexandrou 2012). This basilica occupied the area of a city block near the heart of the Late Antique town (Childs 1988, 127, 2008, 69). Only the foundations remain, but fragments of marble columns and decorative stone sculpture, painted wall plaster, mosaic, and bronze lighting fixtures hint at its interior decoration (Papalexandrou 2012). The layout of the original basilica (Figure 4.2) is typical of its time: three aisles were divided from one another by colonnades and terminated at the east in three apses (the vaulted, semicircular spaces that normally project from the east wall of a church). A narrow vestibule, or narthex, preceded the naos (the main body of the church) to the west. The naos consisted of the area outside the sanctuary where the congregation assembled for services. A large, open courtyard to the south separated the building from what seems to have been an area of workshops. A series of long, narrow buildings of undetermined function abutted the church to the east, and a lamp kiln operated below the south apse earlier during the Roman period.

Multiple phases of construction and use are evident at the E.F.2 basilica. It is likely that the original building sustained damage sometime after the seventh century, if not before, and subsequent campaigns of rebuilding or remodeling lasted as late as the eleventh century. Piers or buttresses at regular intervals along the interior walls attest to replacement of the original columns and wooden roof with masonry walls that supported barrel vaults overhead (Childs 1988, 127–128; Ćurči 1999, 75).

The E.F2 basilica is typical of Early Christian churches in its accommodation of a number of burials inside the building (see also Fox et al. this volume). At least ten graves were sunk into the interior floors, including two in the center aisle and four in the narthex. These were lined with stone and sealed with cover slabs. In addition, three large tombs were built into the south aisle, immediately before the apse and adjacent to the south wall of the building (Figure 4.2). A smaller stone-lined child's grave was located west of these tombs. The three large tombs were lined with a smooth coat of plaster, and one was covered by large marble slabs. Two were fashioned as a stepped shaft so that the body rested in a narrow cavity at the base of the shaft, covered by slabs. The tombs in the south aisle contained Late Roman red-slipped wares (fifth to seventh centuries). The occupant of the middle tomb was buried with an impressive bronze cross and a coin dating to the fifth or sixth century (Papalexandrou 2012). The placement of these tombs, the quality of their construction, and the types of grave goods indicate that they belonged to individuals who were privileged or held in high esteem. The bronze cross, for example, suggests that the person in the middle tomb was a member of the clergy. At some point

Figure 4.2. Aerial view (from the west) of the E.F2 excavation area showing the basilica at the upper left. Note the three aisles terminating in apses at their east ends. Three tombs along the interior of the basilica's south wall are evident. Princeton Cyprus Expedition archive.

after the basilica was constructed, an open porch was added immediately to the south. Graves were eventually dug into the floor of this area as well (Buck 1993, Fig. 2).

After the decline of the surrounding workshops, the area outside the basilica (especially to its south and east) was used as a cemetery. Activity at the church and its cemetery appears to have waned after the eighth century; evidence of use gradually decreases until its eventual abandonment. A minimum of 140 individuals was excavated from graves in and around the E.F2 church through 1993, 82 of which contained sufficiently preserved and undisturbed skeletons to be described by their excavators (Buck 1993, 44). Excavations since 2000 have added to the number of graves known outside the church. Twelve disturbed skeletons and five disturbed tombs that each contained an articulated and a disturbed, disarticulated skeleton were also described by Buck (1993, 41), who implied that the graves were not marked. Standing stones found at two graves excavated in 1988, one engraved with a cross, show that markers did exist for at least some burials. Because most of these burials were neither formally organized nor regularly spaced and have not been disturbed, it is

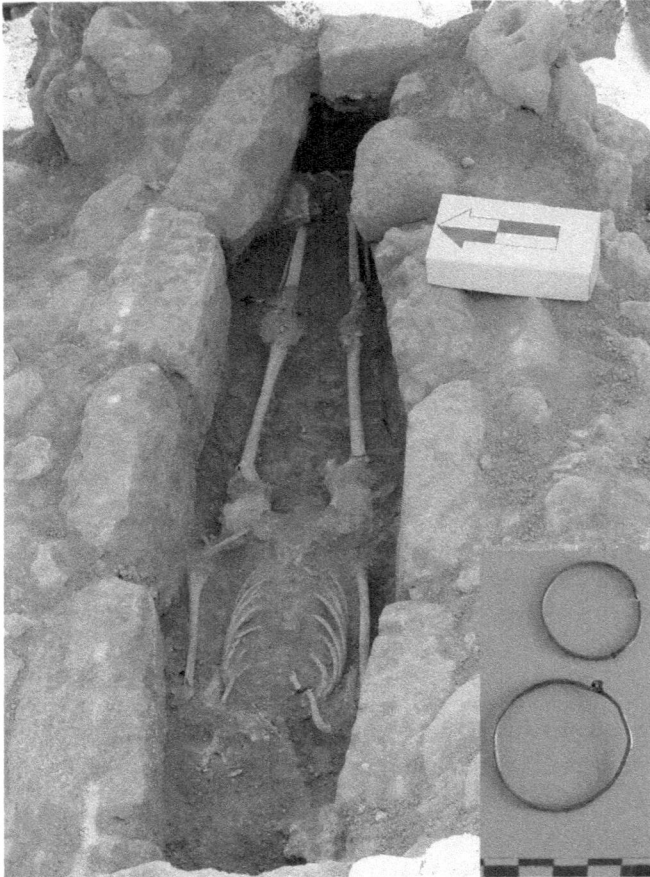

Figure 4.3. A cist tomb in the E.F2 cemetery (Trench e10, Burial 2005.3) contained a teenaged girl with silver hoop earrings at each side of the skull, the larger on the right. The earrings (inset) are shown after cleaning by conservators (R47220/BR1671; R47221/BR1672). Tomb photo by Brenda J. Baker; inset photo, Princeton Cyprus Expedition archive.

likely that all or most were marked. Those containing both an articulated and a disarticulated skeleton were graves that appear to have been reopened for interment of a second individual (the articulated skeleton). In these graves, the first individual (the disarticulated skeleton) was pushed aside to accommodate the new interment.

Most graves outside the E.F.2 church are not as well constructed or furnished as those inside the basilica. Simple subsurface pits with few or no lining stones predominate; occasionally these graves are covered by limestone slabs. More costly cist tombs of ashlar (squared stone) masonry and limestone cover slabs are infrequent. Graves are oriented on a roughly east-west axis with minor variation likely due to seasonal alignment with the rising and setting sun. Almost all bodies were in a supine, extended position with the head to the west and feet to the east, though Buck (1993, 41) indicated that two were placed on their right sides. Tritsaroli (2008) noted similar positioning of one individual in the early Christian (seventh century) Greek cemetery of Akraiphnio, Boeotia, the region northeast of the Gulf of Corinth. Although Tritsaroli (2008) suggested that placement on the right side was a Muslim tradition, Islamic burials would also face Mecca. Interment on the right side could simply reflect variability in body positioning during this period. Grave goods accompanying E.F.2 burials are not common. These include some illegible coins; pectoral crosses of metal, stone, ivory, and picrolite (a soft green to blue-green stone); three finger rings; seven earrings; a beaded necklace; terra-cotta lamp fragments; and a large amount of broken glass. More utilitarian items, like a bone needle fashioned from the dorsal spine of a catfish, are found in a few graves (Baker, Terhune, and Papalexandrou 2012).

Two cist tombs excavated 22 meters to the southwest of the church in 2005 were among the more elaborate graves in the cemetery. One of these tombs (Trench e10, Burial 2005.1), housed an older adult male 50–60 years of age (based on the auricular surfaces) accompanied by a coin and a possible slingshot stone. The nearby tomb (Trench e10, Burial 2005.1) contained the skeleton of a girl 13–15 years old (based on epiphyseal fusion and dental development) who was buried with two silver hoop earrings (Figure 4.3). The absence of iron nails and the fact that the space between the skeleton and the stone blocks is insufficient indicate that the occupants of these carefully constructed tombs were not placed in wooden coffins within them. In contrast, the presence of iron nails in simple subsurface pits indicates that individuals in these graves were frequently interred in coffins (Papalexandrou 2012).

The E.G0 Basilica

The church in the E.G0 excavation area is located at the edge of a bluff overlooking the Mediterranean Sea at the edge of the town, a short walk to the north from the E.F2 basilica (Figure 4.1). This basilica differs in plan from its neighbor and has a much more complicated use history. Its

Figure 4.4. Aerial view (from the west) of the partially excavated E.G0 basilica showing graves inside the church and the multiple-burial repositories. The longest facility is evident at the bottom left, just west of the apse in the north wall. Princeton Cyprus Expedition archive.

southern portion lies under a modern building used by the project. The northern portion, representing less than half of this basilica, was excavated intermittently during field seasons between 1996 and 2006 (Najberg, Nicklies, and Papalexandrou 2002; Papalexandrou 2012). The excavated area shows that, like the E.F2 church, it was originally a three-aisled basilica with a narthex to the west (Figure 4.4). It is somewhat larger than the E.F2 basilica. Its estimated dimensions are 30 × 14.5 meters. Its initial construction may predate the E.F2 basilica; fragments of mosaic floors and imported marble architectural elements suggest a date slightly earlier in the fifth century (Najberg, Nicklies, and Papalexandrou 2002; Papalexandrou 2012).

This basilica is distinguished by repositories for multiple burials that were integrated into its design or added soon after construction, suggesting it may have been founded as a funerary church (Papalexandrou 2012). These subsurface constructed pits are evident along the north wall and turn the corner at the northeast (Figure 4.4). There are seven repositories outside the north wall and two more along its interior. All but the longer repository to the west of the small apse in the middle of the north wall measured approximately 1 × 2 meters and 1.5 to 3 meters deep (Najberg, Nicklies, and Papalexandrou 2002, 147). Although not uniform in terms of construction, most of the external repositories are similar in size and contained vertically aligned holes in one end of their long walls. The intended function of these holes is unclear, although they may have served as niches to hold terra-cotta lamps; one lamp was found directly below a niche. Lamps that dated to the seventh century were found in most of the repositories. All bore signs of burning, and some were intact. All the repositories contained commingled remains of multiple disarticulated skeletons; up to 30 adults and children were found in the long western repository. Grave goods in this repository were abundant and included coins dating to the fourth or fifth as well as the seventh centuries, rings and earrings (some of which are gold), and several bronze belt buckles. Charcoal fragments, lime, and an oily consistency of the soil were also recorded, perhaps attesting to attendant rituals. The contents of this repository were thought by the excavators to be deposited all at once rather than accumulating over multiple episodes, in contrast to the Early Bronze II–III charnel houses (communal burial structures) at Bab edh-Dhra', Jordan, which were used continuously over a period of approximately 500 years (see Ullinger et al. this volume). Grave offerings in the other repositories of the E.G0 basilica were similar. Belt buckles dating to the seventh century appear in several of them and a coin found near bedrock in one indicates that its contents were deposited after the mid-seventh century.

The absence of later grave goods suggests that the Early Christian church was used into the seventh century and was subsequently abandoned, at least for a time (Najberg, Nicklies, and Papalexandrou 2002, 149). The burial repositories were not reused, though only one had any cover stones. Sometime after the ninth century, the basilica was rebuilt as a vaulted structure with frescoed walls and a gray mortar floor that covered remnants of the Late Antique mosaic pavement and the internal burial repositories (Najberg, Nicklies, and Papalexandrou 2002, 152). The walls and roof of this church later collapsed onto the mortar floor, creating a level of rubble approximately 40 centimeters thick that was used as packing for a thick concrete subfloor over which thin paving stones were laid. A coin found between the subfloor and the pavers dates between 1460 and 1473, indicating this final structure was built after this time.

During the later medieval period, from the thirteenth century, the interior of the church was again used for burials that accorded with usual practices of the time. These graves were dug into the rubble layer. The greatest concentration was in the narthex, though the naos was also used. The last burials occurred during the Venetian period, as is evidenced by a grave in the area of the north aisle (E.G0:g11, Tomb 2) that was excavated in 1996. This grave contained a man in his 40s (based on auricular surface morphology). A bowl imported from Italy was placed on his chest and a coin had been inserted in his mouth (Papalexandrou 2007), which stained the right side of the mandible green. The copper coin (R 20545, NM 1181) was identified by Alan Stahl (personal communication 2006) as the issue of Doge Girolamo Priuli of Venice and dates to 1559–1567. While bowls are common in late Byzantine graves in Cyprus, placement on the chest is unusual. For example, at Soloi (a town with two basilicas east of Polis), only 7 percent of those interred with bowls dating to the late thirteenth to fourteenth centuries had one on the chest (Ivison 1993, I:242).

Most burials in the narthex were accompanied by glazed vessels that date to the fourteenth and fifteenth centuries placed by the head or legs/feet. Interments containing open vessels that date from the thirteenth to sixteenth centuries have commonly been termed "bowl burials" (Ivison 1993, I:240–241). As with the burials in and around the E.F2 basilica, the

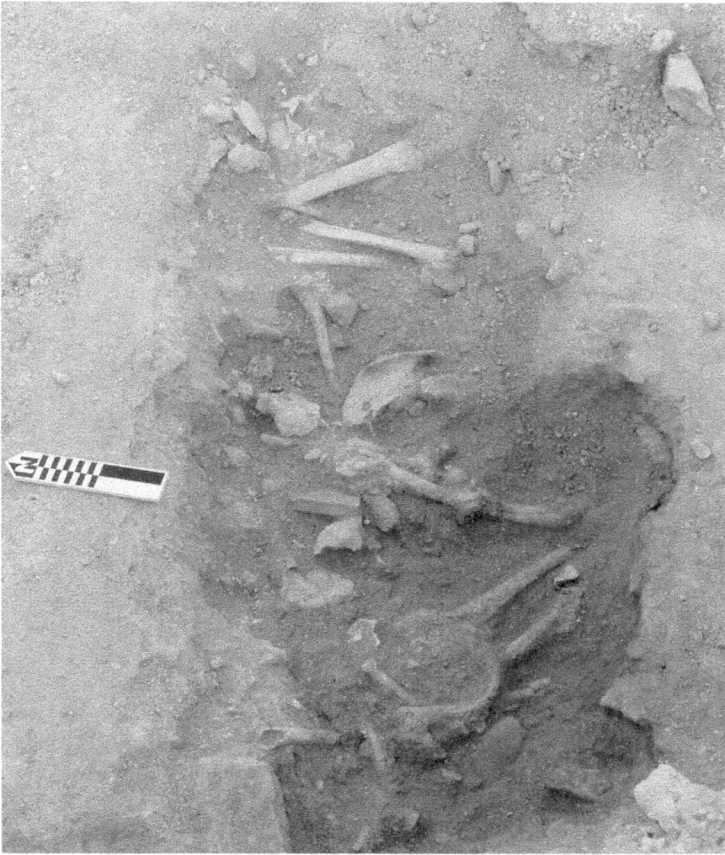

Figure 4.5. The Burial 34 grave fill in the E.G0 narthex contained commingled skeletal remains of at least five individuals. An articulated right leg at the bottom of the deposit was not disturbed by the intrusion of Burial 34A to its north. Photo by Brenda J. Baker.

primary interments in these graves are laid in supine, extended positions with the feet to the east and the head to the west. A significant difference, however, is that the graves in the E.G0 narthex were typically reused or cut into by later burials, a practice that often jumbled the remains of multiple individuals and the rubble fill (Figure 4.5). It is possible that graves dug under the floor were not marked above ground.

While some of the graves within the narthex are cist tombs, many are simply subsurface pits that lack lining stones or cover slabs. The absence of cover slabs undoubtedly contributed to the disturbance of prior burials

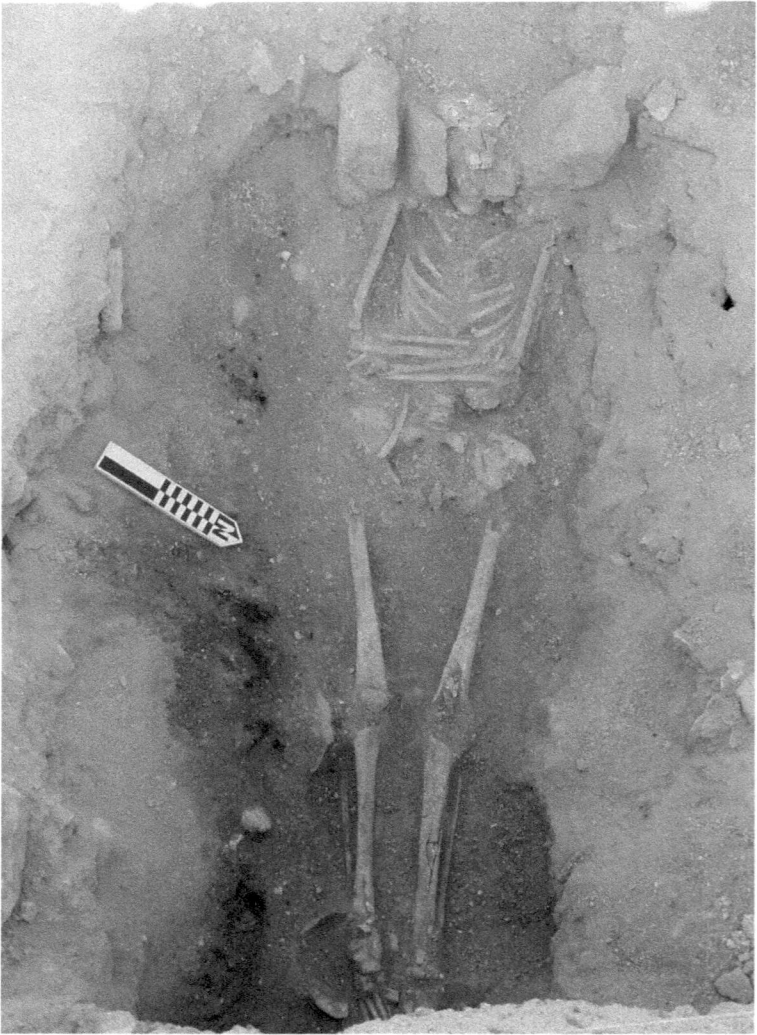

Figure 4.6. The skull of Burial 34A, an older adult female, rested on a fragment of roof tile and had support stones on each side. A vitreous glaze bowl was placed at the right foot and a piece of another was found by the right knee. The southern portion of the Burial 34 grave, where an articulated right leg was located, is under the north arrow that points to the dark line of carbonized coffin wood from that individual's coffin. Photo by Brenda J. Baker.

over time. As in the E.F2 area, iron nails indicate that wooden coffins were sometimes used. Charred remnants of a wooden coffin found at the base of a narthex grave (Burial 34) that was disturbed by a later inhumation (Burial 34A) have been identified as juniper that dates to the fourteenth century or later (Sturt Manning, personal communication 2009). Many individuals, including those in cist tombs, were interred without coffins. Instead, stones were placed at each side of the head, and stones or other items, such as ceramic roof tile, were placed under the head (Figure 4.6). Head supports were not found in the E.F2 graves excavated by the authors and are not mentioned by Buck (1993), suggesting that they mark a later custom in Cyprus (i.e., dating from the 1200s or later) that coincides with the inclusion of bowls. "Stone pillows" are also noted in Cyprus at Episkopi in three graves, two from Chrysanayiotissa Site I, Layer 1 (ca. 1550 to 1571) and one from Chrysanayiotissa Site II, which dates from the fifteenth or sixteenth century, in which the arms of the deceased were extended by their sides rather than crossed over the chest (Ivison 1993, II:145–47). At Polis, those interred with head supports in the E.G0 narthex include adults of both sexes whose arms tend to be folded across the waist. Stones were placed to level the head and maintain the face in an upright position (i.e., looking upward). In one case (Burial 35), a large stone was also set under a man's chin to keep the head from collapsing onto his chest. Similar head support stones have been found among Frankish burials at Corinth dating from the mid-thirteenth century to the second decade of the fourteenth century (Barnes 2003).

Bioarchaeological Research at Polis

The divergent functions and periods of use of the two churches provide new insight into medieval Cypriot burial practices and changes in these practices over time, as demonstrated by the variability outlined above in grave types and their inclusions. Yet to be understood is whether certain grave types or items included with the deceased are reserved for specific segments of the population or are distributed widely across age, sex, or socioeconomic groups. For example, were cist tombs typically reserved for men rather than women or for older adults rather than children? Were certain grave inclusions associated only with particular age groups or only one sex (e.g., pectoral crosses, coins, ceramics)? Buck (1993, 43) found that only 20 of the 80 graves included in her study of the E.F2 basilica and environs had at least one cover slab and only five had evidence of a coffin, but she did not detect any association of cover slabs, coffins, or the occurrence of grave goods with the age of the deceased. The increased sample size for the E.F2 cemetery and the addition of burials from the E.G0 basilica will permit a thorough analysis of relationships among age, sex, grave location, type of grave, and various accoutrements.

How Do the Mortuary Treatment and Identity of Individuals from the Two Basilicas Compare?

Demographic profiles of all those buried inside both basilicas and those in the E.F2 external cemetery are not yet available but will be compiled to compare the age and sex composition and mortality rates of those in differing contexts. The possibility that certain areas of the cemetery were reserved for those of a particular sex or age group will also be evaluated. For example, it has been observed that burials of children were concentrated to the east of the E.F2 basilica and that their bodies were consistently buried at higher elevation than others, indicating that the cemetery may have been restricted to children during its final period of use. Alternatively, children's graves may simply have been shallower than those of adults. The proportion of children to adults interred in this area of the cemetery and comparison of the depths of these graves with those of children buried elsewhere must be assessed to substantiate this suggestion.

Because of their placement, it is possible that those interred inside the E.F2 basilica and the naos of the E.G0 basilica had important roles in the community, though some individuals in cist tombs in the E.G0 narthex and the E.F2 cemetery (e.g., Burials 1 and 3 in Trench e10; Figure 4.3) may also be special in some way. Burial 37, in the southwest corner of the E.G0 narthex, was located in a defined space that was further demarcated by stones along the grave's top perimeter (Figure 4.7). The tomb contained the skeleton of a young woman (age 18–24, based on multiple indicators) and the disarticulated remains of an infant (7–11 months old) along her left thigh and arm. The presence of a fetal metacarpal or metatarsal and phalanx recovered from the level of skeletal remains indicates that the woman was pregnant at the time of death. The woman's head rested on a piece of limestone, and limestone blocks framed the top of the skull, one forming a ledge at the northwest corner of the grave on which an intact glazed bowl rested. A second bowl was found in two pieces at the left

Figure 4.7. Burial 37, located in the southwest corner of the narthex in the E.G0 basilica, during excavation in July 2006 (viewed from above, south). This grave is outlined by 15 limestone and sandstone slabs. Stones support either side of the young woman's skull at the west end of the grave, with one providing a ledge on which a vessel was placed. Cranial bones of an infant are evident atop the woman's left shoulder and next to her left elbow. Photo by Brenda J. Baker.

knee. These ceramics were identified as products of a Paphos workshop and dated to the thirteenth century or the first half of the fourteenth century (Demetra Bakirtzis, personal communication 2006). Fragments of wood in the thoracic cavity above the scapulae, some with bright yellow and orange-red coloration, suggest that an icon may have been placed on the chest.

Graves such as this one illustrate the significant changes in burial rituals and treatment of the dead from Late Antiquity to the later Middle Ages. The later burials include bowls containing matter that was burned, in one case charring and preserving part of the coffin of a previous burial into which the grave cut (Figure 4.6). Ivison (1993, I:247; see also Ivison 2000) discussed this "radical departure from previous Byzantine burial customs" as "a change in attitudes to the needs of the dead" that "coincides with the Latin conquest of Byzantium." He suggested a Frankish origin for these new practices, which included placement of vessels containing charcoal and aromatic plants and herbs, including frankincense. Aromatics were believed to reduce the odor of decomposition and keep demons away (Ivison 1993, I:248–249). Charcoal is also an excellent odor absorber.

The fact that Cyprus was controlled by foreign rulers during this period raises the question of origin of the individuals buried within the E.G0 basilica. Were these people local elites, or could some have been colonizers from the Frankish or Venetian heartland who were transplanted to control the island's resources and populace? Stable isotope analysis of human remains provides a means of investigating this question. Garvie-Lok's (2008) study of residential mobility in Frankish Corinth illustrates the potential of using stable isotopes to distinguish between local and nonlocal individuals in burial assemblages of this era. Results of her preliminary investigation identified two of 17 individuals with oxygen isotope values indicative of birth outside the Aegean region. In combination with stable carbon and nitrogen analyses, Garvie-Lok (2008) was able to determine that one individual had immigrated to Corinth from a hot, arid (i.e., desert) region in North Africa or the Middle East, while the other had grown up in an area with a climate that was similar to that of Corinth but had a dramatically different diet than that of local residents, which suggested divergent subsistence practices. While much evidence (written sources as well as archaeological finds) attests to the presence of westerners in the larger cities of medieval Cyprus (villages and remote areas are thought to have been occupied mainly by the native, Orthodox population), these assumptions have yet to be tested directly using the physical remains of the people themselves.

Why Does the E.G0 Basilica Include Burial Repositories that Contain Commingled Remains?

Of the two Late Antique basilicas, only that in area E.G0 contained adjoining repositories used for interment of multiple individuals. It may, then, have been intended as a funerary church and it may also have provided services to a different group of people than the neighboring basilica. Deposition of the human remains in repositories, or at least the ritual activity associated with their deposit, occurred no later than the first half of the seventh century. The presence of coins from the fourth or fifth centuries, however, suggests the possibility of a much earlier primary burial or redeposition of prior burials. The large numbers of adults and children commingled in these repositories could be due to mass death, perhaps from plague, earthquake, or an Arab incursion on the town, all of which are well documented for Cyprus during the period between the basilica's construction in the late fifth century and its later abandonment (see also Fox et al. this volume, who report a deposit of nine individuals in a cistern due to a catastrophic event around the mid-seventh century at Kalavasos-Kopetra). The possibility that the repositories were built as family tombs or as ossuaries to house burials removed from an earlier cemetery must also be considered. Future analysis of the skeletal remains from these repositories, as delineated in the following sections, will address these alternative hypotheses.

The Conflict Hypothesis

Between 600 and 800, Cyprus was a battleground between the Byzantine government and Arab caliphs, who attacked the island at least 24 times (Hackett 1972). The recovery of belt buckles and spear tips from some of the E.G0 repositories, as well as the location of the church near a possible watch tower, led Najberg, Nicklies, and Papalexandrou (2002, 149, 153–154) to suggest that the basilica may have served a local garrison during its earliest phase of use. This hypothesis is fortified by two inhumations near the easternmost repository. These burials, just north and east of the main apse, included bronze javelins or pikes and an iron spear point next to the bodies with an associated coin dating to the early or mid-seventh century (Papalexandrou 2012). This apparent military presence during the period of Arab invasions promotes the hypothesis originally advanced by Najberg, Nicklies, and Papalexandrou (2002) that these repositories contained victims of conflict.

In the case of a conflict, one would expect the age and sex profile of those interred within the repositories to be skewed toward adult males who guarded the town, but it would also likely include women and children who were victims of a raid on the town (i.e., a "catastrophic" mortality profile discussed below and also by Gauld in this volume). The extent to which individual skeletons are represented will be critical in evaluating this hypothesis, as incomplete remains of multiple individuals would not be expected unless the dead were mutilated and dismembered by their attackers. The crucial test of this hypothesis, however, lies in examination of the skeletal remains for evidence of violent perimortem trauma. A high frequency of violent trauma would be expected if conflict resulted in large numbers of dead who were deposited simultaneously in these repositories.

The Plague Hypothesis

Bubonic plague swept the Byzantine empire in periodic outbreaks between 541 and 750 (Little 2006). Thus, mass graves of this era may have functioned as plague pits during this Justinianic pandemic (McCormick 2006), similar to those found throughout Europe during the Black Death. The possibility that the E.G0 repositories contained the dead from an epidemic of plague was raised by Papalexandrou (2012), who pointed out that partial articulation of the skeletons would be expected, although the excavators indicated that the remains were completely disarticulated and commingled.

In epidemics or natural disasters such as an earthquake, one would expect to find both sexes and all age groups. Waldron (2001) concluded that the age and sex distribution in a London plague pit established in 1349 did not differ from those of an overlying attritional cemetery "control group." McCormick (2009, 298), however, noted better representation of infants and juveniles in Waldron's (2001) plague sample than in the cemetery sample, which he contended more closely resembled expected "normal" mortality of these age groups. Age-at-death distributions caused by catastrophic events do, in fact, mirror the age distribution of the living population and include "a greater number of older children, adolescents, and young adults than typical mortality profiles" (Paine 2000, 181). Violent perimortem trauma (especially sharp force injuries) should not be apparent in the skeletal remains, though blunt trauma and crush injuries would be expected in the case of an earthquake. When catastrophes strike, there are often few left to bury the huge numbers of dead. For example, sources during the Justinianic pandemic attest to mortality so high that corpses were often piled up in streets and would remain there for days (Morony 2006, 73). In such situations, decomposition will ensue before burial, so lime and charcoal would be likely additions to mass graves to reduce the stench of putrefaction. For example, bodies covered by quicklime were described at a small potential plague pit in Naples (McCormick 2006, 298–299).

Family Tombs

The possibility that these repositories were originally intended to serve as family tombs was considered by Najberg, Nicklies, and Papalexandrou (2002). Only the western interior repository in the north aisle contained a primary burial that was undisturbed and in its original location, as would be expected in a family tomb. This individual was interred within a stone-lined cist tomb at the bottom of the repository that was covered by slabs and sealed with mortar. Disarticulated remains of other individuals were found in the corner areas around the tomb. Typically, when tombs are reopened for the addition of another body, the earlier remains are pushed aside to make room. Thus, disarticulation and commingling of earlier skeletons often occurs, but the last individual placed in the grave should be articulated and found near the top of the deposit if a large number of interments preceded it.

Again, analysis of skeletal remains can aid in evaluating this hypothesis. If these repositories were family tombs that were reused for as long as one or two centuries, multiple interments and commingling would be expected and would include infants, children, and adults of both sexes. The degree of representation of each individual should be nearly complete, even if earlier remains were pushed aside as new corpses were added. Although soldiers could be interred in family tombs, evidence of perimortem trauma (or at least that attributable to violence) should be uncommon. Because these skeletal signals are similar to those expected for plague deposits, the date ranges for artifacts within the repositories is critical for determining whether or not the repositories were reopened frequently over time or used only briefly to bury a large numbers of people at once.

Reburial of Earlier Interments

A final hypothesis is that the repositories were intended for secondary burials that were removed from their previous location and redeposited within or near the basilica. Papalexandrou (2012) suggested that these facilities may have been intended to accommodate transfer of burials from a preexisting cemetery, perhaps from an earlier church that was destroyed or enlarged by the new structure.

If these are secondary burials, complete disarticulation and only partial representation of skeletons is expected. Small bones of the hands and feet, the sternum, ribs, and other thin or fragile bones should be significantly underrepresented in the repositories. Teeth will also be poorly represented, as they could easily fall out during transfer. Remains of infants and children would likely be the most incomplete, though the age and sex profile should represent a demographic cross-section.

In addition to analysis of the skeletal remains, testing these alternative hypotheses must involve careful examination of photographic records to assess the degree of disarticulation evident. Hasty burials of victims of a raid or epidemic would be at least partly articulated even if bodies were somewhat decomposed prior to burial. Long use of family tombs or gathering of earlier burials for redeposit in these facilities, however, would promote complete disarticulation.

What Was Everyday Life Like in Medieval Polis?

Study of the skeletal remains also provides direct evidence of the health and lifestyles of the populace of Polis in the Late Antique to Venetian periods. The health status of most individuals from the E.G0 basilica has not yet been assessed. The large portion of the E.F2 sample documented by Buck (1993) provides a basis for comparison with other samples in the Eastern Mediterranean region.

Infection

In a small sample of 14 variably preserved (but fairly complete) individuals from the interior (late medieval phase) of the E.G0 basilica examined by Baker through 2007, nonspecific infectious disease is evident in only two (14.3 percent). Buck (1993) found no evidence of chronic infection in the large sample she analyzed from the interior and immediate vicinity of the E.F2 basilica. Periosteal reaction, caused by inflammation that raises the outer covering of bone and stimulates new bone formation, typically reflects localized or systemic infection and sometimes biomechanical stress (e.g., shin splints). The inflammation causes plaque-like deposits to form, leaving striations on the bone's outer surface when healed. The absence of such lesions in the Late Antique sample from E.F2 contrasts sharply with a sample from a basilica at Elaiussa Sebaste on the Turkish coast that dates from the mid-sixth century to the mid-seventh century that was examined by Paine and coworkers (2007). In that sample, 19 percent of adults and 18 percent of subadults exhibited periosteal reaction (Paine et al. 2007, 178). Periosteal reaction in contemporaneous samples from Eleutherna, Crete, and Messene in the Peloponnese affected 6 percent and 9.5 percent of the samples, respectively; at Messene, a case of osteomyelitis (a pus-producing, severe bone infection) and rib lesions indicative of respiratory infection were also evident (Bourbou 2003). At Sourtara Galaniou Kozanis, a cemetery dating to the sixth and seventh centuries in northern Greece, periosteal reaction occurred in only two individuals; the affected bones represented 3.2 percent of the observable left fifth metatarsals and 1.4 percent of the right fibulae (Bourbou and Tsilipakou 2009, 125). In a rural cemetery sample at Korytiani in western Greece (late tenth century to early eleventh century), periosteal reaction affected 6.6 percent of the lower extremities but none of the upper extremities (Papageorgopoulou and Xirotiris 2009, 207).

The rare occurrence of infection in the Polis skeletal remains is an important factor in interpreting the population distribution and life tables produced by Buck (1993, 54–60), which show increased mortality in adolescents and young adults, particularly compared to other contemporaneous samples (e.g., Sourtara [Bourbou and Tsilipakou 2009, 122–123]). A spike in these age groups would be expected in populations with high rates of tuberculosis, and one probable case was discovered in a male approximately 17 years old from the E.G0 sample during the summer of 2010. Buck (1993, 58–59) considered the effects of immigration, but higher mortality in these age groups could also be explained by deaths from conflict, occupational hazards, and the risks of childbearing.

Dental Pathology

The most pervasive conditions observed thus far by Baker in Polis skeletons from both basilicas are dental pathology and osteoarthritis, followed by trauma. In her E.F2 sample, Buck (1993, 65–68) also found a high frequency of individuals (67 percent) with dental pathology, including caries (cavities), calculus (calcified plaque or tartar), and periodontal disease. Additionally, she reported that 44 of 56 individuals (79 percent) displayed one or more enamel hypoplasias. These lesions occur in childhood during tooth formation. When enamel deposition is interrupted, then resumed, a linear groove across the surface of a tooth crown marks the episode of stress. These lesions can be caused by illness, nutritional deficiency, trauma, and other conditions but provide evidence that the childhood stress was survived. At Polis, Buck (1993) found an average of six hypoplasias per individual. In contrast, hypoplasias in the Korytiani sample affected only 17 individuals (9.6 percent), though the mean number per person was 11.24 (Papageorgopoulou and Xirotiris 2009, 202).

Unfortunately, the prevalence of caries, periodontal disease, and other dental pathology at Polis is not directly comparable to most studies that report frequencies based only on tooth count but do not also report them by individual. For example, caries was found in 20 percent of the total number of permanent teeth present from the cemetery at Sourtara that dates to the sixth and seventh centuries (Bourbou and Tsilipakou 2009); 16.8 percent from a rural Byzantine site at Sa'ad, Jordan (Albashaireh and Al-Shorman 2010); and 10.7 percent from Korytiani in the late tenth to early eleventh centuries (Papageorgopoulou and Xirotiris 2009). Nonetheless, the Polis rates seem high and point to a cariogenic diet comprised mainly of carbohydrates, fruit, and vegetables that promoted caries, abscesses, periodontal disease, and antemortem tooth loss.

This pattern contrasts with dietary data from the early sixth century through the mid-seventh century at St. Stephen's monastery in Jerusalem, where adults consumed considerable protein derived from cheese, milk, eggs, and potentially meat (Gregoricka and Sheridan, this volume). Similarly, at an eleventh-century cemetery at Kastella in Heraklion, Crete, isotopic analyses corroborated literary evidence for a diet that included a large proportion of dairy products and fish rather than reliance on grains (Bourbou and Richards 2007). Trace element analyses of a contemporaneous sample from Korytiani in northern Greece confirmed a diet high in plant foods and low in marine foods (Papageorgopoulou and Xirotiris 2009), but Garvie-Lok (2001) found evidence for some consumption of marine resources by Middle Byzantine island inhabitants, including a ruling family on Mitilini and a group of burials from a basilica at Petras, near Siteia, Crete. While island samples suggest a high proportion of protein and fish consumption, Garvie-Lok (2001) found that the medieval diet of the region was generally based on C_3 grains (wheat, barley), olive oil, wine, and a substantial amount of animal products, including dairy, eggs, and some meat. The contribution of fish or animal products to the diet of past Cypriots is thus far unknown, but the high rate of dental pathology suggests that starchy foods were the staple of the Late Antique and Byzantine population of Polis.

Osteoarthritis and Activity-Related Indicators

Osteoarthritis is present in all of the more complete adult skeletons examined by Baker from both the E.F2 and E.G0 basilicas. Buck (1993, 76–77), however, reported it in only 18 of 140 individuals (13 percent) in her E.F2 sample. The greatest frequency was in hand phalanges, followed by the temporomandibular joint, the elbow, and the spine.

In the Late Antique sample from Sourtara, only 2–3 percent of specific elements were affected, all in men over 46 years of age (Bourbou and Tsilipakou 2009, 124). Those at Eleutherna more commonly displayed moderate to severe osteoarthritis in the upper rather than the lower extremities, with higher frequencies (61 percent) observed in all major joints of young adults (18–35 years) than in older adults (Bourbou 2003, 306). Similarly, Paine and co-workers (2007, 178) found the highest frequency in the right shoulder (65 percent) in the Late Antique burials at Elaiussa Sebaste. One third of the sample from Korytiani, dating to the late tenth century to the early eleventh century, displayed osteoarthritis in at least one long bone joint, most often in the knee, followed by the right elbow, the hip, and the shoulder (Papageorgopoulou and Xirotiris 2009, 205–206).

Vertebral degenerative disease occurred in 16.2 percent of the Eleutherna sample, 4.6 percent at Messene sample (Bourbou 2003, 306), and 11 percent (80 of 728 preserved vertebrae) at Sourtara (Bourbou and Tsilipakou 2009, 124), all similar to the 6 percent frequency of vertebral osteophytosis (bony outgrowths) in the E.F2 sample at Polis (Buck 1993, 77). In the somewhat later group from Korytiani, vertebral osteophytosis was evident in 11.6 percent of 809 observable adult vertebrae, and osteoarthritis of vertebral joints occurred in 24.7 percent (Papageorgopoulou and Xirotiris 2009, 203). At Late Antique Elaiussa Sebaste, however, 14 of the 16 adults with vertebrae (87.5 percent) were affected (Paine et al. 2007, 178–179).

Clearly, some of the disparity is due to how frequencies are reported (e.g., percentages of observable elements affected versus the number of individuals with observable elements affected). It would appear, however, that the Early Christian group at Elaiussa Sebaste performed different types of work than those buried at the other locations, while those interred in the E.F2 basilica and cemetery at Polis did more work involving the hands than others.

The manual labor in which the Polis population engaged is exemplified by a woman buried in the E.F2 cemetery who has been identified as a seamstress (Baker, Terhune, and Papalexandrou 2012). Muscle attachments and facet development on the woman's hand bones are consistent with occupational stress attributed to tailors, while alterations in the hips, legs, and feet indicate habitual kneeling, sitting, and squatting (see also Ullinger et al. this volume). Grooves and wear on the lateral aspects of the upper second incisors arose from drawing thread through them, indicating involvement in textile or clothing production. To date, 15 of 45 adults (33.3 percent) with observable dentitions, including 11 women and 4 men, show alterations of the anterior teeth consistent with their use as tools (Baker 2011). Three patterns of use wear consisting of grooves and notches have been identified, indicating different ways of using the anterior dentition in daily work (Baker and Moramarco 2011). Use of teeth in fiber and textile production predominates among women (11 of 16, or 68.8 percent, of adult females are affected compared to 4 of 27, or 16.7 percent, of males). Thus, of the 15 affected, nearly 73.3 percent are women (Baker 2011).

Participants in fiber production (spinning using the mouth) were also identified at the Venetian period cemetery of Athienou-Malloura, where 5 of 35 adults presented a pattern of notches, grooves, and lingual wear on the maxillary teeth nearly identical to that of the woman from the E.F2 cemetery in Polis (Harper and Fox 2008, 19). These individuals also had squatting facets, ischial rugosity from long periods of sitting on hard surfaces, and expanded metacarpal shafts from repetitive motion of the hands (ibid.). Erdal (2008) also attributed mesiodistally directed (transverse) grooves crossing the occlusal surfaces of incisors from five tenth-century females in a small sample from Kovuklukaya, near the Black Sea in northern Anatolia, to use of the mouth for spinning yarn. The orientation and position of grooves in the anterior teeth of these women differ significantly in direction and position from those documented in Cyprus (side to side across the biting surface of the top front teeth rather than back and forth along the sides of the adjacent incisor teeth).

Trauma

At Polis, Buck (1993, 69–70) found trauma in only two left ulnae, a right tibia, one rib, a left clavicle, and a hand phalanx, all of which were healed or in the process of healing. Only one of the left ulnae exhibited a parry fracture. Transverse fractures below (distal to) the midshaft of this bone that do not involve the adjacent radius typically result from raising the forearm to protect the face and may be used as an indicator of interpersonal violence (Judd 2008).

Evidence of trauma in the smaller sample observed by Baker since 2005 is more frequent, affecting 13 of 40 (32.5 percent) of relatively complete adults (mostly from the E.G0 basilica) thus far analyzed for pathology (Baker 2011). Trauma in this group is largely accidental and more common in males (9 of 22, or 40.9 percent, affected), who often exhibit multiple healed fractures. An example is an older adult male, 45–50 years old (based on pubic symphysis and auricular surface morphology), who survived a fall that caused a compression fracture in one lumbar vertebra and broke the spinous processes of those below it, fractured his left clavicle, and subsequently developed severe osteoarthritis in the left shoulder and neck (Figure 4.8). Also affected was the Venetian period man buried with the bowl on his chest and the coin in his mouth (E.G0:g11, Tomb 2). This man had lost all his lower teeth (the upper jaw was not preserved) well before dying at 40–49 years of age. Rugged muscle attachments in the hands and upper arms are accompanied by a healed fracture of a right rib and the left fifth metacarpal (the outer bone in the palm) and injury to the right wrist and left shoulder with subsequent osteoarthritis in that joint and the thoracic region of his spine. Taken together, these factors indicate that he did not live a life of ease. In contrast, only three of 16 females (18.8 percent) examined to date display trauma. In two cases, including a woman with well-healed cranial depression fractures (E.G0:f11, Tomb 15, Individual 1) and another with a parry fracture of the right ulna and broken ribs (E.G0:d13, Burial 34A), the injuries are consistent with violence (Baker 2011).

Fractures vary in frequency in other medieval samples from the eastern Mediterranean region, as do the proportions attributable to violence. For Late Antique samples, only five cases were found in 151 individuals (3.3 percent) at Eleutherna, all in adult males and confined to two fractures at the wrist end of the radius that were caused by bracing during a fall (Colles' fractures), two fifth metatarsal fractures on the outside of the foot, and one parry fracture of the ulna (Bourbou 2003, 308). At Sourtara, trauma was even less frequent (Bourbou and Tsilipakou 2009), and no fractures were reported for Messene Bourbou (2003, 308). In contrast, Paine et al. (2007, 179) observed trauma in a minimum of 21 percent of

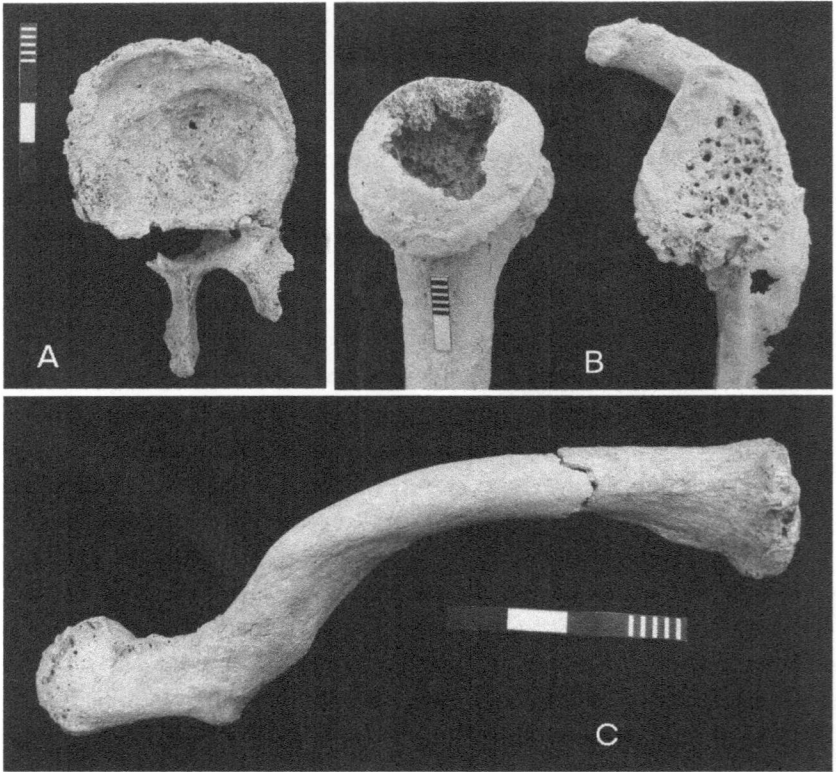

Figure 4.8. Trauma in an older man, age 45–50 (E.G0:g11 Tomb 1, Individual 2 [1996]). A: Compression fracture of the third lumbar vertebra, superior view. B: Severe osteoarthritis of the left shoulder joint, probably from a partial dislocation, with marginal lipping of the humerus head (left) and the porous and irregular surface of the glenoid fossa of the scapula (right). Postmortem damage obscures observation of the articular surface of the humerus head. C: Healed fracture of the lateral (shoulder) portion of the left clavicle shaft causing misalignment (at bottom left), superior view. All photos by Brenda J. Baker.

the Elaiussa Sebaste adults, including several healed cranial fractures, a healed mandible fracture, and a number of stab/cut wounds. The rate of trauma at this coastal urban center is similar to that at Kastella, an eleventh-century urban cemetery in Crete documented by Bourbou (2009), where 10 of 35 adults (28.5 percent) displayed one or more fractures, seven of which were males. Evidence of violence included sharp force and blunt force cranial fractures in two men, respectively, and a cut to the left scapula of another. Three individuals sustained multiple fractures. Bourbou compared trauma patterns at Kastella with those at two other Middle Byzantine sites in the rural western part of Crete and found that fracture frequencies were much lower in the two rural samples; frequencies for particular bones ranged from 6.2 to 13.3 percent at Pemonia and 4.2 to 6.2 percent at Stylos. While most fractures were attributed to accidents, one individual at each of the rural sites had a parry fracture of the right ulna. The rural site of Korytiani, which dates from the end of the tenth and the beginning of the eleventh century, like the rural sites in Crete, had a low rate of trauma. Only four of 131 adults (3 percent) exhibited fractures—three fibula fractures and one ulnar parry fracture (Papageor-gopoulou and Xirotiris 2009). Interestingly, the pattern of trauma in the Late Antique Polis sample analyzed by Buck (1993) resembles the rural samples reported by others, despite the evidence that it was a town of some importance at this time.

Anemia

Lesions attributable to hereditary or acquired anemia are of great interest in this region. Acquired anemia can result from iron deficiency due to a diet poor in iron, the malabsorption of iron due to infection or parasite load, or other nutritional deficiencies such as rickets and scurvy. Heredi-tary anemias, including thalassemia (also known as Cooley's anemia) and sickle-cell anemia, are genetic conditions found in areas where malaria was or remains prevalent.

Thalassemia today is a major health concern in Cyprus. Approximately 15 percent of the population carries the gene for beta-thalassemia and 10 percent carries the gene for alpha-thalassemia (Ashiotis et al. 1973; Book 1980). This frequency is among the highest known. Fetuses that are homo-zygous for alpha-thalassemia (inheriting one thalassemia allele from each parent) are typically stillborn. One of 166 newborns is homozygous for beta-thalassemia (thalassemia major) with an incidence of approximately five per 1,000 live births (Ashiotis et al. 1973). Without medical treatment, homozygous individuals generally do not live beyond the second year (Lagia, Eliopoulos, and Manolis 2007, 281). Those who inherit only one allele for beta-thalassemia (thalassemia minor) do not have medical prob-lems. Individuals with an intermediate expression, however, may exhibit bone changes but usually live longer than homozygous individuals (Book 1980, 61–62, 67; Lagia, Eliopoulos, and Manolis 2007, 272). The most se-vere skeletal pathology is found in the skull. The diploë (the spongy bone between the inner and outer tables of the cranial vault) expands, causing thickening of the skull bones and destruction of the external table (porotic hyperostosis). In radiographs, a "hair-on-end" appearance (Ortner 2003, 365) is seen, which may also occur in severe cases of acquired anemia. In homozygous individuals, the facial bones are affected and growth and maturation are retarded (Book 1980; Lagia, Eliopoulos, and Manolis 2007; Ortner 2003, 365). Tubular bones of the limbs, ribs, vertebrae and hip bones are affected in homozygous and heterozygous individuals, mainly due to reduced bone density and porosity, often accompanied by frequent pathological fractures.

Thalassemia undoubtedly affected past populations of Cyprus (Angel 1966). At Polis, however, gross evidence of hereditary or acquired anemia is uncommon. Among individuals Baker examined from the E.G0 basilica, cribra orbitalia (manifested as irregular new bone formation in active cases and pinprick porosity when healed) is present in the orbital roofs of only one adult (healed) and no children and in one adult male (healed) from the E.F2 cemetery, indicating acquired anemia in all cases. Buck (1993, 81) observed only two instances in the 75 frontal bones present (2.7 percent) in her E.F2 sample, but radiographs of nine crania that were deemed thicker than normal revealed two with the diagnostic "hair-on-end" appearance and five others with expanded diploë, though none showed porosity on the external table. Because it is difficult to differentiate between acquired and hereditary anemias, Buck did not specify which condition was most likely responsible for the cranial pathology.

Bourbou (2003, 306) found three cases of cribra orbitalia in 51 subadults (5.9 percent) at Eleutherna, in two of 19 subadults (10.5 percent) and 6 of 55 adults (10.9 percent) at Messene, and one case of porotic hyperostosis, also suggesting acquired anemia, in the entire sample of 74 individuals (1.4 percent). Frequencies at Sourtara (northern Greece) are reported by bone; four of 13 frontals (13 percent) exhibit cribra orbitalia (two in subadults) and 5–8 percent of parietal and occipital bones display porotic hyperostosis (Bourbou and Tsilipakou 2009, 124). Papageorgopoulou and Xirotiris (2009, 218) found no evidence of metabolic or anemic conditions at Korytiani, also in northern Greece. At Elaiussa Sebaste on the Turkish coast, however, 20 percent of the 42 with preserved cranial elements had porotic hyperostosis or cribra orbitalia (Paine et al. 2007, 182).

Summary

From this preliminary analysis of skeletal pathology, it is apparent that Polis resembles rural populations from other parts of the eastern Mediterranean in many ways but differs in dietary staples that may have led to increased dental disease and nutritional stress in infancy and childhood. The low frequency of infectious disease and trauma attributable to interpersonal violence contrasts with the urbanized sample from Elaiussa Sebaste. Patterns of osteoarthritis and musculoskeletal stress in the Polis sample reveal that most people were performing work that used the upper body. In addition, 15 of 45 adults (33.3 percent) with observable dentitions analyzed to date show alterations of the anterior teeth consistent with their use as tools, including 11 women and 4 men (Baker 2011). Three patterns of use wear consisting of grooves and notches have been identified, indicating different ways of using the anterior dentition in daily work (Baker and Moramarco 2011).

Systematic analysis of pathology in all the post-Classical skeletal remains at Polis will permit comparison of those from each basilica and among different periods. Thorough analysis will also reveal patterns of health among age groups or differences between males and females or high versus lower status interments. This research is necessary to discern differences in risk or susceptibility to various conditions based on age, sex, or socioeconomic status and will also facilitate comprehensive comparisons with other Late Antique and Byzantine skeletal samples in the region.

Conclusion

A recent review of Cypriot bioarchaeology by Harper and Fox (2008) highlighted the paucity of such research in general, but especially on the Late Antique and medieval inhabitants of the island. Ivison (1996, 99) contended that "the dismissive perception of Byzantine graves by classical archaeologists" led to their underutilization in understanding key aspects of change in settlement and society, and other investigators (e.g., Bourbou 2003; Bourbou and Tsilipakou 2009; Papageorgopoulou and Xirotiris 2009; Paine et al. 2007) have lamented the lack of attention the later periods have received and decry the scattered comparative material available for the entire eastern Mediterranean region.

This chapter highlights the potential that bioarchaeological research holds for interpreting the later history of Cyprus and the lives of the people who created it. The bioarchaeological approach to the investigation of burials associated with the two medieval basilicas excavated by the Princeton team in Polis, Cyprus, integrates aspects of mortuary variability and ideology with biological data gleaned from the skeletal remains of the deceased. As analysis of the skeletal collection proceeds, information on age and sex, pathology present, indicators of skeletal stress, and metric and nonmetric variation related to biological affinities and relatedness will be obtained through nondestructive observation of preserved bone. In addition, isotopic research requiring destructive sampling may be used in the future at Polis to reconstruct the diet and to assess the possibility that some individuals may have immigrated into the town during different periods. An interdisciplinary perspective that incorporates bioarchaeology will thus augment archaeological research at Polis in multiple ways, enriching our understanding of its past peoples.

Acknowledgments

We are grateful to the Department of Antiquities of Cyprus and to William A. P. Childs, director of the Princeton University Archaeological Expedition to Polis, who have supported this work and provided access to previously excavated material. We also wish to thank Nancy Serwint, assistant director; Alexandros Koupparis, the expedition foreman; Nancy Corbin, project registrar; and many past and present project members who have contributed to the excavation and curation of the Polis burials. We also thank Sidney Rempel for drafting Figure 4.1. Any errors of interpretation are our own.

References Cited

Albashaireh, Z. S. M., and A. A. Al-Shorman
2010   The Frequency and Distribution of Dental Caries and Tooth Wear in a Byzantine Population of Sa'ad, Jordan. *International Journal of Osteoarchaeology* 20:205–213.
Angel, J. Lawrence
1966   Porotic Hyperostosis, Anemias, Malarias, and Marshes in the Prehistoric Eastern Mediterranean. *Science* 153:760–763.

Ashiotis, Th., Z. Zachariadis, K. Sofroniadou, D. Loukopoulos, and G. Stamatoyan-
nopoulos
1973   Thalassaemia in Cyprus. *British Medical Journal* 2(5857):38–42.
Baker, Brenda J.
2011   Skeletal Evidence for the Sexual Division of Labor in Medieval Arsinoë. Paper
        presented at the Annual Meeting of the American Schools of Oriental Re-
        search, San Francisco.
Baker, Brenda J., and Michael W. Moramarco
2011   Groovy Teeth: Unraveling Patterns of Dental Use Wear in a Medieval Sample
        from Polis, Cyprus. *American Journal of Physical Anthropology* 144(Suppl.
        52):80.
Baker, Brenda J., Claire E. Terhune, and Amy Papalexandrou
2012   Sew Long? The Osteobiography of a Woman from Medieval Polis, Cyprus.
        In *The Bioarchaeology of Individuals,* edited by Ann L. W. Stodder and Ann
        Palkovich, pp. 151–161. University Press of Florida, Gainesville.
Bakirtzis, Charalambos
1999   Early Christian Rock-Cut Tombs at Hagios Georgios, Peyia, Cyprus. In *Me-
        dieval Cyprus. Studies in Art, Architecture, and History in Memory of Doula
        Mouriki,* edited by Nancy Patterson Ševčenko and Christopher Moss, pp. 35–
        48. Department of Art and Archaeology, Princeton University Press, Princ-
        eton, N.J.
Barnes, Ethne
2003   The Dead *Do* Tell Tales. In *Corinth, The Centenary: 1896–1996,* pp. 435–443.
        Vol. 20 of *Corinth.* American School of Classical Studies, Athens.
Book, Patricia A.
1980   *Thalassemia: An Anthropological Study of 86 Patients and Their Families in
        Cyprus.* Ph.D. dissertation, University of Connecticut. University Microfilms,
        Ann Arbor.
Bourbou, Chryssi
2003   Health Patterns of Proto-Byzantine Populations (6th–7th centuries AD) in
        South Greece: The Cases of Eleutherna (Crete) and Messene (Peloponnese).
        International Journal of Osteoarchaeology 13:303–313.
2009   Patterns of Trauma in a Medieval Urban Population (11th Century A.D.) from
        Central Crete. In *New Directions in the Skeletal Biology of Greece,* edited by
        Lynne A. Schepartz, Sherry C. Fox, and Chryssi Bourbou, pp. 111–120. Hespe-
        ria Supplement 43. American School of Classical Studies at Athens, Princeton,
        N.J.
Bourbou, Chryssi, and Michael P. Richards
2007   The Middle Byzantine Menu: Palaeodietary Information from Isotopic Analy-
        sis of Humans and Fauna from Kastella, Crete. *International Journal of Osteo-
        archaeology* 17:63–72.
Bourbou, Chryssi, and Agathoniki Tsilipakou
2009   Investigating the Human Past of Greece during the 6th–7th Centuries A.D. In
        New Directions in the Skeletal Biology of Greece, edited by Lynne A. Schepartz,

Sherry C. Fox, and Chryssi Bourbou, pp. 121–136. Hesperia Supplement 43. American School of Classical Studies at Athens, Princeton, N.J.

Buck, Stacey A.

1993   Life on the Edge of the Empire: Demography and Health in Byzantine Cyprus. Unpublished master's thesis, Department of Anthropology, Arizona State University, Tempe.

Buikstra, Jane E., and Douglas H. Ubelaker (editors)

1994   *Standards for Data Collection from Human Skeletal Remains.* Arkansas Archeological Survey Research Series no. 44. Arkansas Archeological Survey, Fayetteville.

Childs, William A. P.

1988   First Preliminary Report on the Excavations at Polis Chrysochous by Princeton University. *Report of the Department of Antiquities, Cyprus* 1988:121–130.

2008   Polis Chrysochous: Princeton University's Excavations of Ancient Marion and Arsinoe. *Near Eastern Archaeology* 71:64–75.

Constas, Nicholas

2006   Death and Dying in Byzantium. In *Byzantine Christianity,* edited by Derek Krueger, pp. 124–145. Fortress Press, Minneapolis.

Ćurčić, Slobodan

1999   Byzantine Architecture on Cyprus: An Introduction to the Problem of the Genesis of a Regional Style. In *Medieval Cyprus: Studies in Art, Architecture, and History in Memory of Doula Mouriki,* edited by Nancy Patterson Ševčenko and Christopher Moss, pp. 71–91. Department of Art and Archaeology, Princeton University Press, Princeton, N.J.

Garvie-Lok, Sandra J.

2001   *Loaves and Fishes: A Stable Isotope Reconstruction of Diet in Medieval Greece.* Ph.D. dissertation, University of Calgary. University Microfilms, Ann Arbor.

2008   Population Mobility at Frankish Corinth: Evidence from State Oxygen Isotope Ratios of Tooth Enamel. In *New Directions in the Skeletal Biology of Greece,* edited by Lynne A. Schepartz, Sherry C. Fox, and Chryssi Bourbou, pp. 245–256. Hesperia Supplement 43. American School of Classical Studies at Athens, Princeton, N.J.

Hackett, John

1972 [1901]   *A History of the Orthodox Church of Cyprus.* Philosophy and Religious History Monographs 103. Burt Franklin, New York.

Harper, Nathan K., and Sherry C. Fox

2008   Recent Research in Cypriot Bioarchaeology. *Bioarchaeology of the Near East* 2:1–38.

Ivison, Eric A.

1993   Mortuary Practices in Byzantium (c950–1453): An Archaeological Contribution. 2 vols. Unpublished Ph.D. dissertation, Centre for Byzantine and Modern Greek Studies, School of Antiquity, University of Birmingham, Birmingham, England.

1996   Burial and Urbanism at Late Antique and Early Byzantine Corinth (*c.* AD 400–700). In *Towns in Transition: Urban Evolution in Late Antiquity and the Early Middle Ages,* edited by Neil Christie and S. T. Loseby, pp. 99–125. Scolar Press, Hants, England.

2000   "Supplied for the journey to heaven": A Moment of West-East Cultural Exchange: Ceramic Chalices from Byzantine Graves. *Byzantine and Modern Greek Studies* 24:147–193.

Judd, Margaret A.

2008   The Parry Problem. *Journal of Archaeological Science* 35:1658–1666.

Lagia, A., C. Eliopoulos, and S. Manolis

2007   Thalassemia: Macroscopic and Radiological Study of a Case. *International Journal of Osteoarchaeology* 17:269–285.

Little, Lester K. (editor)

2006   *Plague and the End of Antiquity: The Pandemic of 541–750.* Cambridge University Press, New York.

McCormick, Michael

2006   Toward a Molecular History of the Justinianic Pandemic. In *Plague and the End of Antiquity: The Pandemic of 541–750,* edited by Lester K. Little, pp. 290–312. Cambridge University Press, New York.

Morony, Michael G.

2006   "For Whom Does the Writer Write?" The First Bubonic Plague Pandemic According to Syriac Sources. In *Plague and the End of Antiquity: The Pandemic of 541–750,* edited by Lester K. Little, pp. 59–86. Cambridge University Press, New York.

Najberg, Tina, Charles Nicklies, and Amy Papalexandrou

2002   Princeton University Excavations at Polis/Arsinoe: Preliminary Report on the Roman and Medieval Levels. *Report of the Department of Antiquities, Cyprus* 2002:139–154.

Ortner, Donald J.

2003   *Identification of Pathological Conditions in Human Skeletal Remains.* 2nd ed. Academic Press, San Diego.

Paine, Richard R.

2000   If a Population Crashes in Prehistory, and There Is No Paleodemographer There to Hear It, Does It Make a Sound? *American Journal of Physical Anthropology* 112:181–190.

Paine, Robert R., R. Vargiu, Alfredo Coppa, C. Morselli, and E. E. Schneider

2007   A Health Assessment of High Status Christian Burials Recovered from the Roman-Byzantine Archeological Site of Elaiussa Sebaste, Turkey. *HOMO—Journal of Comparative Human Biology* 58:173–190.

Papageorgopoulou, Christina, and Nikolaos I. Xirotiris

2009   Anthropological Research on a Byzantine Population from Korytiani, West Greece. In *New Directions in the Skeletal Biology of Greece,* edited by Lynne A. Schepartz, Sherry C. Fox, and Chryssi Bourbou, pp. 193–221. Hesperia Supplement 43. American School of Classical Studies at Athens, Princeton, N. J.

Papalexandrou, Amy

2007   Contextualizing the Tomb: "Bowl Burials" from Polis, Cyprus. Abstracts of Papers, 33rd Annual Byzantine Studies Conference, Toronto, October 11–14, p. 46. Available electronically at http://www.bsana.net/conference/archives/2007/BSCAbstracts2007.pdf.

2012   Polis/Arsinoë in Late Antiquity: A Cypriot Town and Its Sacred Sites. In *Approaches to Byzantine Architecture and Its Decoration: Studies in Honor of Slobodan Ćurčić,* edited by Mark J. Johnson, Robert Ousterhout, and Amy Papalexandrou, pp. 27–46. Ashgate, Farnham, Surrey, UK.

Prokopiou, Eleni

1995   Amathous. Eastern Necropolis. Tomb Ossuary of the 7th Century AD. *Report of the Department of Antiquities, Cyprus* 2002:249–279. In Greek.

Purcell, H. D.

1968   *Cyprus.* Frederick A. Praeger, New York.

Sapin, Christian

1999   Architecture and Funerary Space in the Early Middle Ages. Translated and revised by Biley K. Young. In *Spaces of the Living and the Dead: An Archaeological Dialogue,* edited by Catherine E. Karkov, Kelley M. Wickham-Crowley, and Bailey K. Young, pp. 39–60. American Early Medieval Studies 3. Oxbow, Oxford.

Tritsaroli, Paraskevi

2008   Biocultural Approaches to the Study of Mortuary Practices in the Early Byzantine Populations from Greece; the Cases of Akraiphnio, Boeotia and Maroneia, Thrace. *American Journal of Physical Anthropology* 135(Suppl. 46):209–210.

Waldron, H. A.

2001   Are Plague Pits of Particular Use to Palaeoepidemiologists? *International Journal of Epidemiology* 30:104–108.

5

Condemned to *Metallum*?

Illuminating Life at the Byzantine Mining Camp at Phaeno in Jordan

MEGAN A. PERRY, DREW S. COLEMAN, DAVID L. DETTMAN,
AND ABDEL HALIM AL-SHIYAB

The region of Khirbet Faynan in southern Jordan was the site of major mining and smelting operations from at least the fifth millennium BC. Exploitation of copper from the mines became a major industrial operation under Roman and Byzantine rule (Hauptmann 2000; Grattan, Gilbertson, and Hunt 2007; Mattingly et al. 2007). In 1996, a cemetery associated with the Byzantine period occupation at the site, the Southern Cemetery of the third to sixth centuries AD, was excavated by the British Institute in Amman for Archaeology and History (now the Council for British Research in the Levant) and Yarmouk University (Findlater et al. 1998; Mattingly et al. 2007). The 45 skeletons excavated from graves sampled from across the Southern Cemetery are a subset of the estimated 1,000 graves that the cemetery originally held. However, even this small sample can provide a valuable cross-section of the individuals living and working at an imperial mining camp in the Byzantine province of *Palaestina Tertia*. Here we focus on presenting multiple chemical indicators of the origins of these individuals, their level of exposure to toxic environments produced by smelting operations, and their health and disease levels to provide a profile of the mining camp residents and the level of imperial control over such operations.

Historical Background

Byzantine Phaeno, modern Khirbet Faynan, is located at the confluence of Wadis Shegar, Ghuwayr, and Dana in southwestern Jordan (Figure 5.1). The main settlement was explored extensively by the Council for British Research in the Levant, who documented a number of churches, industrial and domestic complexes, water catchment and storage works, and extensive agricultural fields (Freeman and McEwan 1998; Hunt, Gilbertson, and el-Rishi 2007; Mattingly et al. 2007). They also identified three cemeteries contemporary with Roman and Byzantine occupation, including the Southern Cemetery to the southeast of the site. The excavated graves have a uniform interment style similar to that found in other Late Roman and Byzantine cemeteries in Jordan (Ibrahim and Gordon 1987; Perry 2007a), although two graves, one containing an individual 10 years old ±30 months (Grave 105) and another with a female 30–39 years old (Grave 107), contained a notably diverse array of artifacts (Findlater et al. 1998).

Historical sources identify some individuals who occupied Faynan and were possibly buried in the southern cemetery. This includes Christian martyrs and heretics sent to Phaeno during the early fourth century AD who were documented by Eusebius (*Ecclesiastical History* VIII.8, 10; *Martyrs of Palestine* 7.4, 8.1, 13.1–3), Athanasius (*Historia Arianorum* 60), and other early Christian church historians. Khirbet Faynan also likely contained criminals charged with crimes other than religious ones, local mine laborers (often under hereditary contracts), and local and nonlocal administrators (Healy 1978; Millar 1984; Pharr 1952, 10.19.15). Other individuals involved in support operations, such as farmers, church officials, merchants, and craft specialists, also would have been buried in the cemetery. Our bioarchaeological interpretations thus must consider the reality that some of these groups are not represented in our sample of 45 individuals.

Stable Isotopes and Human Migration

First, we explored the presence of immigrants to the site—criminals condemned to *metallum* (the mines) or laborers lured by economic opportunities—using strontium and oxygen isotope analysis of human dental enamel. The ratio of ^{87}Sr to ^{86}Sr is unique to the underlying bedrock and

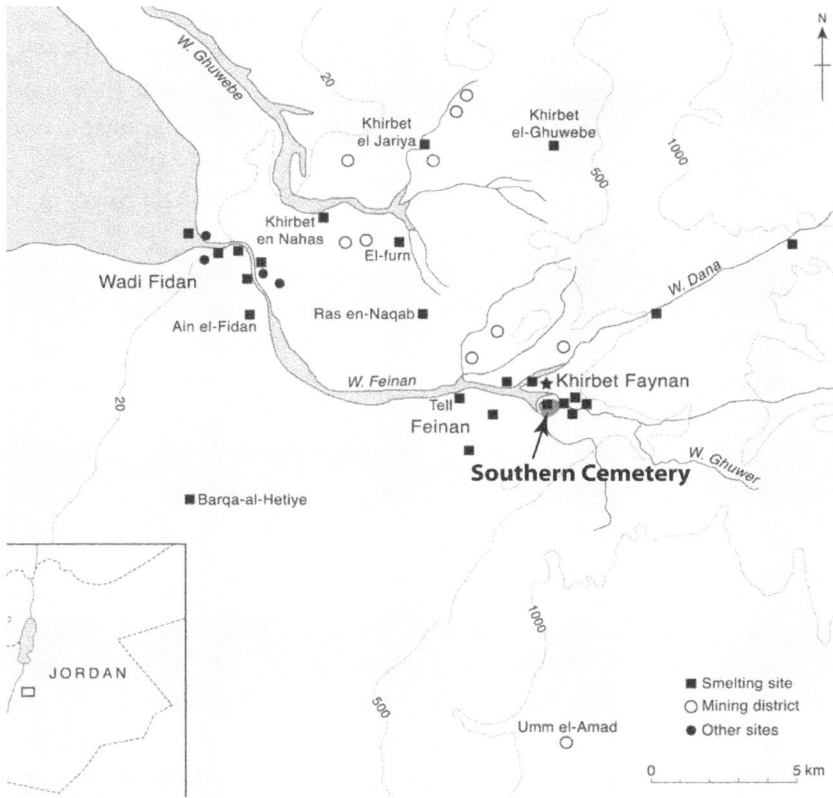

Figure 5.1. Sites located in the vicinity of Khirbet Faynan and Wadi Fidan (from Grattan et al. 2007).

soils of a particular region (Faure 1986; Faure and Powell 1972). Humans and other animals ingest strontium through the consumption of plants, water, and other animals that reflect the geology of the origin of these resources (Bentley 2006; Ericson 1985; Price, Burton, and Bentley 2002). Oxygen isotopes reflect environmental water, including precipitation, surface water bodies, and groundwater (Dansgaard 1964). Oxygen isotope values vary regionally based on distance from the ocean, elevation, evaporation, and a number of climatic variables (Gat and Dansgaard 1972). Humans absorb oxygen isotopes primarily through drinking water, although water in food can slightly influence body water $\delta^{18}O$ (Kohn, Schoeninger, and Valley 1996; Luz, Kolodny, and Horowitz 1984; Luz and Kolodny 1989). Isotopes in human dental enamel become absorbed during childhood enamel formation and do not change during the life-time of an individual and therefore provide a permanent record of the geology and water sources of the area where they spent their childhood (see Dupras and Schwarcz 2001; Ericson 1985, 1989; Ezzo, Johnson, and Price 1997; Evans, Chenery, and Fitzpatrick 2006; Price et al. 1994; Price, Grupe, and Schröter 1998; Price, Burton, and Bentley 2002; Prowse et al. 2007; White, Longstaffe, and Law 2004).

The local strontium isotope value at Faynan was established using fau-nal dental enamel and snail shells recovered from the nearby and geo-logically similar site of Fidan (see Perry et al. 2009). The expected local oxygen isotope value was estimated using published data on groundwater and precipitation oxygen isotope values (Bajjali and Abu-Jaber 2001; Gat and Dansgaard 1972) and by testing the two main water sources at the site: the Wadi Dana and the Wadi Ghuweir springs.

Bioaccumulation of Lead and Copper

Previous studies have indicated that the Roman and Byzantine inhabitants at Faynan lived in an environment contaminated by mining and smelting activities (Grattan et al. 2005; Grattan, Gilbertson, and Hunt 2007; Pyatt et al. 2000). The toxicity of the environment is reflected in elevated lead and copper levels discovered in many of the skeletons from the Southern Cemetery (Grattan et al. 2002; Grattan, Condon et al. 2003; Grattan, Hux-ley, and Pyatt 2003b; Grattan et al. 2005; Pyatt et al. 1999; Pyatt et al. 2000; Pyatt et al. 2005). Published information on lead and copper levels were compared with isotopic indicators of immigration to determine if locally born individuals or immigrants had greater exposure to lead and copper, presumably from working in the mines.

Health and Disease Levels

Finally, we incorporated published data on skeletal pathologies collected by Lotus Abu Karaki and Mahmoud El-Najjar (Abu Karaki 2000; El-Naj-jar and al-Shiyab 1998), and new information was collected by the lead author (Perry) in 2005 to clarify the quality of life of Faynan residents. Historical sources mention the high morbidity and mortality in the mines and the arduous life of many mine workers. First, information on joint osteoarthritis and vertebral osteophytosis (degeneration) was used to see if the Faynan individuals had higher levels of arthritis due to the heavy labor involved in mining compared with levels in regional contemporary populations. These conditions are caused by a combination of normal aging processes and a number of systemic and localized agents such as joint location, sex, genetics, body morphology, and previous injury (Jurmain 1999; Moskowitz 1997; Peyron 1986). Clinical studies have not proven a direct association between joint stress through increased activity and degeneration, although occasionally this can result in greater-than-expected severity over time.

Second, indicators of health and disease levels in this sample were assessed using rates of cribra orbitalia and porotic hyperostosis and the prevalence of dental enamel hypoplasias (DEHs). Textual data provides evidence that the individuals at Faynan were presumed to have poorer health and higher disease loads than other populations. Cribra orbitalia and porotic hyperostosis result in crania porosity and usually are thought to reflect iron-deficiency anemia resulting from consuming iron-poor foods, infectious disease, weanling diarrhea, and parasites (El-Najjar et al. 1976; Stuart-Macadam 1987, 1992; Sullivan 2005). Similar skeletal responses can occur from congenital anemias such as sickle-cell anemia and thalassemia prevalent in areas where malaria is endemic (Angel 1966). Cranial inflammation, taphonomy, and metabolic conditions such as Vitamin C or D deficiency can produce cranial changes that are similar to those caused by iron-deficiency anemia (see Ortner and Putschar 1985; Ortner et al. 2001; Wapler, Crubézy, and Schultz 2004). Careful diagnosis is necessary to distinguish iron-deficiency anemia from these conditions (e.g., Jacobi and Danforth 2002; Sullivan 2005; Wapler, Crubézy, and Schultz 2004).

DEHs form through a cessation and resumption of enamel growth due to a period of physiological or psychological stress during childhood (Goodman and Rose 1990; Goodman, Armelagos, and Rose 1980). Many different types of stress can cause DEH formation (Cuttress and Suckling 1982), but they generally consist of malnutrition, localized trauma, disease, and hereditary anomalies (Goodman and Armelagos 1985; Sarnat and Schour 1941; Sweeney, Saffir, and de Leon 1971). Dental enamel of different teeth forms at essentially set periods during childhood; therefore, the location of the defect from the cemento-enamel junction (CEJ) can indicate the approximate age that the insult occurred (Goodman and Rose 1990; Goodman, Armelagos, and Rose 1980).

Materials and Methods

The Faynan Southern Cemetery sample contains 45 individuals (Table 5.1). Age and sex of the individuals were assessed using Buikstra and Ubelaker's standards (Buikstra and Ubelaker 1994). Sex could be estimated for 20 individuals, 14 females and 6 males. Another six individuals were children aged between 3 years (±12 months) and 10 years (±12 months). Age and/or sex information were not available for the other 19 individuals. Observations of health and disease indicators also followed standard protocol. The central maxillary incisor and mandibular canines were observed for DEHs, since these teeth are more susceptible to DEH formation (Goodman and Armelagos 1985). In addition, presence, degree, location, and activity of porotic hyperostosis and cribra orbitalia and osteoarthritis and vertebral osteophytosis had been observed macroscopically in individuals with cranial remains by Abu Karaki (2000) and El-Najjar and al-Shiyab (1998).

The archaeological human and faunal dental enamel samples for strontium and oxygen isotope analysis were processed and mechanically cleaned in the Bioarchaeology Laboratory at East Carolina University. The human and faunal dental enamel and snail shell samples were subjected to chemical cleaning through repeated washing with distilled water and cleaning with glacial acetic acid at approximately 80°C for 10 hours. After cleaning, the tooth enamel was dissolved in 500 μL of twice-distilled 7N nitric acid (HNO_3) and then evaporated and redissolved in 250 μL of 3.5N HNO_3. Strontium extraction from the sample was accomplished using Eichrom Sr-Spec resin. The sample was dried, then redissolved with 2 μL of 0.1 M dihydrogen phosphate (H_2PO_4)and 2 μL of tantalum pentachloride ($TaCl_5$) and loaded onto rhenium filaments. Isotopic ratios were measured on a VG Micromass Sector-54 thermal ionization mass spectrometer in quintuple-collector dynamic mode at the Isotope Geochemistry Laboratory in the Department of Geosciences at the University of North Carolina at Chapel Hill, using the internal ratio $^{86}Sr/^{88}Sr$ = 0.1194 to correct for mass fractionation. The UNC-Chapel Hill ratios are reported relative to a value of 0.710270 ±0.000014 (2σ) for the NBS 987 standard. Internal precision for strontium runs is typically ±0.000012 to 0.000018 percent (2σ) standard error based on 100 dynamic cycles of data collection.

Table 5.1. Demographic profile of the Southern Cemetery sample from Khirbet Faynan (Phaeno)

Age Category	Indeterminate sex	Males	Females	Total
Birth–1.9 years	0	—	—	0
2–4.9 years	2	—	—	2
5–12.9 years	4	—	—	4
13–19.9 years	0	—	—	0
20–34.9 years	0	5	6	11
35–49.9 years	1	1	7	9
50+ years	0	0	1	1
Adult	3	0	0	3
Indeterminate age	15	0	0	15
Total	25	6	14	45

Oxygen ($\delta^{18}O$) and carbon ($\delta^{13}C$) isotope analysis of enamel carbonate from the archaeological human dental samples was performed at the Stable Isotope Laboratory in the Department of Geosciences at the University of Arizona using a Finnegan MAT 252 mass spectrometer with a Kiel III automated carbonate sampling device. Samples were reacted with dehydrated phosphoric acid at 70°C, and the oxygen isotope fractionation due to the acid release of CO^2 is assumed to be identical to that of calcite. Samples were normalized using NBS 18 and NBS 19. NBS 19 has a reproducibility of ±0.08 percent (1σ) for $\delta^{13}C$ and ±0.1% for $\delta^{18}O$. University of Arizona oxygen isotope ratios are reported relative to the V-PDB carbonate standard and are expressed in parts per mil (‰) using the standard formula:

$$\delta^{18}O = ((^{18}O/^{16}O_{sample})/^{18}O/^{16}O_{standard})-1) \times 1,000.$$

Diagenesis in the dental enamel was assessed using Fourier transform infrared (FTIR) spectral analysis and Sr content. Fourteen teeth were randomly selected for FTIR study. Because tooth sample quantities remaining after analysis were small, 30 microgram samples were pressed into a 40 mg potassium bromide (KBr) pellet and measured on a Midac Corporation infrared spectrometer. Carbonate/phosphate (C/P) ratios were calculated following Pucéat, Reynard, and Lécuyer (2004), and apatite crystallinity index (CI) was calculated using Weiner and Bar-Yosef (1990).

Both C/P and CI were relatively homogenous for the Faynan teeth enamel samples (Perry et al. 2009). C/P ratio ranged from 0.22 to 0.32 (1σ = 0.027), and CI ranged from 3.7 to 4.3 (1σ = 0.19). For comparison, a modern human tooth was also analyzed six different times between the ancient grave samples to test for instrument accuracy and preservation of the ancient samples. Mean C/P for this tooth was 0.22; CI was 3.17. Although CI was higher in the ancient teeth than in the modern one, the CI values measured are well within normal minimally altered tooth enamel samples reported in the archaeological literature (e.g. Wright and Schwarcz 1996; Weiner and Bar-Yosef 1990) and are similar to some CI values in modern bovid tooth enamel samples (Sponheimer and Lee-Thorp 1999). The absence of outliers in this population suggests that these teeth are minimally altered and that isotopic data is unlikely to be modified by diagenesis.

Results and Discussion

Results of the $^{87}Sr/^{86}Sr$ analysis identified only one individual out of 31 as someone originating from a region geologically different from Faynan based on the fauna-established local $^{87}Sr/^{86}Sr$ range of 0.70793 to 0.70814 (Table 5.2; for details, see Perry et al. 2009). This individual, from Grave 102, a male 30–34 years old, possibly grew up in the coastal region and foothills of the Galilee plain in Israel, although other geologically similar regions outside the Levant are possible points of origin (Figure 5.2; see Perry, Coleman, and Delhopital 2008). The oxygen isotope values, in contrast, are relatively homogeneous, although slightly higher than expected considering the local groundwater sources (Bajjali and Abu-Jaber 2001; Gat and Dansgaard 1972). This could result from ingesting evaporated water sources, such as collected rainwater coming from enriched precipitation (Daux et al. 2008; Levin, Gat, and Issar 1980).

Grattan and Pyatt's published copper and lead levels demonstrate that almost all individuals recovered from the Southern Cemetery had elevated copper and lead levels, including some individuals with notably elevated concentrations (Figure 5.3). Levels of these two heavy metals are not affected by age of the individual. Compared with a reference sample with "normal" copper and lead levels (González-Reimers et al. 2001; González-Reimers et al. 2003), 10 individuals from Faynan had copper levels greater than 2 standard deviations of the reference sample mean (>42 μg/g), and

Table 5.2. $^{87}Sr/^{86}Sr$ and $\delta^{18}O$ values and lead and copper levels of archaeological human dental enamel samples at Faynan

Context	Age	Sex	Tooth sampled[a]	Corrected $^{87}Sr/^{86}Sr$[b]	$\delta^{18}O$ VDPB ‰	Copper (µg/g)[c]	Lead (µg/g)[c]
Grave 5	—	—	—	—	—	278.5	47.6
Grave 10	—	—	—	—	—	17.0	20.7
Grave 11	35–39	F?	RM_1	0.70798	-0.95	9.8	1.8
Grave 12	50+	F	RM_1	0.70787	5.38	8.6	112.3
Grave 22	—	—	—	—	—	13.2	1.6
Grave 25	40–44	M	M^1	0.70785	-1.74	109.1	170.0
Grave 27	—	—	—	—	—	30.7	47.5
Grave 63	35–39	F	LM^1	—	-1.30	—	—
Grave 63	35–39	F	LM_1	0.70799	5.98	—	—
Grave 66	—	—	—	—	—	24.0	55.3
Grave 67	6 yrs. ± 24 mos.	?	PM_1	0.70790	0.69	181	289.2
Grave 69	—	—	RPM_2	0.70798	-2.05	17.1	27.6
Grave 70	25–29	F	RPM^2	0.70785	9.84	5.0	1.0
Grave 71	20–25	F	LM^1	0.70791	-1.39	—	—
Grave 71	20–25	F	PM_2	—	-1.63	—	—
Grave 72	25–29	M	LM^1	0.70801	-0.55	3.0	13.0
Grave 73	30–34	F	PM^2	0.70797	-1.78	296.2	19.1
Grave 75	45–49	F	RPM^1	0.70794	-0.77	7.0	42.0
Grave 78	7–9	?	?	0.70798	2.31	20.0	12.8
Grave 80	35–39	F	RM^1	0.70798	4.38	6.3	37.7
Grave 81	30–35	F	LM^1	0.70801	3.36	7.0	27.9
Grave 83	45–49	F	LPM_2	0.70800	0.69	11.0	28.9
Grave 84	35–39	F	PM	0.70793	-2.05	—	—
Grave 84	35–39	F	LPM_2	—	-2.39	—	—
Grave 85	4 yrs. ± 12 mos.	?	—	—	—	43.7	1.0
Grave 86	—	—	—	—	—	2.4	15.0
Grave 87	30–34	M	LPM^1	0.70801	-0.67	2.4	4.7
Grave 88	Adult	?	LM^2	0.70803	-1.34	135.6	75.6
Grave 89	—	—	—	—	—	2.5	16.0
Grave 91	40–45	F	—	—	—	30.0	26.6
Grave 94	—	—	—	—	—	2.1	9.2
Grave 96	20–25	M	RM^1	0.70784	0.32	90.7	44.2
Grave 97	20–24	F?	PM_1	0.70792	2.20	5.7	13.7
Grave 99	3 yrs. ± 12 mos.	?	Rm^1	0.70795	-0.10	—	—
Grave 100B	3 yrs. ± 12 mos.	?	Lm^1	0.70809	0.35	—	—
Grave 101	—	—	—	—	—	29.2	24.3
Grave 102	30–34	M	PM_1	0.70830	-1.12	27.5	75.6
Grave 104	7 yrs. ± 24 mos.	?	LUc	0.70776	-0.05	43.1	17.01
Grave 105	10 yrs. ± 30 mos.	?	RM_1	0.70801	-1.14	17.9	37.1
Grave 107	30–39	F	RM_1	0.70781	-2.24	—	—
Grave 108	Adult	?	LPM_1	0.70793	-0.38	—	—
Grave 109	25–29	M	LM^1	0.70785	-2.45	—	—
Grave 110	—	—	—	—	—	2.8	8.4
Grave 112	45–49	?	RPM_1	0.70783	-1.11	5.9	14.4
Grave 113	—	—	—	—	—	73.9	46.7
Grave 115	Adult	F	RM_1	0.70791	5.20	—	—
Grave 117	45–49	F	RM^1	0.70791	-1.26	22.4	93.7

Notes: a. Tooth notation includes the side, if available (L or R), the tooth type (Uc = upper deciduous canine, m = deciduous molar, PM = adult premolar, M = adult molar), and the number of the tooth position, if applicable, in superscript for upper dentition and subscript for lower dentition
b. NBS 987 standard running mean = 0.710270σ St. Dev. = 0.000014
c. From Grattan et al. 2002

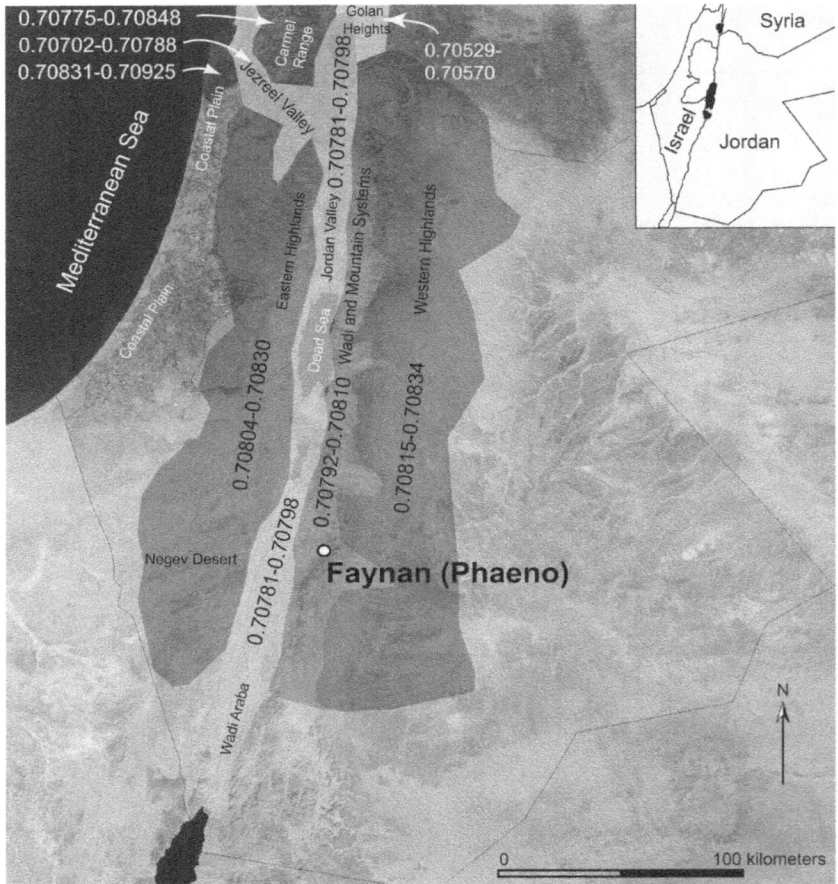

Figure 5.2. Map of the region showing the location of Khirbet Faynan and ^{87}Sr/^{86}Sr variation based on samples of archaeological and modern fauna and modern flora (Perry, Coleman, and Delhopital 2008; Shewan 2004). Unshaded areas of the map indicated insufficient strontium isotope data for these regions.

22 had lead levels more than 2 standard deviations of the reference sample mean (>16.24 μg/g).

Grattan and Pyatt felt that the elevated copper and lead levels in the Faynan residents stemmed from prolonged exposure to a contaminated environment (Grattan et al. 2005; Pyatt et al. 2005). But a comparison of lead and copper concentrations with strontium and oxygen isotope values discovered no relationship between the two. The one definitively nonlocal individual in Grave 102 did have higher-than-average lead levels

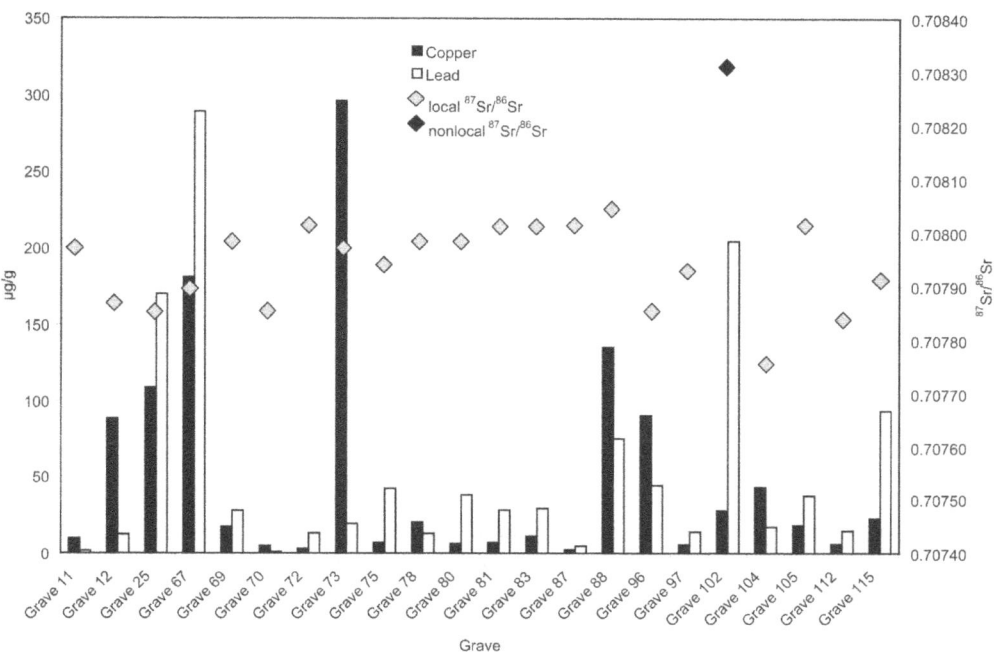

Figure 5.3. Comparison of $^{87}Sr/^{86}Sr$ values and copper and lead skeletal levels in the individuals from Faynan.

but normal copper bioaccumulation. These results confirm Pyatt and Grattan's supposition that living in Faynan's contaminated environment led to bioaccumulation of lead and copper. However, we suspect that the individuals with extremely elevated levels may have had higher exposure because they worked directly in the mines or in smelting activities. Unfortunately other indicators of arduous labor, such as osteoarthritis and vertebral degeneration, cannot be analyzed by individual because of how the data were published.

DEHs provide an indication of childhood health and nutrition levels, as described earlier, and potentially could be used to predict whether or not children with poorer health, and presumably less access to resources, would be more likely to have higher exposure to toxic metals as adults. This does not appear to be the case, for the individuals with DEHs include both those with high and low levels of lead and copper. In fact, a majority of the sample, 83 percent, displayed at least one dental enamel hypoplasia. This is significantly higher than the rate for residents in the Byzantine

Table 5.3. Porotic hyperostosis and dental enamel hypoplasia frequencies from Faynan, Rehovot, and Aila

Site	DEH[1]		Porotic Hyperostosis[2]	
	N	%	N	%
Faynan	15/18	83	17/52	33
Rehovot	35/51	68	16/73	22
Aila	**10/21**	**48**	**3/33**	**9**

Notes: 1. Percentages based on number of individuals with observable central maxillary incisors or mandibular canines.
2. Percentages based on number of individuals with observable parietals and/or frontal bones.
Porotic hyperostosis data for Faynan from El-Najjar and Al-Shiyab (1998) and Abu Karaki (2000). Values in **bold** are significantly different from values at Faynan ($p < 0.05$).

period port city of Aila (48 percent) but not statistically substantially higher than the rate for inhabitants of the Byzantine agricultural village of Rehovot-in-the-Negev (68 percent) (Perry 2002, 2007b) (Table 5.3). Thus, we cannot definitively say that the Faynan individuals were much different in terms of childhood health than residents of other agricultural communities during this period.

However, individuals at Faynan who died as children (less than 15 years of age) had substantially higher oxygen isotope values than individuals who died during adulthood (15 years of age or older) ($p = 0.0192$). In other words, children with enriched $\delta^{18}O$ had greater fragility (see Wood et al. 1992) in terms of death than children who lived into adulthood. The same childhood health patterns emerged when we compared rates of cribra orbitalia and porotic hyperostosis, potential indicators of iron-deficiency anemia that are usually active in children, for the Faynan sample with other samples (Table 5.3). Faynan has higher frequencies of these conditions than Aila (43 percent at Faynan compared to 9 percent at Aila), where substantial seafood consumption may have created a balanced diet even if other minerals and vitamins were lacking (Perry 2002). Using these indicators, childhood health at the agricultural village of Rehovot is similar to the health of the children at Faynan (Perry 2002, 2007b).

One surprising result emerged. The frequencies and patterns of osteoarthritis and vertebral degeneration were different among these three communities (Table 5.4). The Faynan sample had significantly lower frequencies of these degenerative conditions than the agricultural village of Rehovot (Perry 2002). Furthermore, these individuals had similar

Table 5.4. Frequency of osteoarthritis (OA) and vertebral osteophytosis (VO) in total sample from Faynan, Rehovot, and Aila

Site	Total # of Individuals in Sample with OA/VO		Upper Limb OA		Lower Limb OA		Vertebrae VO	
	N	%	N	%	N	%	N	%
Faynan[1]	31/55	56	7/45	16	8/45	18	22/45	49
Rehovot[2]	**63/72**	**88**	195/493	39	**158/493**	**32**	554/1382	40
Aila[2]	28/62	45	19/110	17	8/32	6	**56/221**	**25**

Notes: 1. Percentage of individuals in sample (Abu Karaki 2000; El-Najjar and al-Shiyab 1998).
2. Upper limb, lower limb, and vertebrae by percentage of joints observed (Perry 2002).
Values in **bold** are significantly different from values at Faynan ($p < 0.05$).

frequencies as the residents of the urban port of Aila (ibid.). Since osteoarthritis and vertebral degeneration is an age-related condition, we checked the age distributions of these two populations to make sure that these results are not driven by different age profiles. These three sites had markedly similar mean ages—Faynan = 34.88 years, Aila = 35.32 years, and Rehovot = 39.60 years. The part of the body affected by joint and vertebral degeneration varied among the sites; individuals at Faynan had higher vertebral degeneration rates than residents of Aila and individuals at Rehovot had a higher frequency of joint degeneration in the lower limb than Faynan individuals.

Implications and Conclusions

The Southern Cemetery at Phaeno contained primarily local individuals who filled various roles in an imperial mining operation. The demographic composition of the sample alone would imply that other individuals besides mine laborers resided at the site and were buried in the cemetery. Children approximately three years old, too young to be responsible for crimes they committed according to the Codex Theodosianus (Pharr 1965, 9.13.1) and presumably too young to work in the mines, lived and died at the site.

Only one individual in the sample could be identified as an immigrant based on the dental enamel strontium isotope value. This male of 30–34 years old from Grave 102 had a strontium isotope signature that indicates that he came from a region geologically similar to the northern plain of Jordan, the Judean Hills, the Carmel Range, and the Galilee regions of modern Israel and the West Bank. This individual's oxygen isotope value should provide another indicator of childhood residence, but this value is only slightly below the sample mean of the Faynan locals. Further research on the variation of oxygen isotopes in the Levant may clarify this issue, but at this point we can state that the male in Grave 102 originated from an area that was geologically different from Faynan but had similar enrichment of water sources. This individual had elevated skeletal lead levels, possibly resulting from heightened exposure to smelting and mining processes.

Twenty-one other individuals had lead levels that were significantly higher than those of the rest of the Faynan population, and nine of those also had elevated copper levels. Most of the other Faynan residents also had higher-than-expected levels of lead and copper in their bones, suggesting that simply residing at Faynan led to bioaccumulation of these heavy metals. Studies in modern communities have found that children and adults living in close proximity to smelting operations have elevated lead levels (Carrizales et al. 2006; Gomaa et al. 2002; Paoliello and De Capitani 2007; Paoleillo et al. 2002; Simon, Maynard, and Thomas 2007). Clinical studies of modern smelters also indicate extremely elevated levels of skeletal lead (Börjesson et al. 1997; Christoffersson et al. 1986; Gerhardsson et al. 1993; Gerhardsson et al. 2002; Gerhardsson et al. 2005; Schütz et al. 1987; Schütz et al. 2005), implying that the individuals with elevated lead levels at Faynan also may have been involved in smelting activities.

The relationship between environmental exposure to toxins and skeletal levels of copper is less clear (Baranowska, Czernicki, and Aleksandrowicz 1995; Gerhardsson et al. 2002; Jurkiewicz et al. 2004). Copper toxicity in modern individuals seems to arise from consumption of copper-rich materials or metabolic disorders rather than ambient exposure (Barceloux 1999; Dameron and Harrison 1998; Theophanides and Anastassopoulou 2002). No modern study has found levels of copper in bone similar to those at Faynan (Baranowska, Czernicki, and Aleksandrowicz 1995; Jurkiewicz et al. 2004), suggesting that bone copper levels may reflect contamination rather than bioaccumulation. On the other hand, elevated copper levels in almost all cases coexist with high lead levels—only one individual in the sample has an elevated level of copper but not lead. Therefore, it is possible that differences in ancient and modern mining practices may mean increased pollution and the chance of copper bioaccumulation in the ancient samples. Since the group of locally born individuals contained both highly elevated and only slightly elevated lead and copper levels, locals were exposed to a variety of toxic environments. This implies that factors other than ambient exposure influenced heavy metal concentrations in the skeleton, most likely from working in mining and smelting activities.

Furthermore, children and adults, who would have been living at Faynan for different periods of time, did not have different skeletal copper and lead concentrations. Four out of seven children had very high lead and/or copper levels, some of whom would probably have been too young to work in the mines according to historical evidence. This excessive exposure in very young children may result from the different pathways of bioaccumulation (hand-to-mouth activities and inhalation) and that children's blood absorbs a higher fraction of the lead that is introduced into their systems than adults (Simon, Maynard, and Thomas 2007; Succop et al. 1998). Finally, these levels may represent contamination, as the bone cortex of children is much less dense than that of adults and thus more prone to absorb elements from the soil surrounding the burial.

Analysis of DEHs and immigration status indicates that individuals with elevated lead levels were not necessarily more likely to be immigrants or were poorly nourished or ill during childhood. In fact, the general health of the Faynan population is not substantially poorer than a the health of residents of a typical Byzantine agricultural village, based on similar frequencies of skeletal indicators of iron-deficiency anemia. This sample from Faynan also had lower-than-expected levels of joint degeneration, considering their supposedly hard lifestyle. Degeneration was seen most often in the spine, although at approximately the same levels as residents of an agricultural village. While other factors besides activity and age influence this condition, this may suggest that this sample did not contain many individuals who actually worked in the mines or that working in the mines was not more arduous (in terms of joint degeneration) than working in agricultural fields.

This bioarchaeological data greatly broadens our perspective of the Byzantine period Faynan residents beyond that presented in ancient texts, despite the small sample size. The presence of locally born individuals at the camp, some of whom likely worked directly in mining and smelting operations, has been confirmed. Childhood and adult health was not compromised significantly at the site, and disease and nutrition apparently resembled that of any other Byzantine agricultural village—not that these villages are the picture of good health. The frequency of joint degeneration also was similar to the frequency for residents of an agricultural village, suggesting either that we have individuals who worked in the extensive agricultural fields documented around the site or that working in the mines resulted in similar osteoarthritis profiles.

Acknowledgments

The Faynan South Cemetery excavations were co-sponsored by the Faculty of Archaeology and Anthropology at Yarmouk University and the Council for British Research in the Levant. We would like to thank Fawwaz al-Khraysheh, director-general of the Department of Antiquities of Jordan, for facilitating this research. We also would like to thank Tom Levy and Adolfo Muñiz for providing the faunal samples from Jebel Hamrat Fidan and Tom Levy, Jennifer Ramsey, and Andrew Smith II for collecting the water samples from the Wadi Dana spring. This chapter is dedicated to Dr. Mahmoud Y. El-Najjar (1942–2009), the "father" of modern physical anthropology in Jordan.

References Cited

Abu Karaki, L.
2000   Skeletal Biology of the People of Wadi Faynan: A Bioarchaeological Study. Unpublished master's thesis, Institute of Archaeology and Anthropology, Yarmouk University, Irbid, Jordan.
Angel, J. L.
1966   Porotic Hyperostosis, Anemias, Malarias, and Marshes in the Prehistoric Eastern Mediterranean. *Science* 153:760–763.
Athanasius
1993   *History of the Arians (Historia Arianorum)*. Eastern Orthodox Books, Willits, Calif.
Bajjali, W., and N. Abu-Jaber
2001   Climatological Signals of the Paleogroundwater in Jordan. *Journal of Hydrology* 243:133–147.
Baranowska, I., K. Czernicki, and R. Aleksandrowicz
1995   The Analysis of Lead, Cadmium, Zinc, Copper, and Nickel Content in Human Bones from the Upper Silesian Industrial District. *The Science of the Total Environment* 159:155–162.

Barceloux, D. G.
1999   Copper. *Clinical Toxicology* 37:217–230.
Bentley, R. A.
2006   Strontium Isotopes from the Earth to the Skeleton: A review. *Journal of Archaeological Method and Theory* 13:135–187.
Börjesson, J., L. Gerhardsson, A. Schütz, S. Mattsson, S. Skerfving, and K. Österberg
1997   In Vivo Measurements of Lead in Fingerbone in Active and Retired Lead Smelters. *International Archives of Occupational and Environmental Health* 69:97–105.
Buikstra, J. E., and D. H. Ubelaker
1994   *Standards for Data Collection from Human Skeletal Remains*. Arkansas Archaeological Survey Research Series no 44. Arkansas Archaeological Survey, Fayetteville, Ark.
Carrizales, L., I. Razo, J. I. Téllez-Hernández, R. Torres-Nerio, A. Torres, L. E. Batres, A-C Cubillas, and F. Díaz-Barriga
2006   Exposure to Arsenic and Lead of Children Living Near a Copper-Smelter in San Luis Potosi, Mexico: Importance of Soil Contamination for Exposure of Children. *Environmental Research* 101:1–10.
Christoffersson, J.-O., L. Ahlgren, A. Schütz, S. Skerfving, and S. Mattsson
1986   Decrease of Skeletal Lead Levels in Man after End of Occupational Exposure. *Archives of Environmental Health* 41:312–418.
Cuttress, T. W., and G. W. Suckling
1982   The Assessment of Non-Carious Defects of Enamel. *International Dental Journal* 32:117–122.
Dameron, C. T. ,and M. D. Harrison
1998   Mechanisms for Protection against Copper Toxicity. *American Journal of Clinical Nutrition* 67:1091S–1097S.
Dansgaard, W.
1964   Stable Isotopes in Precipitation. *Tellus* 16:436–468.
Daux, V., C. Lécuyer, M-A. Héran, R. Amiot, L. Simon, F. Fourel, F. Martineau, N. Lynnerup, H. Reychler, and G. Escarguel
2008   Oxygen Isotope Fractionation Between Human Phosphate and Water Revisited. *Journal of Human Evolution* 55:1138–1147.
Dupras, T. L., and H. P. Schwarcz
2001   Strangers in a Strange Land: Stable Isotope Evidence for Human Migration in the Dakhleh Oasis, Egypt. *Journal of Archaeological Science* 28:1199–1208.
El-Najjar, M. Y. and A. H. Al-Shiyab
1998   Skeletal Biology and Pathology of the People of Wadi Faynan in Southern Jordan. *Mu'tah Lil-Buhuth wad-Dirasat* 13:9–39.
El-Najjar, M. Y., D. J. Ryan, C. G. Turner II, and B. Lozoff
1976   The Etiology of Porotic Hyperostosis among the Prehistoric and Historic Anasazi Indians of Southwestern United States. *American Journal of Physical Anthropology* 44:477–488.

Ericson, J. E.
1985   Strontium Isotope Characterization in the Study of Prehistoric Human Ecology. *Journal of Human Evolution* 14:503–514.
1989   Some Problems and Potentials of Strontium Analysis for Human and Animal Ecology. In *Stable Isotopes in Ecological Research*, edited by P. W. Rundel, R. Ehleringer, and K. A. Nagy, pp. 25–29. Springer-Verlag, New York.

Eusebius of Caesarea
1927   *Ecclesiastical History and the Martyrs of Palestine.* Macmillan, New York.

Evans, J. A., C. A. Chenery, and A. P. Fitzpatrick
2006   Bronze Age Childhood Migration of Individuals Near Stonehenge, Revealed by Strontium and Oxygen Isotope Tooth Enamel Analysis. *Archaeometry* 48:309–321.

Ezzo, J. A., C. M. Johnson, and T. D. Price
1997   Analytical Perspectives on Prehistoric Migration: A Case Study from East-Central Arizona. *Journal of Archaeological Science* 24:447–466.

Faure, G.
1986   *Principles of Isotope Geology.* John Wiley & Sons, New York.

Faure, G., and J. L. Powell
1972   *Strontium Isotope Geology.* Springer-Verlag, New York.

Findlater, G., M. El-Najjar, A. H. Al-Shiyab, M. O'Hea, and E. Easthaugh
1998   The Wadi Faynan Project: The South Cemetery Excavation, Jordan 1996: A Preliminary Report. *Levant* 30:69–83.

Freeman, P., and L. McEwan
1998   The Wadi Faynan Survey, Jordan: A Preliminary Report on Survey in Area WF2 In 1997. *Levant* 30:61–68.

Gat, J. R., and W. Dansgaard
1972   Stable Isotope Survey of The Fresh Water Occurrences in Israel and the Northern Jordan Rift Valley. *Journal of Hydrology* 16:177–212.

Gerhardsson, L., A. Akantis, N.-G. Lundström, G. F. Nordberg, A. Schütz, and S. Skerfving
2005   Lead Concentrations in Cortical and Trabecular Bones in Deceased Smelter Workers. *Journal of Trace Elements in Medicine and Biology* 19:209–215.

Gerhardsson, L., R. Attewell, D. R. Chettle, V. Englyst, N-G. Lundström, G. F. Nordberg, H. Nyhlin, M. C. Scott, and A. C. Todd
1993   In Vivo Measurements of Lead in Bone in Long-Term Exposed Lead Smelter Workers. *Archives of Environmental Health* 48:147–156.

Gerhardsson, L., V. Englyst, N.-G. Lundström, S. Sandberg, and G. F. Nordberg
2002   Cadmium, Copper, and Zinc in Tissues of Deceased Copper Smelter Workers. *Journal of Trace Elements in Medicine and Biology* 16:261–266.

Gomaa, A., H. Hu, D. Bellinger, J. Schwartz, T. Shirng-Wern, T. Gonzalez-Cossio, L. Schnaas, K. Peterson, A. Aro, and M. Hernandez-Avila
2002   Maternal Bone Lead as an Independent Risk Factor for Fetal Neurotoxicity: A Prospective Study. *Pediatrics* 110:110–118.

González-Reimers, E., J. Velasco-Vázquez, M. Arnay-de-la-Rosa, V. Alberto-Barrosos, L. Gilando-Martín, and F. Santolaria-Fernández
2003   Bone Cadmium and Lead in Prehistoric Inhabitants and Domestic Animals from Gran Canaria. *The Science of the Total Environment* 310:97–103.

González-Reimers, E., J. Velasco-Vázquez, M. Arnay-de-la-Rosa, F. Santolaria-Fernández, and L. Gilando-Martín
2001   Paleonutritional Analysis of the Pre-Hispanic Population from Fuerteventura (Canary Islands). *The Science of the Total Environment* 264:215–220.

Goodman, A. H., and G. Armelagos
1985   Factors Affecting the Distribution of Enamel Hypoplasias within the Human Permanent Dentition. *American Journal of Physical Anthropology* 68:479–493.

Goodman, A. H., G. Armelagos, and J. C. Rose
1980   Enamel Hypoplasias as Indicators of Stress in Three Prehistoric Populations From Illinois. *Human Biology* 52:515–528.

Goodman, A. H., and J. C. Rose
1990   Assessment of Systemic Physiological Perturbations from Dental Enamel Hypoplasias and Associated Histological Structures. *Yearbook of Physical Anthropology* 33:59–110.

Grattan, J. P., L. Abu Karaki, D. Hine, H. Toland, D. D. Gilbertson, Z. Al Saad, and B. Pyatt
2005   Analyses of Patterns of Copper and Lead Mineralization in Human Skeletons Excavated from an Ancient Mining and Smelting Centre in the Jordanian Desert: A Reconnaissance Study. *Mineralogical Magazine* 69:653–666.

Grattan, J. P., A. Condon, S. Taylor, L. Karaki, F. Pyatt, D. D. Gilbertson, and Z. Saad
2003   A Legacy of Empires? An Exploration and Medical Consequences of Metal Production in Wadi Faynan, Jordan. In *Geology and Health: Closing the Gap*, edited by H. Skinner and A. Berger, pp. 99–105. Oxford University Press, Oxford.

Grattan, J. P., D. D. Gilbertson, and C. O. Hunt
2007   The Local and Global Dimensions of Metalliferous Pollution Derived from a Reconstruction of an Eight Thousand Year Record of Copper Smelting and Mining at a Desert-Mountain Frontier in Southern Jordan. *Journal of Archaeological Science* 34:83–110.

Grattan, J. P., S. I. Huxley, and F. B. Pyatt
2003   Modern Bedouin Exposures to Copper Contamination: An Imperial Legacy? *Ecotoxicology and Environmental Safety* 55:108–115.

Grattan, J. P., S. N. Huxley, L. Karaki, H. Toland, D. D. Gilbertson, A. J. Pyatt, and Z. Saad
2002   "Death More Desirable Than Life . . ."? The Human Skeletal Record and Toxicological Implications of Ancient Copper Mining and Smelting in Wadi Faynan, South West Jordan. *Toxicology and Industrial Health* 18:297–307.

Hauptmann, A.
2000   *Zur frühen Metallurgie des Kupfers in Fenan/Jordanien*. Deutsch Bergbau Museum, Bochum.

Healy, J. F.
1978   *Mining and Metallurgy in the Greek and Roman World*. Thames and Hudson, London.

Hunt, C. O., D. D. Gilbertson, and H. A. El-Rishi
2007   An 8000-Year History of Landscape, Climate, and Copper Exploitation in the Middle East: The Wadi Faynan and the Wadi Dana National Reserve in Southern Jordan. *Journal of Archaeological Science* 34:1306–1338.

Ibrahim, M. M., and R. L. Gordon
1987   *A Cemetery at Queen Alia International Airport*. Harrassowitz, Wiesbaden.

Jacobi, K. P., and M. E. Danforth
2002   Analysis of Interobserver Scoring Patterns in Porotic Hyperostosis and Cribra Orbitalia. *International Journal of Osteoarchaeology* 12:248–258.

Jurkiewicz, A., D. Wiechuła, R. Nowak, T. Gaździk, and K. Loska
2004   Metal Content in Femoral Head Spongious Bone of People Living in Regions of Different Degrees of Environmental Pollution in Southern and Middle Poland. *Ecotoxicology and Environmental Safety* 59:95–101.

Jurmain, R.
1999   *Stories from the Skeleton: Behavioral Reconstruction in Human Osteology*. Gordon Breach, Amsterdam.

Kohn, M. J., M. J. Schoeninger, and J. W. Valley
1996   Herbivore Tooth Oxygen Isotope Compositions: Effects of Diet and Physiology. *Geochimica et Cosmochimica Acta* 60:3889–3896.

Levin, M., J. R. Gat, and A. Issar
1980   Precipitation, Flood- and Groundwaters of the Negev Highlands: An Isotopic Study of Desert Hydrology. In *Arid-Zone Hydrology: Investigations with Isotope Techniques*, pp. 3–22. International Atomic Energy Agency, Vienna.

Luz, B., and Y. Kolodny
1989   Oxygen Isotope Variation in Bone Phosphate. *Applied Geochemistry* 4:317–323.

Luz, B., Y. Kolodny, and M. Horowitz
1984   Fractionation of Oxygen Isotopes Between Mammalian Bone-Phosphate and Environmental Water. *Geochimica et Cosmochimica Acta* 48:1689–1693.

Mattingly, D., P. Newson, O. Creighton, R. Tomber, J. P. Grattan, C. O. Hunt, D. D. Gilbertson, H. el-Rishi, and B. Pyatt
2007   A Landscape of Imperial Power: Roman and Byzantine Phaino. In *Archaeology and Desertification: The Wadi Faynan Landscape Survey, Southern Jordan*, edited by G. Barker, D. D. Gilbertson, and D. Mattingly, pp. 305–348. Oxbow Books, Oxford.

Millar, F.
1984   Condemnation to Hard Labour in the Roman Empire, from the Julio-Claudians to Constantine. *Papers of the British School at Rome* 52:124–147.

Moskowitz, R. W.
1997   Clinical Laboratory Findings in Osteoarthritis. In *Arthritis and Allied Conditions*, edited by W. J. Koopman, pp. 1985–2025. Lea & Febiger, Philadelphia.

Ortner, D. J., W. Butler, J. Cafarella, and L. Mulligan
2001 Evidence of Probable Scurvy in Subadults from Archaeological Sites in North America. *American Journal of Physical Anthropology* 114:343–351.

Ortner, D. J., and W. G. J. Putschar
1985 *Identification of Pathological Conditions in Human Skeletal Remains.* Smithsonian Institution Press, Washington, D.C.

Paoliello, M. M. B., and E. M. De Capitani
2007 Occupational and Environmental Human Lead Exposure in Brazil. *Environmental Research* 103:288–297.

Paoliello, M. M. B., E. M. De Capitani, F. G. da Cunha, T. Matsuo, M. D. F. Carvalho, A. Sakuma, and B. R. Figueiredo
2002 Exposure of Children to Lead and Cadmium from a Mining Area of Brazil. *Environmental Research Section A* 88:120–128.

Perry, M. A.
2002 Health, Labor, and Political Economy: A Bioarchaeological Analysis of Three Communities in Provincia Arabia. Ph.D. dissertation, Department of Anthropology, University of New Mexico, Albuquerque.

2007a A Preliminary Report on the Cemeteries of Bir Madhkur. *Bulletin of the American Schools of Oriental Research* 346:79–93.

2007b Is Bioarchaeology a Handmaiden to History? Developing a Historical Bioarchaeology. *Journal of Anthropological Archaeology* 26:486–515.

Perry, M. A., D. Coleman, and N. Delhopital
2008 Mobility and Exile at 2nd Century A.D. Khirbet Edh-Dharih: Strontium Isotope Analysis of Human Migration in Western Jordan. *Geoarchaeology* 23:528–549.

Perry, M. A., D. Coleman, D. L. Dettman, and A. H. al-Shiyab
2009 An Isotopic Perspective on The Transport of Byzantine Mining Camp Laborers into Southwestern Jordan. *American Journal of Physical Anthropology* 140:420–441.

Peyron, J. G.
1986 Osteoarthritis: The Epidemiologic Viewpoint. *Clinical Orthopedics* 213:13–19.

Pharr, C.
1952 *Codex Theodosianus.* Princeton University Press, Princeton, N.J.

Price, T., J. H. Burton, and R. A. Bentley
2002 The Characterization of Biologically Available Strontium Isotope Ratios for the Study of Prehistoric Migration. *Archaeometry* 44:117–136.

Price, T., G. Grupe, and P. Schröter
1998 Migration of the Bell Beaker Period of Central Europe. *Antiquity* 72:405–411.

Price, T., C. M. Johnson, J. A. Ezzo, J. Ericson, and J. H. Burton
1994 Residential Mobility in the Prehistoric Southwest United States: A Preliminary Study using Strontium Isotope Analysis. *Journal of Archaeological Science* 21:315–330.

Prowse, T., H. P. Schwarcz, P. Garnsey, M. Knyf, R. Macchiarelli, and L. Bondioli
2007   Isotopic Evidence for Age-Related Immigration to Imperial Rome. *American Journal of Physical Anthropology* 132:510–519.
Pucéat, E., B. Reynard, and C. Lécuyer
2004   Can Crystallinity be used to Determine the Degree of Chemical Alteration of Biogenic Apatites? *Chemical Geology* 205:83–97.
Pyatt, A. J., G. W. Barker, P. Birch, D. D. Gilbertson, J. P. Grattan, and D. J. Mattingly
1999   King Solomon's Miners—Starvation and Bioaccumulation? *Ecotoxicology and Environmental Safety* 43:305–308.
Pyatt, F. B., G. Gilmore, J. P. Grattan, C. O. Hunt, and S. J. McLaren
2000   An Imperial Legacy? An Exploration of the Environmental Impact of Ancient Metal Mining and Smelting in Southern Jordan. *Journal of Archaeological Science* 27:771–778.
Pyatt, F. B., A. J. Pyatt, C. Walker, T. Sheen, and J. P. Grattan
2005   The Heavy Metal Content of Skeletons from an Ancient Metalliferous Polluted Area in Southern Jordan with Particular Reference to Bioaccumulation and Human Health. *Ecotoxicology and Environmental Safety* 60:295–300.
Sarnat, B. G., and I. Schour
1941   Enamel Hypoplasia (Chronologic Enamel Aplasia) in Relation to Systemic Disease: A Chronologic, Morphologic, and Etiologic Classification. *Journal of the American Dental Association* 28:1989–2000.
Schütz, A., M. Olsson, A. Jensen, L. Gerhardsson, J. Börjesson, S. Mattsson, and S. Skerfving
2005   Lead in Finger Bone, Whole Blood, Plasma, and Urine in Lead-Smelter Workers: Extended Exposure Range. *International Archives of Occupational and Environmental Health* 78:35–43.
Schütz, A., S. Skerfving, S. Mattsson, J.-O. Christoffersson, and L. Ahlgren
1987   Lead in Vertebral Bone Biopsies from Active and Retired Lead Workers. *Archives of Environmental Health* 42:340–346.
Simon, D. L., E. J. Maynard, and K. D. Thomas
2007   Living in a Sea of Lead—Changes in Blood- and Hand-Lead of Infants Living Near a Smelter. *Journal of Exposure Science and Environmental Epidemiology* 17:248–259.
Sponheimer, M., and J. A. Lee-Thorp
1999   Oxygen Isotopes in Enamel Carbonate and their Ecological Significance. *Journal of Archaeological Science* 26:723–728.
Stuart-Macadam, P.
1987   Porotic Hyperostosis: New Evidence to Support the Anemia Theory. *American Journal of Physical Anthropology* 74:521–526.
1992   Porotic Hyperostosis: A New Perspective. *American Journal of Physical Anthropology* 87:39–47.
Succop, P., R. Bornschein, K. Brown, and C. Tseng
1998   An Empirical Comparison of Lead Exposure Pathway Models. *Environmental Health Perspectives* 106:1577–1583.

Sullivan, A.
2005   Prevalence and Etiology of Acquired Anemia in Medieval York, England. *American Journal of Physical Anthropology* 128:252–272.
Sweeney, E. A., J. A. Saffir, and R. de Leon
1971   Linear Enamel Hypoplasias of Deciduous Incisor Teeth in Malnourished Children. *American Journal of Clinical Nutrition* 24:29–31.
Theophanides, T., and J. Anastassopoulou
2002   Copper and Carcinogenesis. *Critical Reviews in Oncology/Hematology* 42:57–64.
Wapler, U., E. Crubézy, and M. Schultz
2004   Is Cribra Orbitalia Synonymous with Anemia? Analysis and Interpretation of Cranial Pathology in Sudan. *American Journal of Physical Anthropology* 123:333–339.
Weiner, S., and O. Bar-Yosef
1990   States of Preservation of Bones from Prehistoric Sites in the Near East: A Survey. *Journal of Archaeological Science* 17:187–196.
White, C. D., F. J. Longstaffe, and K. R. Law
2004   Exploring the Effects of Environment, Physiology and Diet on Oxygen Isotope Ratios in Ancient Nubian Bones and Teeth. *Journal of Archaeological Science* 31:233–250.
Wright, L. E., and H. P. Schwarcz
1996   Infrared and Isotopic Evidence for Diagenesis of Bone Apatite at Dos Pilas, Guatemala: Palaeodietary Implications. *Journal of Archaeological Science* 23:933–944.

6

Food for Thought

Isotopic Evidence for Dietary and Weaning Practices in a Byzantine Urban Monastery in Jerusalem

LESLEY A. GREGORICKA AND SUSAN G. SHERIDAN

Biochemistry has proven to be a valuable tool for exploring dietary trends, particularly with the use of stable isotope analysis (Dupras 1999; Feasby 1998; Richards, Mays, and Fuller 2002; Richards et al. 2003; Thomas, Chaix, and Richards 2008; see also Chapter 5 [this volume] for the application of biogeochemical techniques to questions of geographic residence). Stable carbon and nitrogen isotopes in bone collagen reflect the consumption of specific plant types and differentiate plant from animal protein intake (Schoeninger and Moore 1992). Isotopes in the bones of infants and young children can also identify the timing and duration of the weaning process (e.g., Dittman and Grupe 2000; Dupras 1999; Herring, Saunders, and Katzenberg 1998; Jay et al. 2008; Schurr and Powell 2005), while carbon isotope ratios can distinguish between various types of weaning foods (e.g., Dupras, Schwarcz, and Fairgrieve 2001; Fuller et al. 2006; Katzenberg, Saunders, and Fitzgerald 1993; Richards et al. 2003). Here we investigate the breast-feeding and weaning trends of subadults interred with the urban monastic community of St. Stephen's in Jerusalem (Figure 6.1) during the Byzantine period (fifth to seventh centuries AD) and their relationship to the diet of the adult members of the monastery. Historical records in this case provide insight into the motives behind dietary regulations and preferences, including childhood feeding guidelines.

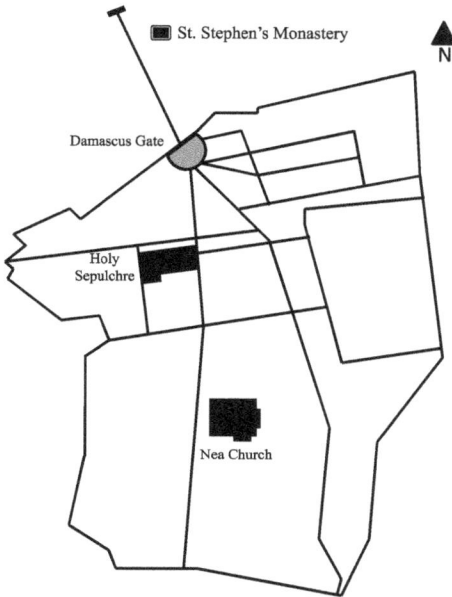

Figure 6.1. The monastery of St. Stephen's and other important Christian sites within the Old City of Jerusalem during the Byzantine period.

Archaeological, Biochemical, and Historical Considerations

St. Stephen's was founded approximately 250 meters north of the Old City of Jerusalem by Empress Eudocia in AD 438–439 (Clark 1982). This urban monastery became an important pilgrimage stop in Jerusalem, given the purported interment of Christianity's first martyr, Stephen, on its grounds and the miracles associated with his remains (Clark 1982; Price and Binns 1991). Several Byzantine-style tombs and two large crypt complexes have been found at the site; the current study focuses on remains from repository six, the largest crypt (Figure 6.2). Barkay and Kloner (1986) dated this crypt to the Iron Age (8th–7th century BC) based on tomb architecture, but others (de Vaux 1886; Lagrange 1894; Vincent and Abel 1926) reported that the Byzantine inhabitants reused the tomb, a common practice in the region (Avni and Greenhut 1996; Barkay, Kloner, and Mazar 1994). Several dating methods corroborate this hypothesis, including the high degree of homogeneity found from fluoride analysis of 600 rib samples, analysis of 202 artifacts commingled with the bones, and radiocarbon dating of a subsample of femora to the Byzantine occupation of the early sixth through mid-seventh centuries AD (Bautch et al. 2000). All of this

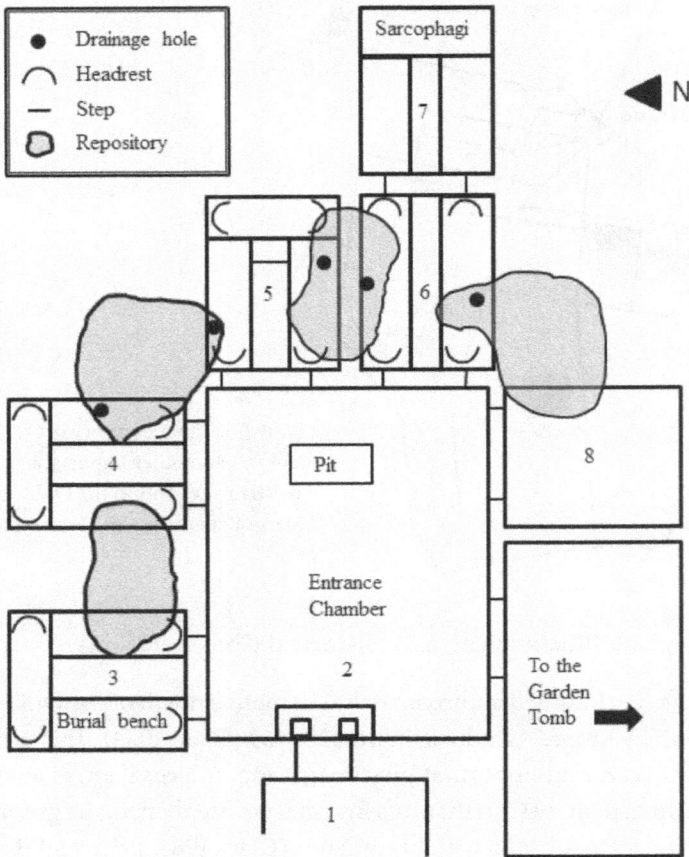

Figure 6.2. St. Stephen's Tomb Complex 1. The skeletal material from reposi-tory six, between chambers six and eight, were analyzed for this study (from Sheridan 1999).

evidence reaffirms that the bones date not to the Iron Age but the Byz-antine period. The most surprising find associated with the St. Stephen's collection was the number of subadult bones (Sheridan 1999). One third of over 15,000 skeletal elements are those of children under 16 years of age. This relatively large number of infants and children provides a unique opportunity to study childhood diet at St. Stephen's and helps identify the reason for their interment at the site.

Stable Isotope Biochemistry

Stable isotopes represent variations in the atomic composition of single elements that have the same atomic number but vary in mass due to the number of neutrons in the nucleus, allowing lighter isotopes to be distinguished from their heavier counterparts (Price et al. 1985). Stable isotope values measure the difference between the isotopic content of a sample and an internationally accepted standard, with a delta symbol (δ) signifying this ratio. The resultant deviation is expressed in parts per mil (‰).

The differences in mass between stable isotopes are important for examining trophic food webs. "Trophic" refers to the relationships between organisms on the food chain and dietary intake (Drucker and Bocherens 2004). As stable carbon isotopes pass through trophic levels, such as from plant to herbivore, they undergo isotope fractionation. This process involves a partial separation between heavier and lighter isotopes as a result of the transition from one trophic level to another so that isotope values change in an identifiable pattern (Hoefs 2004). While $\delta^{13}C$ levels in the atmosphere are consistent at 98.89 percent for ^{12}C and 1.11 percent for ^{13}C, plants discriminate against the heavier ^{13}C isotopes due to preferences for particular biochemical routes (ibid.). Thus, two primary types of fractionation occur as seen in C_3 (Calvin-Benson) and C_4 (Hatch-Slack) photosynthetic pathways.

C_3-based plants discriminate against the heavier ^{13}C isotopes in favor of ^{12}C during photosynthesis (Schwarcz and Schoeninger 1991). These plants fix carbon dioxide (CO_2) into a three-carbon molecule, range in $\delta^{13}C$ values from -33‰ to -22‰, and include fruits, nuts, legumes, wheat, barley, and rice (DeNiro 1987; Smith and Epstein 1971). On the other hand, C_4-based plants fix molecules with four carbons and discriminate less against ^{13}C; accordingly, these plants are significantly more enriched in ^{13}C than the relatively depleted values of C_3 vegetation and thus possess elevated $\delta^{13}C$ values between -16‰ and -9‰ (Schoeninger and Moore 1992). C_4 plants consist of tropical grasses, including maize, sorghum, millet, and sugarcane (DeNiro 1987).

C_3 and C_4 photosynthetic pathways display two isotopically distinct signatures that continue to differ through the food chain, enabling the identification of plant and animal types in an organism's diet. Such biochemical signatures are incorporated into human bone collagen, with $\delta^{13}C$ collagen values derived from the diet differing from the actual foods consumed by approximately +5‰ (van der Merwe and Vogel 1978). Subsequently, the $\delta^{13}C$ values of humans consuming a C_3-dominated diet are approximately -19‰, while those relying on C_4 foodstuffs have values around -5‰ (Dupras, Schwarcz, and Fairgrieve 2001). Diets containing both C_3 and C_4 plants possess $\delta^{13}C$ values falling midway between the two. Diets including a significant marine component display enriched $\delta^{13}C$ values similar to terrestrial C_4 plants due to lessened fractionation in phytoplankton (Richard and Hedges 1999).

As with carbon, nitrogen isotopes also undergo fractionation as they move through trophic levels. Nitrogen isotopes occur naturally in the atmosphere, with ^{14}N comprising 99.64 percent and ^{15}N 0.36 percent (Hoefs 2004). Plants derive nitrogen from the atmosphere, soils, or water, producing varying isotopic values (Price et al. 1985). When these plants are consumed, additional fractionation takes places as nitrogen passes into animal tissue. A predictable, stepwise enrichment of $\delta^{15}N$ values occurs as one moves up the food web from plants to herbivores to carnivores at a rate of approximately 3–4‰ per trophic level (Minagawa and Wada 1984). Subsequently, plants possess depleted nitrogen values, carnivores contain the most enriched amounts, and omnivores tend to possess intermediate values between herbivores and carnivores. Finally, the presence of a larger number of trophic levels in a maritime environment coupled with the fixation of dissolved nitrate by marine plants also results in elevated $\delta^{15}N$ ratios (Richard and Hedges 1999).

Stable Isotopes and Weaning

Infant isotopic values additionally reflect a fractionation process associated with the consumption of breast milk. Initially, a newborn shares nitrogen values comparable to its mother; however, breast-feeding changes an infant's nitrogen composition due to elevated amounts of ^{15}N found in breast milk in relation to the mother's diet (Katzenberg, Herring, and Saunders 1996). Therefore, the infant develops a $\delta^{15}N$ value approximately 2.0–3.6‰ higher than the mother (Steele and Daniel 1978). This gradually decreases once weaning begins, as breast milk is supplemented with new foods. This reduction stems from the lower nitrogen values found in most diets in comparison to breast milk (Schurr 1998).

Although not as enhanced as that of nitrogen, infants also experience a carbon trophic level effect, with ^{13}C-enriched breast milk initiating a rise in $\delta^{13}C$ of approximately 1‰ (Fuller, Richards, and Mays 2003). The infant's slightly elevated carbon isotope value may then follow one of two paths determined by the specific foods used in weaning. First, it may decrease with the introduction of C_3-based plants and animal products, including milk from goats or cows (Fuller et al. 2006). Secondly, the value may increase with the inclusion of C_4-based plants and animal protein into the diet, such as gruel made from maize or sorghum (Katzenberg, Saunders, and Fitzgerald 1993). Both nitrogen and carbon isotopes thus provide an important means of delineating the duration of breast-feeding, the timing and extent of the weaning process, and the weanling diet.

Presence of Children at a Monastery: Differential Diagnosis

The reasons for burial of children at St. Stephen's monastery are unclear from the textual record for the site. Nevertheless, the presence of children in Byzantine monasteries was not unknown during this time, as these establishments commonly served as social welfare institutions. Subsequently, monastic resources frequently targeted neglected children from the surrounding community through public assistance programs.

One aspect of social welfare facilitated by the urban monastic community was the founding of hospitals, particularly those attending to the needs of sick children (Moffatt 1986). However, given the number of hospitals in Jerusalem, it is unlikely that St. Stephen's managed a hospital on its grounds (Miller 1997). Alternatively, it has been postulated that these children may have served as oblates, or monks in training. In the Byzantine period, it was not uncommon for children as young as ten years old to enter monastic life (Boswell 1984). However, there were strict regulations against the inclusion of individuals under the age of five years, and the majority of St. Stephen's subadults were less than three years old. This seems to preclude the possibility that the majority of subadults represented oblates engaged in religious study.

Two other explanations have been posited for the presence of children at St. Stephen's monastery—an orphanage/school or a sacred burial site. During the fourth century AD, Basil of Cappadocia developed a series of regulations regarding the care of orphaned children by the church, directives that encouraged Byzantine monasteries to develop orphanages and schools (Miller 2003). Beginning in AD 540, the "Justinianic Plague" moved through Palestine approximately every 15–20 years, which may have resulted in many orphaned young (Allen 1979; Conrad 1987). Alternatively, it is possible that the subadults were local members of the lay community whose parents wished them to be laid to rest near venerated remains. *Depositio ad sanctos,* or the practice of burying a body in close proximity to holy figures, became increasingly popular during the Byzantine period (Brown 1981). Byzantine children held a unique status as innocents and were regarded as innately holy, permitting their interment in a monastery (Leyerle 2002). However they came to be interred at St. Stephen's, the prevalence of subadult bones offers us the opportunity to study aspects of childhood health in Byzantine Jerusalem.

Breast-Feeding and Weaning in the Byzantine Near East

Many of the procedures practiced during the Byzantine period regarding breast-feeding and weaning originated in Roman thought. Children were weaned based on their ability to begin taking in solid foods; this was generally held to a minimum age of six months old (Garrison 1923). The first-century AD physician Soranus of Ephesus recommended that infants be kept on a diet of breast milk alone for at least six months, followed by the introduction of appropriate soft foods such as porridge and milk (Soranus, *Gynecology* XXI[XLI]; Fildes 1986). Soranus condemned abrupt weaning in favor of the continued supplementation of breast milk with new foods until around one and a half to two years old, when the child proved capable of processing harder foods (Soranus, *Gynecology* XXI[XLI]). Claudius Galen, a second century AD Roman physician, also advised that infants exclusively consume breast milk until around six months of age; caregivers should then initiate the weaning process only with the eruption of the child's front teeth (Galen, *De sanitate tuenda,* Chapter X). He advocated the gradual introduction of solid foods, beginning with softer breads before moving on to vegetables and meat. However, Galen recommended a somewhat later weaning completion date than Soranus, at around three years of age (Fildes 1986).

Records regarding the feeding of infants exist from the Byzantine era as well, providing valuable evidence in estimating the age children were weaned. Soranus and Galen heavily influenced these medical works; in fact, Byzantine physicians went so far as to copy whole chapters from Roman practitioners into their own prescriptions (Still 1931). In his medical encyclopedia, the fourth-century physician Oribasius of Pergamum advocated the complete cessation of breast-feeding at around two years of age (Oribasius, *Oribasii Collectionum Medicarum Reliquiae* IV–V; Lascaratos and Poulakou-Rebelakou 2003). Similarly, Aetios of Amida, a sixth-century obstetrician, suggested that mothers wean their children at 20 months (Aetios 1950; Fildes 1986). The seventh-century doctor Paulus Aeginata agreed with Galen's recommendation of commencing weaning only after the teeth first begin to erupt at around six or seven months old (Aeginata 1844, section IX). As with Soranus and Galen, he recommended softened cereals as fitting introductory solid foods, contending that complete weaning should not occur until two years of age (ibid., section V; Fildes 1986; Lascaratos and Poulakou-Rebelakou 2003).

Recommendations by medical experts were reinforced by religious authorities. The Byzantine church encouraged lengthy breast-feeding and criticized mothers who weaned too early, going so far as to assign penances to these women (Lascaratos and Poulakou-Rebelakou 2003). Therefore, based on the opinions of some of the most prolific medical minds in the Roman and Byzantine world, an acceptable weaning period from approximately six months to two years old was the probable norm for the era.

Wet nurses played various roles in breast-feeding, weaning, and general child care during the Roman and Byzantine periods. Nurses commonly took over the task of breast-feeding from women who wanted to wean their children but were prohibited from doing so because of the Byzantine church (Lascaratos and Poulakou-Rebelakou 2003). It is difficult to determine whether or not wet nurses were available for infants and young children who were under monastic care. Miller (2003) has speculated that wet nurses must have been made available to feed infants at monasteries.

Even though pediatric weaning guidelines that date from the Roman era persisted into the Byzantine period, an interesting shift occurred in the use of wet nurses during the latter period. Beginning in the second century AD and continuing into early Byzantium, wet nurses were fairly common, particularly in the affluent portion of the population (Moffatt 1986). However, evidence for the use of wet nurses is scarce for the sixth and seventh centuries AD and may have become a last resort in the case of the impairment or death of a mother. It seems that maternal breast-feeding became more highly valued, reflecting a change in the way wet-nursing was perceived socially (Abrahamse 1979).

The Monks of St. Stephen's: Adult Diet

If the children buried in the tomb complex at St. Stephen's were living at the monastery, they were probably eating weaning foods similar to those available to the monks. Therefore, the adult diet may offer evidence of subadult nutrition. According to historical texts, the monastic diet in Byzantine Palestine was monotonous by design, consisting primarily of bread in both urban and rural settings (Hirschfeld 1996; Rautman 2006). Gardening was a basic activity of monks as a means of food production as well as physical labor. Thus, vegetables often supplemented the cereal grains used to make bread, such as wheat and barley. Beans, lentils, peas, onions, carrots, cabbage, and chickpeas were among the commonly cultivated plants in the Byzantine Near East (Hirschfeld 1992; Kislinger 1999; Talbot 2002, 2007). Orchard fruits are another possible source of nutrition, including figs, olives, carobs, and grapes, although rules about their consumption varied greatly among monasteries (Harlow and Smith 2001; Kislinger 1999; Talbot 2002). Meat, often associated with luxury and indulgence, was generally taboo in the monastic setting except for the sick and on rare feast days (McGowan 1999).

As one of the most easily manipulated aspects of daily life, dietary intake has been a common source of social control throughout history (Miles 1995). Monastic life in the Byzantine period was governed by rules, many of which focused on which foods were acceptable for everyday consumption. Despite the fact that dietary asceticism was mandated, the practical application of these monastic instructions in day-to-day life may have differed significantly, and reports of austere food intake may have been exaggerated as a means of enhancing a monastery's status and reputation (Patrich 1995). Thus, the veracity of reports in historical texts has been challenged; it is not clear that such texts depict the true nature of monastic eating habits. In the urban setting of Jerusalem, the adult monks of St. Stephen's may have engaged in more flexible dietary practices, despite textual records of asceticism.

Materials and Methods

The total subadult sample consisted of 55 individuals, ranging from newborn to approximately 19 years old. Here, subadult is defined by the presence of both unfused proximal and distal femoral diaphyses. Because of the commingled nature of the remains, right proximal femora were sampled to prevent duplication. All femoral samples came from unfused diaphyses and included no epiphyses. Age ranges were determined based on total length of the femoral diaphysis (Scheuer and Black 2000, 393–395; Ubelaker 1999, 71), and its midpoint was taken (Schurr 1997). The total adult sample consisted of 54 left distal male femora.

Sample preparation was drawn from Schurr (1998); a general overview of isotope mass spectrometry can be found in Katzenberg (1992). Isotope values in bone collagen reflect protein ingested (Ambrose and Norr 1993), not the total dietary composition (carbohydrates, lipids, proteins). As both plants and animals contain protein, this represents an acceptable medium from which to assess dietary intake in the past. No associated faunal remains dating to the Byzantine were available for analysis; while faunal material that is not contemporaneous was present, the possibility of temporal isotopic variability as a result of changes in diet or subsistence practices precluded their use in this study. The absence of animal baselines limits the conclusions that can be made about general dietary intake and trophic level and must be treated with caution. Nevertheless, comparisons within results (e.g., comparing the dietary patterns of adults and subadults) are valid. The nonparametric Mann-Whitney U-test was used for comparisons among these ordinal data.

Results

The stable isotope data are presented in Table 6.1. Extraction percentage yields and carbon-to-nitrogen (C/N) ratios were used to evaluate collagen preservation. All subadult (n = 55) and 52 (of 54) adult samples displayed acceptable extraction percentage yields above 2 percent, while 49 (of 55) subadult and all adult C/N ratios fell within or near the expected range for collagen at 2.9–3.6 (DeNiro 1985). Six subadult and two adult samples were not excluded in the subsequent analysis because of unacceptable extraction percentage yields. Figure 6.3 shows a bivariate plot of stable carbon and nitrogen isotope values for adults and subadults. When evaluated against the adults of St. Stephen's monastery, whose $\delta^{13}C$ values ranged from -20.6 to -17.7‰ (n = 52; $\bar{X}$ = -19.0±0.6‰), the subadult $\delta^{13}C$ values are not significantly different (U = 2339.0; z = -1.09; p = 0.28). However, subadults under two years of age exhibit statistically significant differences from both adults (U = 166.5; z = -3.36; p = 0.0008) and subadults

Table 6.1. Stable carbon and nitrogen isotope values of subadults and adults from St. Stephen's monastery

Sample #	$\delta^{13}C$	$\delta^{15}N$	C/N ratio	Extraction Yield (%)	Age (years)[a]
22.291	-17.7	12.3	3.4	12.2	0.2
17.139	-18.8	13.8	3.3	16.9	0.4
24.267	-17.2	13.7	3.2	12.7	0.6
J.449[b]	-31.1	3.9	5.5	22.0	0.7
7.125	-18.2	13.5	3.2	17.8	0.8
2.527	-18.1	12.9	3.2	13.2	0.8
9.71	-18.3	13.0	3.4	12.8	0.8
9.300	-18.6	11.6	3.3	11.7	0.8
21.308[b]	-27.9	6.6	4.8	18.0	0.8
21.438	-17.9	12.4	3.2	13.6	0.8
2.214	-18.9	11.0	3.3	18.7	0.9
11.824	-18.6	13.0	3.5	6.7	1.1
15.139	-19.5	10.3	3.4	12.0	1.1
12.647	-18.0	12.5	3.2	7.8	2.1
18.206	-19.1	11.6	3.3	11.3	2.1
7.118	-19.0	11.6	3.4	30.6	2.5
9.235	-19.1	10.6	3.3	3.6	2.5
28.166	-19.1	10.0	3.5	20.0	2.5
1.382	-19.3	10.4	3.3	9.1	2.8
8.137	-18.0	12.0	3.2	12.0	2.9
23.377	-18.4	9.6	3.2	6.5	2.9
3.133	-19.2	9.2	3.4	18.9	3.0
5.278	-18.5	11.4	3.2	17.4	3.0
6.364[b]	-19.1	9.7	4.1	34.0	3.0
9.319	-19.8	9.8	3.5	6.3	3.0
12.92	-19.2	9.7	3.3	4.4	3.0
15.217	-19.3	10.3	3.2	14.6	3.0
16.135	-19.2	9.1	3.2	19.5	3.0
27.310	-18.8	9.8	3.2	9.1	3.0
4.223	-18.9	9.5	3.3	29.7	3.2
19.108	-18.8	9.2	3.2	3.5	3.2
3.148	-19.8	10.8	3.6	4.1	3.3
11.422	-18.6	9.4	3.3	7.1	3.3
1.41	-18.4	9.7	3.4	19.5	3.8
1.172	-19.9	9.2	3.5	7.2	3.8
7.85	-19.1	10.5	3.7	14.7	3.8
11.384	-19.4	8.0	3.3	3.2	4.3
25.232	-19.1	10.2	3.3	8.6	4.3
12.317	-19.3	9.8	3.2	5.1	4.9
27.228	-19.3	8.7	3.6	25.8	5.1
12.152[b]	-20.0	8.3	4.6	16.0	5.3
2.174	-18.3	8.9	3.2	13.7	6.0
7.170	-19.0	8.6	3.3	10.5	6.0
J.441	-18.8	9.0	3.2	11.3	6.0

Sample #	$\delta^{13}C$	$\delta^{15}N$	C/N ratio	Extraction Yield (%)	Age (years)[a]
1.149	-18.8	9.2	3.3	12.4	6.8
6.16	-19.3	8.3	3.3	28.3	6.8
11.236	-18.2	9.3	3.2	11.5	6.8
25.241	-20.4	8.3	3.5	31.4	6.8
25.120[b]	-20.1	9.6	4.9	26.5	10.0
1.373	-19.2	8.9	3.4	19.0	10.3
3.134	-19.4	6.9	3.4	8.2	11.0
1.206[b]	-22.3	8.5	3.8	13.7	11.1
23.350	-18.6	8.9	3.2	8.0	11.4
4.122	-19.3	8.7	3.7	27.5	17.8
1.263	-19.6	8.4	3.7	23.6	19.3
6.318	-19.6	7.5	3.5	9.5	Adult
3.118	-19.2	9.6	3.6	5.4	Adult
22.382	-18.6	9.7	3.5	7.3	Adult
12.134	-18.3	11.6	3.5	7.1	Adult
6.228	-20.6	11.0	3.6	5.9	Adult
22.86	-19.8	9.3	3.7	4.1	Adult
3.114	-19.6	9.3	3.4	13.6	Adult
1.33	-19.3	7.8	3.6	19.7	Adult
6.238	-19.2	9.7	3.6	10.4	Adult
1.359	-19.1	10.6	3.4	15.5	Adult
27.255	-19.1	9.0	3.5	10.9	Adult
1.409	-19.0	9.9	3.4	5.2	Adult
2.287	-19.0	10.6	3.5	6.5	Adult
4.4296	-18.9	9.0	3.4	13.9	Adult
6.135	-18.9	8.2	3.4	6.6	Adult
7.436	-18.8	9.7	3.4	19.6	Adult
21.166	-18.6	9.4	3.6	19.0	Adult
4.206	-18.6	9.3	3.5	11.9	Adult
1.358	-18.3	11.1	3.4	14.6	Adult
10.865	-17.7	11.9	3.5	6.1	Adult
12.601	-20.6	7.3	3.4	11.4	Adult
6.261	-19.9	9.1	3.5	6.0	Adult
1.36	-19.9	7.6	3.5	12.2	Adult
4.360	-19.9	10.2	3.5	10.7	Adult
11.674	-19.8	7.8	3.4	5.5	Adult
1.199	-19.8	8.1	3.5	6.2	Adult
3.154	-19.6	8.5	3.5	14.6	Adult
25.239	-19.4	12.6	3.5	5.0	Adult
5.433	-19.4	11.5	3.3	14.3	Adult
1.376	-19.3	9.4	3.5	6.3	Adult
1.47	-19.2	10.6	3.6	23.7	Adult
3.144	-19.1	8.5	3.3	9.7	Adult
3.127	-19.1	8.9	3.4	8.9	Adult
8.77	-19.1	9.6	3.5	8.9	Adult
6.175	-19.0	8.0	3.4	8.8	Adult

(continued)

Table 6.1.—*Continued*

Sample #	δ¹³C	δ¹⁵N	C/N ratio	Extraction Yield (%)	Age (years)[a]
1.146	-19.0	8.9	3.3	14.1	Adult
1.325	-19.0	9.1	3.6	5.4	Adult
9.325	-18.9	9.9	3.5	11.4	Adult
2.167	-18.9	10.4	3.6	5.1	Adult
4.174	-18.9	10.0	3.5	9.6	Adult
2.282	-18.9	9.8	3.4	17.9	Adult
3.117	-18.8	10.8	3.6	5.1	Adult
4.169	-18.8	10.0	3.5	8.4	Adult
1.407[c]	-18.7	9.0	3.6	1.9	Adult
22.201	-18.7	11.5	3.5	8.8	Adult
1.38	-18.7	10.0	3.4	8.8	Adult
5.163	-18.7	11.0	3.4	13.0	Adult
3.131	-18.7	10.8	3.4	12.1	Adult
1.125	-18.7	9.3	3.5	10.0	Adult
2.171	-18.6	11.2	3.4	5.2	Adult
6.321	-18.6	8.7	3.3	12.5	Adult
6.122[c]	-18.5	10.3	3.5	0.5	Adult
2.166	-18.5	9.2	3.4	5.0	Adult
4.186	-18.2	8.5	3.3	20.9	Adult

Notes a. Subadult ages were calculated from femoral diaphyseal lengths, following Ubelaker 1999 and Scheuer and Black 2000.
b. Excluded due to unacceptable C/N ratio.
c. Excluded due to low extraction yields.

over the age of two (U = 147.5; z = -3.05; p = 0.002). Correspondingly, adults and subadults over the age of two do not differ discernibly (U = 1754.5; z = 0.20; p = 0.83).

Figure 6.4 displays δ¹⁵N values throughout breast-feeding and the weaning process. They become increasingly elevated after birth, continuing until the values peak at around six months old. Such a peak illustrates the end of a diet composed entirely of breast milk, followed by the introduction of new foods. The gradual decline in δ¹⁵N values reflects a change in sources of dietary protein from breast milk to weaning foods, and these subadult isotopic values continue to diminish as supplementary foods progressively play a larger role in nutrition. The complete cessation of breast-feeding and the end of the weaning process occurred between two to three years of age. As with carbon, δ¹⁵N values of subadults under the age of two differ significantly from those of both adults (U = 610.6; z = 4.67; p < 0.0001) and subadults over the age of two (U = 464.5; z = 4.53; p < 0.0001).

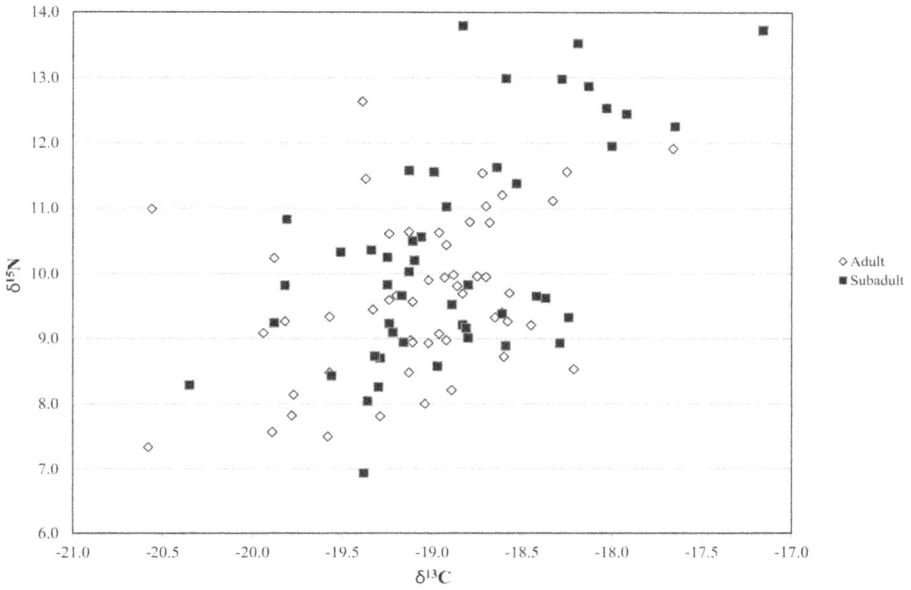

Figure 6.3. Bivariate plot of $\delta^{13}C$ and $\delta^{15}N$ values for the adults and subadults of St. Stephen's.

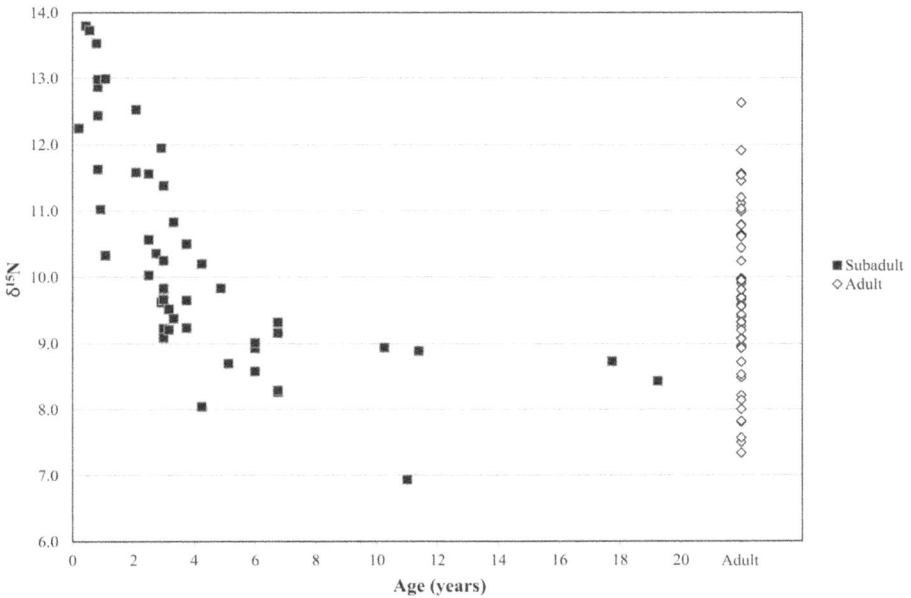

Figure 6.4. Age profile of $\delta^{15}N$ for the subadults of St. Stephen's.

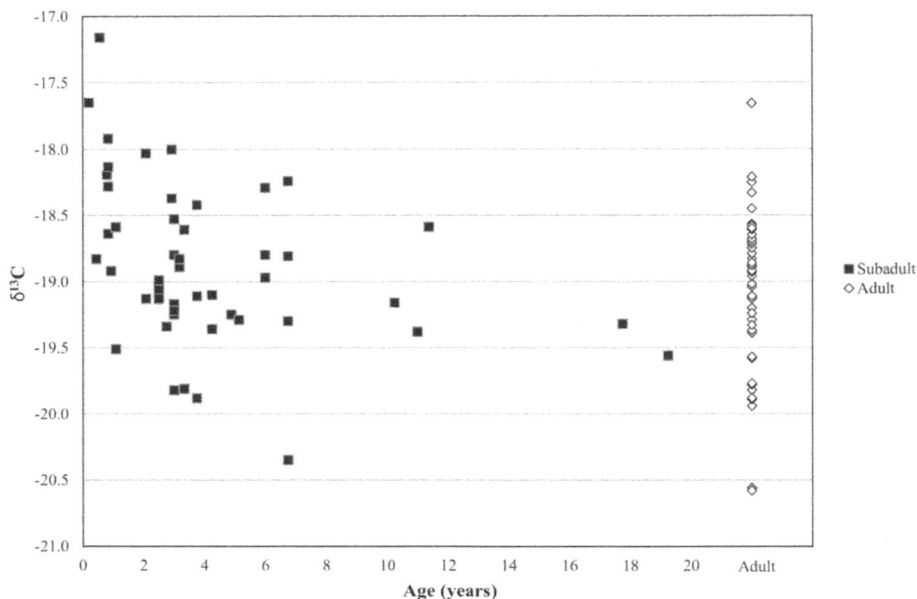

Figure 6.5. Age profile of δ¹³C for the subadults of St. Stephen's.

Figure 6.5 illustrates the relationship between age and $\delta^{13}C$ values for the St. Stephen's subadults. As with $\delta^{15}N$ values, the $\delta^{13}C$ values for this age profile reflect patterns of breast-feeding and weaning. The first portion depicts an initial rise in carbon levels, signifying the onset of breast-feeding with a diet composed of only breast milk. These values peak at around six months of age. Although more variably scattered than the fairly uniform path of the $\delta^{15}N$ values, $\delta^{13}C$ values after this peak gradually decline, indicative of the supplementation of breast milk with new foods and hence the commencement of the weaning process. Breast milk continued to play a role in the diet of these children until the second or third year of life, when complete weaning occurred.

Discussion

Unexpectedly enriched $\delta^{15}N$ values in the adult profile suggest the habitual consumption of protein derived from secondary animal products such as cheese, milk, eggs, and perhaps meat. Such animal protein intake contradicts historical references to the dietary asceticism espoused in the patristic literature. While secondary animal products were permitted on feast days at some monasteries, these items would have had to be consumed on a regular basis in order to attain the elevated $\delta^{15}N$ values seen in the adults. Moreover, such "luxury" items would have been expensive and difficult to come by for monks living a reportedly abstinent lifestyle. However, St. Stephen's monastery was affluent both because of its urban location and income from patron donations and pilgrims (Binns 1994; Caner 2002; Patrich 1995; Thomas and Hero 2000), and it may have had greater access to animal protein resources. This would explain the high $\delta^{15}N$ values.

It is important to note that in arid, drought-susceptible regions, both plant and animal tissues (including those of humans) generally have higher $\delta^{15}N$ values, a product of ^{15}N enrichment in desert soils as well as ^{14}N depletion during increased urea excretion as part of water conservation (Ambrose 1991). However, paleoclimatic studies suggest that the Byzantine period was a time of plentiful rainfall and elevated humidity in the Near East, resulting in centuries of agricultural prosperity (Hirschfeld 2004). Nevertheless, additional isotopic analyses on faunal remains from this period and region must be performed to determine if ^{15}N enrichment plays a role in this trophic system.

The depleted $\delta^{13}C$ values associated with the St. Stephen's adults indicate a primarily terrestrial diet dominated by C_3-based foods. These results are consistent with textual evidence that emphasizes the importance of bread made from C_3 cereals in addition to other C_3 garden produce. Only a few adult individuals display slightly elevated $\delta^{13}C$ values that might correspond to the intake of marine protein such as fish when associated with enriched $\delta^{15}N$ values.

Among the subadults, $\delta^{13}C$ and $\delta^{15}N$ values effectively demonstrate the trophic level effect of breast-feeding. The average $\delta^{13}C$ value of children under the age of two was -18.3‰, and for those over two it was -19.0‰ (Table 6.2). A difference of 0.7‰ between these means may reflect ^{13}C enrichment due to a trophic-level effect during the consumption of breast milk by the infant (Katzenberg, Saunders, and Fitzgerald 1993; Katzenberg, Herring, and Saunders 1996; Wright and Schwarcz 1998). Moreover, subadults under two years of age have an average $\delta^{15}N$ value of 12.5‰, 2.9‰ greater than the mean $\delta^{15}N$ of 9.6‰ for their older counterparts. This difference falls into the expected enrichment range of 2.0–3.6‰ because of an increase in ^{15}N, a product of the nitrogen trophic-level effect

Table 6.2. Means and ranges of stable carbon and nitrogen isotope values of subadults and adults from St. Stephen's monastery

	N	$\delta^{13}C$ (‰)			$\delta^{15}N$ (‰)		
		Mean	SD	Range	Mean	SD	Range
Adults	52	-19.0	0.6	-20.6 to -17.7	9.6	1.2	7.3 to 12.6
Subadults	49	-18.9	0.6	-20.4 to -17.2	10.3	1.7	6.9 to 13.8
Subadults under 2	11	-18.3	0.5	-19.5 to -17.2	12.5	1.1	10.3 to 13.8
Subadults over 2	38	-19.0	0.6	-20.4 to -18.0	9.6	1.2	6.9 to 12.5

between a mother and an infant fed with breast milk. This demonstration of the trophic-level effect in both carbon and nitrogen stable isotope ratios illustrates that the children interred at St. Stephen's were indeed breastfed, either by their natural mothers or by wet nurses, and that they underwent a gradual, steady weaning process as opposed to a sudden transition to new foods.

In addition to illustrating the isotopic effects on the bone collagen of breast-feeding infants, stable isotope ratios contribute to our understanding of how Byzantine peoples dealt with the weaning process. This was not an unorganized, hasty event but instead was a culturally prescribed practice in which infants were introduced to foods after an allotted period of time. Furthermore, weaning did not end abruptly but continued for a year and a half to two years before a total cessation of breast-feeding. Roman physicians such as Soranus and Galen as well as the later Byzantine physicians Aetios, Paulus Aeginata, and Oribasius appear to have had significant influence over the appropriate implementation of this process. The fact that mothers followed their recommendations about the timing and duration of weaning is reflected in both the stable carbon and nitrogen isotopic values of the subadults of St. Stephen's.

Although historical accounts are corroborated by the breast-feeding and weaning profiles, it is important to recognize that these profiles do not represent the diet of a single individual. Instead, they reflect the food intake of 49 separate subadults at the time of their deaths. Subsequently, the weaning curve produced cannot be thought of as a blanket depiction of the weaning process for the children of St. Stephen's. While the profiles generated by stable carbon and nitrogen isotope ratios do give meaningful insight into generalized patterns of breast-feeding and weaning, each individual value corresponds to a single point in time on 49 different weaning curves. The variability seen in these profiles suggests that the weaning process was not entirely uniform but differed somewhat among individuals, an indication of a heterogeneous sample in which most (but not all) subadults were weaned during the second and third years of life. Although cultural records give credence to an interpretation that breast-feeding ended at two to three years of age, the biochemical data are more variable, pointing to a more diverse representation of subadult weaning practices.

Immediately after peaking when the infants were six months old, $\delta^{13}C$ values decline, indicating that infants were likely consuming a predominantly C_3-based diet of plants and/or animal protein, which would produce lower $\delta^{13}C$ values due to the depleted levels of ^{13}C in these food sources. Such foods likely included softened breads made from wheat or barley, porridge, vegetables, eggs, and milk, as recommended by Roman and Byzantine physicians. This corresponds with historical data on the foods consumed by monks and more generally by Near Eastern populations during the Byzantine period. While adult and (all) subadult $\delta^{13}C$ values do not differ significantly from one another, suggesting that the children interred at St. Stephen's consumed a C_3-based diet that was similar to that of the monks upon weaning, more detailed analyses of subadults under the age of two indicate that some differences did in fact exist and are likely attributable to a slight enrichment of ^{13}C as a result of breast-feeding.

The biocultural implication of this similarity is that the women who were breast-feeding the infants shared a diet similar to that of the monks. Thus, these children may have been cared for in a monastic hospital or orphanage by wet nurses who consumed a diet isotopically comparable to monastic dietary intake. Alternatively, the subadults may have been breastfed by their mothers in the community, who also consumed a C_3-based diet, and were simply buried at the monastery. The latter theory is supported by textual references to a movement away from wet-nursing and toward maternal breast-feeding by the sixth and seventh centuries AD. However, despite this maternally oriented trend, wet nurses were still socially permitted in extreme cases, which would indeed hold if the children of St. Stephen's were orphans cared for by the monastery.

Subadult nitrogen and carbon isotope values are generally correlated for the infants and young children. Nevertheless, variation within each age class suggests variability in weaning diets, particularly some disparity in C_3 products consumed. A portion of the subadults may have eaten weaning foods such as goat's milk or eggs while others may have been weaned with wheat porridges or vegetables. These differences may point to multiple origins for the children interred at St. Stephen's or to health differences that warranted differential feeding. Sick or dying children may have been given foods that were not typically consumed by their healthier counterparts, diets that may have produced the variability seen here. Characteristic of the challenge set forth by the osteological paradox, it is imperative to keep in mind the notion of selective mortality, in which individuals experience varying degrees of health, potentially resulting in morbidity and mortality that is not necessarily made evident in the skeleton (Wright and Yoder 2003). Illness that was recognized during the end of life would have been treated in culturally prescribed ways that may have included changes to diet.

Subadult mortality appears to peak in children under the age of one and corresponds to the highest values of both $\delta^{13}C$ and $\delta^{15}N$ at around six months of age. This may suggest that infants were introduced to nutritionally inadequate weaning foods or to food-related pathogens during this period (Cook 1981). With decreased consumption of the resistance factors found in breast milk, including the immunoglobulins IgA, IgG, and IgM as well as T and B lymphocytes and antistaphylococcal factor (Hayward 1986; King and Ulijaszek 1999; Popkin et al. 1986), the immature immune systems of infants and young children were more susceptible to disease.

Mortality diminishes between one and two years of age, then peaks again during the second and third years of life, after weaning foods had been established in the diet for some time. This is consistent with the ages at which the weaning process was completed as measured by $\delta^{13}C$ and $\delta^{15}N$ values, again raising the possibility that these subadults were exposed to pathogen-containing foods. The loss of passive immunity from breast milk may have been a contributing factor, but increased exposure to external pathogens is the more likely causative agent (Katzenberg, Herring, and Saunders 1996). It is important to stress that the imprecise nature of determining age from the midpoints of age ranges derived from femoral measurements may have skewed the relationship presented here between mortality and age at death (Schurr 1997). In addition, too little is known about how the children came to be present in the St. Stephen's monastery to be certain that the mortality profile of the sample accurately represents that of the contributing population.

Summary and Conclusions

Stable isotope data can add much to our knowledge of past diet. At St. Stephen's, adult isotopic values indicate the consumption of C_3 plants, consistent with historical reports of grains and produce available to monasteries during the Byzantine period. However, the presence of elevated nitrogen values suggests the inclusion of animal protein in the diet, "luxury" goods that were prohibited by religious mandate and/or too were expensive for an ascetic monastic community. St. Stephen's rather unique position as a wealthy monastery in the urban center of Jerusalem may have afforded the city-dwelling monks access to these products.

Subadult isotope values provide an index of the timing and duration of weaning but also facilitate the identification of specific photosynthetic pathways used by different kinds of plants (and accordingly, animal products) consumed by young children. Both stable carbon and nitrogen isotope values show agreement between biochemical signatures and historical reports regarding the length of the weaning interval. Historical sources stipulated that weaning should begin at around six months old and end when the child was between two and three years old. However, the variability of isotopic values in the age profile suggests that this was a generalized pattern that contained individual variation.

Using stable carbon isotopes, we can discriminate between particular weaning diets and put forth ideas about the relationship between the diets of these children and their adult counterparts. Subadults had depleted carbon isotope values indicative of a C_3-based diet that was isotopically similar to that of the adult monks. Based on textual evidence that Byzantine monasteries cared for young children, it is possible that St. Stephen's provided wet nurses to feed them and that these nurses and children consumed food that was also available to the monks. More generally, however, diet in the Byzantine Near East was largely composed of C_3-based foods and only occasional animal protein, making it difficult to distinguish between children cared for outside the monastic grounds and those cared for within the monastery. This portrait of childhood diet in the Byzantine period becomes even more complex with the possibility that the lay community may have used the St. Stephen's tombs as a sacred place to bury their young.

The children of St. Stephen's do not fit a simplistic model of orphans fed a rigid diet, but it is evident that their caregivers did follow culturally determined ideas about appropriate infant feeding practices. Taken together, this study indicates the utility of synthesizing the biochemical and historical evidence for a more holistic glimpse of childhood at this large and important urban monastery in Jerusalem.

Acknowledgments

Thanks to the Center for Environmental Science and Technology at the University of Notre Dame for the use of its mass spectrometer, particularly to Professor Mark Schurr and Dennis Birdsell for their supervision of sample preparation and isotopic analyses. This research was supported by the National Science Foundation Research Experiences for Undergraduates (SES #0244096) and the Notre Dame Institute for Scholarship in the Liberal Arts. Special thanks to the L'École Biblique et Archéologique Française de Jérusalem/Coûvent Saint-Étienne for access to the St. Stephen's collection.

References Cited

Abrahamse, Dorothy
1979   Images of Childhood in Early Byzantine Hagiography. *Journal of Psychohistory* 6:497–517.
Aeginata, Paulus
1844   *The Seven Books of Paulus Aeginata, with a Commentary.* Vol. 1. Translated by F. Adams. Sydenham Society, London.
Aetios of Amida
1950   *Aetios of Amida: The Gynaecologya and Obstetrics of the VIth Century, A.D. (Aetii Medici).* Translated by J. V. Ricci. The Blakistan Company, Philadelphia.
Allen, Paul
1979   The "Justinianic" Plague. *Byzantion* 49:5–20.
Ambrose, Stanley H.
1991   Effects of Diet, Climate and Physiology on Nitrogen Isotope Abundances in Terrestrial Foodwebs. *Journal of Archaeological Science* 18:293–317.
Ambrose, Stanley H., and Lynette Norr
1993   Experimental Evidence for the Relationship of the Carbon Isotopes Ratios of Whole Diet and Dietary Protein to Those of Bone Collagen and Carbonate. In *Prehistoric Human Bone: Archaeology at the Molecular Level,* edited by Joseph B. Lambert and Gisela Grupe, pp. 1–37. Springer-Verlag, New York.
Avni, Gideon, and Zvi Greenhut
1996   *The Akeldama Tombs: Three Burial Caves in the Kidron Valley, Jerusalem.* Israeli Antiquities Authority, Jerusalem.

Barkay, Gabriel, and Amihai Mazar

1986   Jerusalem Tombs from the Days of the First Temple. *Biblical Archaeology Review* 12:22–39.

Barkay, Gabriel, Amos Kloner, and Amihai Mazar

1994   The Northern Necropolis of Jerusalem during the First Temple Period. In *Ancient Jerusalem Revealed,* edited by H. Geva and J. Shadur, pp. 119–127. Israel Exploration Society, Jerusalem.

Bautch, K., R. Bautch, G. Barkay, and S. Sheridan

2000   "The Vessels of the Potter Shall Be Broken": The Material Culture from a Burial Cave at St. Etienne's Monastery, Jerusalem. *Revue Biblique* 107(4):561–590.

Binns, John

1994   *Ascetics and Ambassadors of Christ: The Monasteries of Palestine, 314–631.* Clarendon Press, Oxford.

Boswell, John E.

1984   Expositio and Oblatio: The Abandonment of Children and the Ancient Medieval Family. *The American Historical Review* 89(1):10–33.

Brown, Peter R. L.

1981   *The Cult of the Saints: Its Rise and Function in Latin Christianity.* University of Chicago Press, Chicago.

Caner, Daniel

2002   *Wandering, Begging Monks: Spiritual Authority and the Promotion of Monasticism in Late Antiquity.* University of California Press, Berkeley.

Clark, Elizabeth A.

1982   Claims on the Bones of Saint Stephen: The Partisans of Melania and Eudocia. *Church History* 51(2):141–156.

Conrad, Lawrence I.

1987   The Plague in Bilad al-Sham in Pre-Islamic Times. In *Proceedings of the Symposium on Bilad al-Sham during the Byzantine Period,* vol. 2, edited by M. Bakhit and M. Asfour, pp. 143–163. University of Jordan, Amman.

Cook, Della C.

1981   Mortality, Age-Structure and Status in the Interpretation of Stress Indicators in Prehistoric Skeletons: A Dental Example from the Lower Illinois Valley. In *The Archaeology of Death,* edited by Robert Chapman, Ian Kinnes, and Klavs Randsborg, pp. 133–144. Cambridge University Press, London.

DeNiro, Michael J.

1985   Postmortem Preservation and Alteration of In Vivo Bone Collagen Isotope Ratios in relation to Palaeodietary Reconstruction. *Nature* 317:806–809.

1987   Stable Isotopy and Archaeology. *American Scientist* 75:182–191.

de Vaux, L.

1886   Découvertes récentes a Jérusalem. *Revue Archéologique* 7:371–374.

Dittman, Karola, and Gisela Grupe

2000   Biochemical and Palaeopathological Investigations on Weaning and Infant Mortality in the Early Middle Ages. *Anthropologischer Anzeiger* 58(4):345–355.

Drucker, D., and H. Bocherens
2004   Carbon and Nitrogen Stable Isotopes as Tracers of Change in Diet Breadth during Middle and Upper Palaeolithic in Europe. *International Journal of Osteoarchaeology* 14:162–177.

Dupras, Tosha L.
1999   Dining in the Dakhleh Oasis, Egypt: Determination of Diet Using Documents and Stable Isotope Analysis. Ph.D. Dissertation, Department of Anthropology, McMaster University, Hamilton, Ontario.

Dupras, Tosha L., Henry P. Schwarcz, and Scott I. Fairgrieve
2001   Infant Feeding and Weaning Practices in Roman Egypt. *American Journal of Physical Anthropology* 115:204–212.

Feasby, Rebecca S. G.
1998   Stable Isotope Evidence for Dietary Patterns and Environmental Conditions at Tell Leilan, Syria, ca. 1900–2900 BC. Ph.D. dissertation, Department of Anthropology, University of Alberta, Edmonton.

Fildes, Valerie A.
1986   *Breasts, Bottles and Babies: A History of Infant Feeding.* Edinburgh University Press, Edinburgh.

Fuller, B. T., T. I. Molleson, D. A. Harris, L. T. Gilmour, and R. E. M. Hedges
2006   Isotopic Evidence for Breastfeeding and Possible Adult Dietary Differences from Late/Sub-Roman Britain. *American Journal of Physical Anthropology* 129:45–54.

Fuller, B. T., M. P. Richards, and S. A. Mays
2003   Stable Carbon and Nitrogen Isotope Variations in Tooth Dentine Serial Sections from Wharram Percy. *Journal of Archaeological Science* 30:1673–1684.

Galen
1951   *A Translation of Galen's Hygiene (De sanitate tuenda).* Translated by R. M. Green. Charles C. Thomas, Springfield, Ill.

Garrison, Fielding H.
1923   A System of Pediatrics: History of Pediatrics. In *Pediatrics,* edited by I. Abt, pp. 1–170. W. B. Saunders Company, London.

Harlow, Mary, and Wendy Smith
2001   Between Fasting and Feasting: The Literary and Archaeobotanical Evidence for Monastic Diet in Late Antique Egypt. *Antiquity* 75:758–768.

Hayward, Anthony R.
1986   Immunity Development. In *Human Growth,* edited by Frank Faulkner and J. M. Tanner, pp. 377–390. Plenum Press, New York.

Herring, D. Ann, S. R. Saunders, and M. A. Katzenberg
1998   Investigating the Weaning Process in Past Populations. *American Journal of Physical Anthropology* 105:425–439.

Hirschfeld, Yizhar
1992   *The Judean Monasteries in the Byzantine Period.* Yale University Press, New Haven, Conn.

1996   The Importance of Bread in the Diet of Monks in the Judean Desert. *Byzantion* 66:143–155.

2004   A Climatic Change in the Early Byzantine Period? Some Archaeological Evidence. *Palestine Exploration Quarterly* 136(2):133–149.

Hoefs, Jochen

2004   *Stable Isotope Geochemistry.* Springer, Berlin.

Jay, Mandy, B. T. Fuller, Michael P. Richards, Christopher J. Knüsel, and Sarah S. King

2008   Iron Age Breastfeeding Practices in Britain: Isotopic Evidence from Wetwang Slack, East Yorkshire. *American Journal of Physical Anthropology* 136(3):327–337.

Katzenberg, M. Anne

1992   Advances in Stable Isotope Analysis of Prehistoric Bones. In *Skeletal Biology of Past Peoples: Research Methods,* edited by S. Saunders and M. Katzenberg, pp. 105–119. Wiley-Liss, New York.

Katzenberg, M. Anne, D. Ann Herring, and Shelley R. Saunders

1996   Weaning and Infant Mortality: Evaluating the Skeletal Evidence. *Yearbook of Physical Anthropology* 39:177–199.

Katzenberg, M. Anne, Shelley R. Saunders, and William R. Fitzgerald

1993   Age Differences in Stable Carbon and Nitrogen Isotope Ratios in a Population of Prehistoric Maize Horticulturalists. *American Journal of Physical Anthropology* 90:267–281.

King, Sarah E., and Stanley J. Ulijaszek

1999   Invisible Insults During Growth and Development: Contemporary Theories and Past Populations. In *Human Growth in the Past: Studies from Bone and Teeth,* edited by Robert D. Hoppa and Charles M. Fitzgerald, pp. 161–182. Cambridge University Press, Cambridge.

Kislinger, Ewald

1999   Christians of the East: Rules and Realities of the Byzantine Diet. In *Food: A Culinary History from Antiquity to the Present,* edited by Albert Sonnenfeld, pp. 194–206. Columbia University Press, New York.

Lagrange, M.-J.

1894   *Saint Étienne et son sanctuaire a Jerusalem.* Alphonse Picard, Paris.

Lascaratos, J., and E. Poulakou-Rebelakou

2003   Oribasius (Fourth Century) and Early Byzantine Perinatal Nutrition. *Journal of Pediatric Gastroenterology and Nutrition* 36:186–189.

Leyerle, B.

2002   Children and Disease in a Sixth Century Monastery. In *What Athens Has to Do with Jerusalem: Essays on Classical, Jewish, and Early Christian Art and Archaeology,* edited by Leonard V. Rutgers, pp. 349–372. Peeters, Leuven.

McGowan, Andrew

1999   *Ascetic Eucharists: Food and Drink in Early Christian Ritual Meals.* Clarendon, Oxford.

Miles, Margaret R.
1995   Religion and Food: The Case of Eating Disorders. *Journal of the American Academy of Religion* 63:549–564.

Miller, Timothy S.
1997   *The Birth of the Byzantine Hospital.* Johns Hopkins University Press, Baltimore, Md.
2003   *The Orphans of Byzantium: Child Welfare in the Christian Empire.* Catholic University of America Press, Washington, D.C.

Minagawa, Masao, and Eitaro Wada
1984   Stepwise Enrichment of ^{15}N along Food Chains: Further Evidence and the Relation between δ^{15}N And Animal Age. *Geochimica et Cosmochimica Acta* 48:1135–1140.

Moffatt, Ann
1986   The Byzantine Child. *Social Research* 53(4):705–723.

Oribasius
1926   *Oribasii Collectionum Medicarum Reliquiae.* Vols. 4–5. Translated by Joannes Raeder. Teubner, Leipzig-Berlin.

Patrich, Joseph
1995   *Sabas, Leader of Palestinian Monasticism: A Comparative Study in Eastern Monasticism, 4th to 7th Centuries.* Dumbarton Oaks Research Library & Collection, Washington, D.C.

Popkin, Barry M., Tamar Lasky, Judith Litvin, Deborah Spicer, and Monica E. Yamamoto
1986   *The Infant-Feeding Triad: Infant, Mother, and Household.* Gordon and Breach Science Publishers, New York.

Price, R. M., and John Binns
1991   *Lives of the Monks of Palestine by Cyril of Scythopolis.* Cistercian Publications, Kalamazoo, Mich.

Price, T. Douglas, Margaret J. Schoeninger, and George J. Armelagos
1985   Bone Chemistry and Past Behavior. *Journal of Human Evolution* 14:419–447.

Rautman, Marcus
2006   *Daily Life in the Byzantine Empire.* Greenwood Press, Westport, Conn.

Richards, M. P., and R. E. M. Hedges
1999   Stable Isotope Evidence for Similarities in the Types of Marine Foods Used by Late Mesolithic Humans at Sites along the Atlantic Coast of Europe. *Journal of Archaeological Science* 26(6):717–722.

Richards, M. P., S. Mays, and B. T. Fuller
2002   Stable Carbon and Nitrogen Isotope Values of Bone and Teeth Reflect Weaning Age at the Medieval Wharram Percy Site, Yorkshire, UK. *American Journal of Physical Anthropology* 119:205–210.

Richards, M. P., J. A. Pearson, T. I. Molleson, N. Russell, and L. Martin
2003   Stable Isotope Evidence of Diet at Neolithic Çatalhöyük, Turkey. *Journal of Archaeological Science* 30:67–76.

Scheuer, Louise, and Sue Black
2000   *Developmental Juvenile Osteology*. Academic Press, San Diego.

Schoeninger, Margaret J., and Katherine Moore
1992   Bone Stable Isotope Studies in Archaeology. *Journal of World Prehistory* 6(2):247–296.

Schurr, Mark R.
1997   Stable Nitrogen Isotopes as Evidence for the Age of Weaning at the Angel Site: A Comparison of Isotopic and Demographic Measures of Weaning Age. *Journal of Archaeological Science* 24:919–927.
1998   Using Stable Nitrogen-Isotopes to Study Weaning Behavior in Past Populations. *World Archaeology* 30:327–342.

Schurr, Mark R., and Mary L. Powell
2005   The Role of Changing Childhood Diets in the Prehistoric Evolution of Food Production: An Isotopic Assessment. *American Journal of Physical Anthropology* 126:278–294.

Schwarcz, Henry P., and Margaret J. Schoeninger
1991   Stable Isotope Analyses in Human Nutritional Ecology. *Yearbook of Physical Anthropology* 34:283–321.

Sheridan, Susan G.
1999   "New Life the Dead Receive": The Relationship Between Human Remains and the Cultural Record for Byzantine St. Stephen's. *Revue Biblique* 106(4):574–611.

Smith, Bruce N., and Samuel Epstein
1971   Two Categories of $^{13}C/^{12}C$ Ratios for Higher Plants. *Plant Physiology* 47:380–384.

Soranus
1956   *Soranus' Gynecology*. Translated by Owsei Temkin. Johns Hopkins University Press, Baltimore, Md.

Steele, K. W., and R. M. Daniel
1978   Fractionation of Nitrogen Isotopes by Animals: A Further Complication to the Use Of Variations in the Natural Abundance of ^{15}N For Tracer Studies. *Journal of Agricultural Science* 90:7–9.

Still, George F.
1931   *The History of Paediatrics: The Progress of the Study of Diseases of Children up to the End of the XVIIIth Century*. Oxford University Press, London.

Talbot, Alice-Mary
2002   Byzantine Monastic Horticulture: The Textual Evidence. In *Byzantine Garden Culture*, edited by A. Littlewood, H. Macquire, and J. Wolschke-Bulmahn, Dumbarton Oaks, Washington, D.C.
2007   Mealtime in Monasteries: The Culture of the Byzantine Refectory. In *Eat, Drink, and Be Merry (Luke 12:19): Food and Wine in Byzantium*, edited by L. Brubaker and K. Linardou, pp. 109–125. Ashgate, Aldershot, England.

Thomas, John, and Angela C. Hero
2000   *Byzantine Monastic Foundation Documents*. Dumbarton Oaks Research Library and Collection, Washington, D.C.

Thomas, A. H., L. Chaix, and M. P. Richards

2008   Stable Isotopes and Diet at Ancient Kerma, Upper Nubia (Sudan). *Journal of Archaeological Science* 35(2):376–387.

Ubelaker, Douglas H.

1999   *Human Skeletal Remains: Excavation, Analysis, Interpretation.* Taraxacum, Washington, D.C.

van der Merwe, Nikolaas J., and J. C. Vogel

1978 ^{13}C Content of Human Collagen as a Measure of Prehistoric Diet in Woodland North America. *Nature* 276:815–816.

Vincent, H., and F. M. Abel

1926   *Jérusalem: Reserches de Topographie, d'archéologie et d'histoire. Tome 2: Jérusalem Nouvelle.* Gabalda, Paris.

Wright, L. E., and Schwarcz, H. P.

1998   Stable Carbon and Oxygen Isotopes in Human Tooth Enamel: Identifying Breastfeeding and Weaning in Prehistory. *American Journal of Physical Anthropology* 106:1–18.

Wright, Lori E., and Cassady J. Yoder

2003   Recent Progress in Bioarchaeology: Approaches to the Osteological Paradox. *Journal of Archaeological Research* 11(1):43–70.

7

Buccal Dental Microwear as an Indicator of Dietary Habits of the Natufian People of El-Wad and El-Kebarah

MOHAMMAD ALROUSAN AND ALEJANDRO PÉREZ-PÉREZ

The subsistence strategies of human populations are important biological and social indicators of human adaptation and evolution. The Natufian period in the Near East (13,000–10,300 BP), for example, saw the biological changes resulting from an increased reliance on agriculture for subsistence concurrent with the social changes that accompanied life in permanent settlements. Scholars assume that Natufian period sites across the Near East shared similar shifts in subsistence. This investigation explores homogeneity in human diet through dental microwear analysis of human dentition from two Natufian sites: El-Wad and El-Kebarah.

Diet and dietary-related behaviors result from the interaction between food availability in the surrounding environment and food procurement and processing technologies. Biological anthropologists use evidence for diet in skeletal tissues to understand and reconstruct past lifeways. Dental microwear analysis, for example, allows direct reconstruction of dietary composition based on the amount of abrasives chewed with food particles. Microwear analyses of tooth enamel surfaces have explored many research issues, from the reconstruction of the dietary behavior of ancient human populations (Molleson and Jones 1991; Molleson, Jones, and Jones 1993; Pérez-Pérez, Lalueza, and Turbon 1994; Larsen et al. 2001, 84–86; Schmidt 2001; Organ, Teaford, and Larsen 2005; Mahoney 2006; Romero and De Juan 2007; Alrousan and Pérez-Pérez 2008; Alrousan, Pérez-Pérez, and Molleson 2009) to primate ecology and diet (Galbany and Pérez-Pérez 2004; Galbany et al. 2009) and is a method that is being continually tightened and improved (Teaford and Oyne 1989; Grine, Ungar, and Teaford 2002; Galbany et al. 2005). Both occlusal microwear (focusing on the bite surface of the teeth) (Molleson and Jones 1990; Molleson, Jones, and Jones 1993; Schmidt 2001; Organ, Teaford, and Larsen 2005; Mahoney 2006; Ungar, Lalueza, and Turbon 2006; El Zaatari 2008) and buccal microwear (on the cheek side of the back teeth) (Pérez-Pérez, Lalueza, and Turbon 1994, 2003; Lalueza et al. 1996; Polo-Cerdá et al. 2007; Romero et al. 2007; Alrousan and Pérez-Pérez 2008; Estaberanz et al. 2009) have been explored in dental microwear studies.

The main causes of dental microwear on occlusal and buccal surfaces are abrasive particles in the diet. The source of these particles is either intrinsic or extrinsic to the foodstuffs consumed. Intrinsic sources include the opal phytoliths present in plant tissues (Lalueza et al. 1994), especially in cereals, and the extrinsic sources result from the contamination of food items with dust, ash, or sand during food processing (Mahoney 2006; Alrousan and Pérez-Pérez 2008). Abrasives in the diet cause pits and scratches to form on occlusal tooth crown surfaces (Schmidt 2001) but will cause only striations on the vestibular or buccal surfaces (Pérez-Pérez et al. 2003). In addition, a mainly carnivorous diet tends to be correlated with a large number of vertical striations on the buccal surfaces, whereas a mainly vegetarian diet tends to correlate with higher densities of horizontal striations (Lalueza et al. 1996). The buccal microwear pattern is a reliable, nondestructive, and accurate method for dietary reconstruction because it can reflect dietary changes over the long term rather than provide evidence about the "last supper." This allows researchers to differentiate between masticatory and nonmasticatory uses of teeth (e.g., as a tool) and identify seasonal changes (Pérez-Pérez, Lalueza, and Turbon 1994, 184–185; Pérez-Pérez 2004; Romero et al. 2009).

The Natufian period, which lasted from 13,000 to 10,300 BP (Bar-Yosef 1998; Eshad, Gopher, and Herskovitz 2006), is an important span in human history, although its culture and biology are still poorly known. The first signs of this culture were excavated from the site of Wadi en-Natuf, and for this reason it is known as the Natufian (Garrod 1932, 20). This period is considered to be the threshold of agricultural practices and cereal consumption (Bar-Yosef 1998). By the end of the last glacial period and before the Neolithic "revolution," the subsistence economy was highly dependent on animal foods, especially large mammals such as gazelle, as well as on gathering wild plant foods, mainly wild cereals (Henry

1989, 215; Bar-Yosef 1998, 167; Munro and Bar-Oz 2005). Marine foods contributed little to the diet in the Natufian (Bar-Yosef and Sillen 1993, 207–208). The primary dietary reliance on plants and cereals and meat is represented by the huge number of tools for hunting and gathering that have been excavated from Natufian sites, including many sickles, pestles, and mortars (Bar-Yosef 1998, 165; Henry 1989, 195).

In contrast to the high precipitation rates and the expansion of wood-lands that characterized the Natufian period (Van Zeist and Bottema 1977, 187; Hillman 1996, 188), a sudden drop in the rainfall around 9,000–8,000 BP resulted in a dry and cold period known as the Younger Dryas (Hillman 1996, 168). As a result, the traditional hunter-gatherer economy vanished and was replaced by transitional agricultural populations who relied heavily on domestic cereals as a major source of food. However, the nature of this Natufian transition in different populations in the Near East has not been well documented.

The present study analyzes the buccal dental microwear patterns of the Natufian populations from the sites of El-Wad and El-Kebarah to shed some light on dietary adaptation and habits during the Natufian period. We also compare these two Natufian sites with later Neolithic groups and with modern hunter-gatherer populations. These two Natufian populations represent similar environmental conditions, and thus dietary variability between Natufian groups should be controlled for in broader comparisons. Finally, the results are discussed within a broad archaeological context of the Natufian populations.

Materials and Methods

Samples

The studied sample consisted of 129 teeth belonging to 31 individuals from the Natufian sites of El-Kebarah (N = 17 individuals, 80 teeth) and El-Wad (N = 14 individuals, 49 teeth). The original teeth are stored at the Peabody Museum in Boston, Massachusetts. Only teeth with well-preserved enamel surfaces and no associated dental pathologies were studied.

The Natufian sites of El-Wad (Mugharet el-Wad) and El-Kebarah (Mugharet el-Kebarah) are located in the Mediterranean basin. El-Kebarah is located about 15 km south of El-Wad (Turville-Petre 1932a, 271) and was first dated to the Natufian period by Turville-Petre (1932a, 20, 1932b,

276) and then more precisely dated using ^{14}C analysis to 12,470±180 BP by Bar-Yosef and Sillen (1993, 205). The Natufian site of El-Wad, which dates from 12,950 to 10,680 BP based on relative and ^{14}C dating techniques (Garrod 1932, 20; Weinstein-Evron 1991, 97), is characterized by a remarkable series of constructions, including limestone pavement slabs and stone walls (Garrod 1932, 20). El-Kebarah did not contain similar architectural features (Smith 1972).

Specimen Preparation and Buccal Microwear Analysis

The dental enamel surfaces were gently cleaned with pure acetone and then rinsed with 70 percent ethanol using cotton ear swabs. Molds of the original teeth were obtained with colténe Regular Body PRESIDENT microSystems™ polyvinylsiloxane (Galbany et al. 2006; Ungar et al. 2006, 84). Positive casts of tooth molds were obtained using a two-component epoxy resin (Epo-Tek 301, manufactured by Química del Aditivo), with a two-stage centrifugation procedure to prevent the formation of air bubbles.

Before examining the casts under a scanning electron microscope (SEM), they were mounted on aluminum stubs with hot-melt glue and the mold was connected to the aluminum stub with a colloidal silver stain. Then the casts were coated with a 400 Å gold layer for SEM examination with a (Leica) Cambridge S-360 SEM at the Serveis Cientificotècnics of the University of Barcelona. The SEM observation settings were 15 KV, secondary electrons with 0° tilt angle.

A total of 14 individuals from El-Kebarah (4 of which were subadults under 18 years old) and 10 individuals from El-Wad (2 of which were under 18 years old) showed well-preserved enamel microwear with clear buccal microwear traces under SEM observation. Age estimation was done according to Buikstra and Ubelaker (1994) based on the morphology of the pubic symphysis and dental eruption. Only the adult samples are analyzed in this study (subadults individuals do not have fully attained microwear patterns; see Pérez-Pérez, Lalueza, and Turbon 1994, 184), and a single post-canine tooth was chosen to represent each individual (Lalueza et al. 1996, 317; Pérez-Pérez et al. 2003, 499; Alrousan and Pérez-Pérez et al. 2008, 48). Postmortem erosion of enamel surfaces and which surfaces were unpreserved were determined according to microwear standards (Teaford 1988; Martinez and Pérez-Pérez 2004; Pérez-Pérez et al. 2003, 502). Teeth with unpreserved enamel were eliminated from the study. Thus, only 17 individuals that fulfilled the criteria of buccal dental microwear analysis were included in this study: 10 from El-Kebarah and 7 from El-Wad.

All the SEM micrographs were taken at 100X magnification, and the images were cropped to cover an area of exactly 0.56 mm^2 on the medial third of buccal surface of the cast, avoiding the cement-enamel junction and the occlusal rim of the cusps. The measure of the side border of each square micrograph was 748.33 μm (Figure 7.1) (Pérez-Pérez et al. 2003, 503–504; Alrousan and Pérez-Pérez 2008, 50).

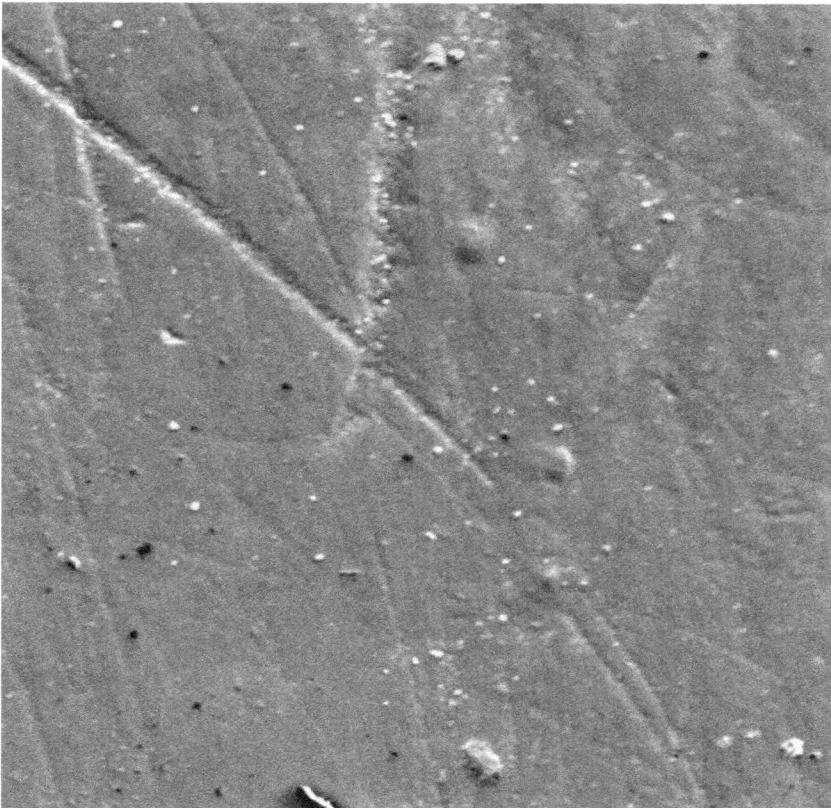

Figure 7.1. SEM image (0.56 mm^2) of the buccal enamel surface of the upper right premolar (URP4) of one individual from El-Kebarah. Striations of various lengths and orientations are clearly visible.

Before analyzing the microwear patterns, each micrograph was processed with Adobe Photoshop CS8 by applying a high-pass (50 pixels) filter and automatic level enhancement. The SigmaScan Pro 5 (SPSS) package was used to quantify the buccal dental microwear (striation density and length). The slope and the length of all the striations in each micrograph were measured. The orientations of the striations were measured according to Pérez-Pérez, Lalueza, and Turbon (1994, 179; 2003, 504) and Lalueza et al. (1996, 372). The orientation was measured from 0° to 180° (degrees) and classified into angle categories as follows:

1. Vertical (V): angle > 67.5° and < 112.5°
2. Mesio-occlusal to disto-cervical (MD): from 112.5° to 157.5° for the upper left and the lower right teeth
3. Disto-occlusal to mesio-cervical (DM): from 22.5° to 67.5° for the upper right and lower left teeth
4. Horizontal (H): angle > 0° and < 22.2° and angle > 157.5° and < 180°

For all orientation categories (V, MD, DM, and H) and for the total number of striations (T), the density (N), average length (X), and standard deviation of the length (S) of the striations were computed. Thus, a total of 15 microwear variables were derived for each analyzed tooth (Pérez-Pérez, Lalueza, and Turbon 1994). The normality of the frequency distributions of the 15 variables was tested with the Kolmogorov-Smirnov test for goodness of fit. Then, a one-factor ANOVA test was used to compare all 15 variables for the two sites studied. All the statistical analyses were done using SPSS 15.0. Then, the NH/NV index (Lalueza et al. 1996, 372) was computed to further characterize the dietary differences between the two sites and to compare them to other human populations that have been studied. This index varies based on the amount of plant material and meat in the diet because meat creates more vertical enamel striations, while cereals and vegetable foods create more horizontal striations. The index thus can be used to loosely classify populations as agriculturists, hunter-gatherers of mixed food, carnivores, or pastoralists.

According to the prevailing environmental conditions in the area and the archaeological context of the two sites, no significant differences between the microwear patterns of the populations at El-Wad and El-Kebarah are expected, as their dietary adaptations and habits are likely to have been similar.

Results

Kolmogorov-Smirnov normality tests showed that none of the 15 variables studied differed significantly from normality for the two sites considered. Therefore, parametric statistical tests could be applied to the raw data. The descriptive statistics of the 15 variables and the NH/NV index derived for the two samples are shown in Table 7.1.

No statistically significant differences in the buccal microwear pattern variables were discovered between the two sites, except for the standard deviation of all the striations (ST) (Table 7.1). The sample from El-Kebarah shows a larger ST value (ST = 80.47) than the sample from El-Wad

Table 7.1. Summary statistics of the pattern of buccal microwear in the two samples studied[a]

| | El-Wad(N = 7) | | El-Kebarah (N = 10) | | ANOVA | |
	Mean	SD[b]	Mean	SD	F-score	p-value
NH[c]	35.29	14.93	28.50	15.20	0.833	0.376
XH	83.04	40.22	89.57	19.72	0.199	0.662
SH	59.09	46.07	76.05	38.28	0.685	0.421
NV	30.14	19.65	42.30	30.43	0.857	0.369
XV	79.09	22.98	111.88	36.05	4.467	0.052
SV	66.24	23.14	98.65	49.69	2.551	0.131
NMD	66.57	39.14	38.60	27.43	3.028	0.102
XMD	60.63	13.07	75.87	30.06	1.565	0.230
SMD	35.06	10.60	62.46	42.80	2.703	0.121
NDM	44.00	14.67	51.80	27.98	0.451	0.512
XDM	61.19	17.52	68.92	23.35	0.546	0.471
SDM	41.13	15.62	52.17	20.23	1.462	0.245
NT	176.00	63.77	161.20	74.40	0.182	0.675
XT	70.65	21.25	85.13	22.49	1.783	0.202
ST	55.06	24.31	80.47	23.35	4.716	0.046
NH/NV	1.17		0.67			

Notes: a. Only adult individuals with well-preserved enamel surfaces were included. One-factor ANOVA tests for the 15 studied variables were made to compare the two studied groups. Only ST (standard deviation of all of the striations) showed significant differences ($p < 0.05$) between the two sites, and only XV was close to significance ($p < 0.1$).
b. Standard deviation.
c. NH = horizontal density; XH = average horizontal length; SH = standard deviation of horizontal length; NV = vertical density; XV = average vertical length; SV = standard deviation of vertical length; NMD = mesio-occlusal to disto-cervical density; XMD = average mesio-occlusal to disto-cervical length; SMD = standard deviation of mesio-occlusal to disto-cervical length; NDM = disto-occlusal to mesio-cervical density; XDM = average disto-occlusal to mesio-cervical length; SDM = standard deviation of disto-occlusal to mesio-cervical; NT = total number of striations; XT = average total number of striations; ST = standard deviation of number of striations.

(ST = 55.06). No significant differences in the total number of striations (NT) between the two sites were found (Figure 7.2); complete overlapping occurs in the dispersion of NT. However, the NH/NV index for El-Wad (1.17) was considerably larger than the index for El-Kebarah (0.67), indicating that the El-Wad diet produced a larger proportion of horizontal striations, perhaps indicating the presence of more plant-related abrasives in the diet.

Figure 7.3 shows that the combined Natufian sample has a large total number of striations (NT), significantly more than the number among modern hunter-gatherer populations, even those from arid environments. The higher NH/NV index observed at El-Wad, a site with clear settlement structures, could indicate that the population at El-Wad was more dependent upon consumption of abrasive food items, such as cereals. The NH/NV index in El-Wad resembles the index for some of the hunter-gatherer populations from both arid and tropical environments who largely depend on plant foods.

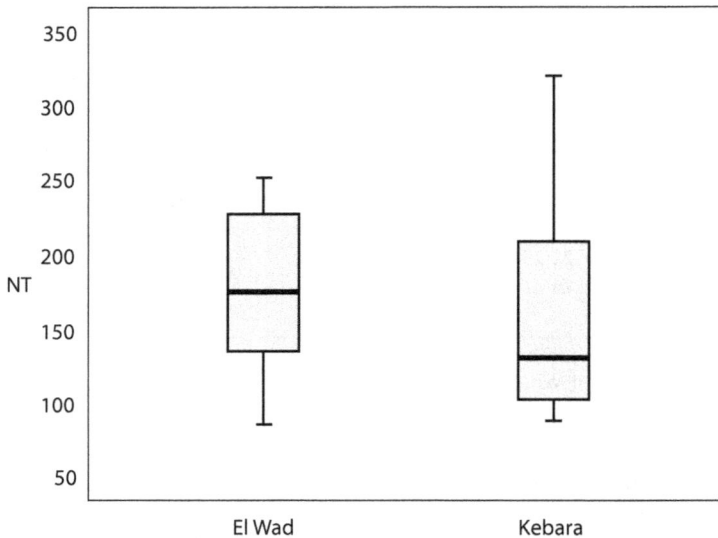

Figure 7.2. Total striation densities (NT) for the two sites studied. Complete overlapping of the dispersion ranges occurs between the two groups since no differences in striation densities are present.

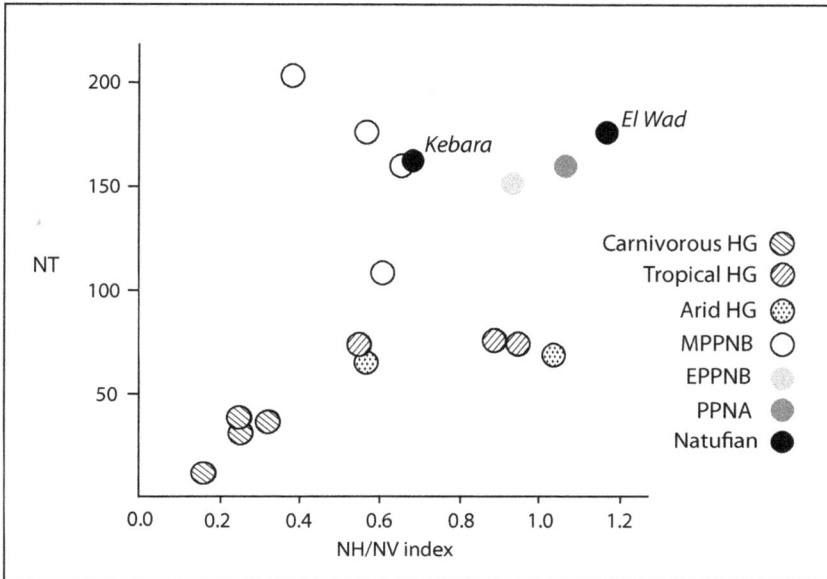

Figure 7.3. NH/NV index (X axis) versus total density of scratches (NT) (Y axis) for the two sites studied compared with other samples. Dots represent average values for the samples studied. HG refers to modern hunting and gathering groups. The MPPNB (Middle Pre-Pottery Neolithic B), EPPNB (Early Pre-Pottery Neolithic B), and PPNA (Pre-Pottery Neolithic A) samples are from Syria and Turkey (8,000–10,000 BP).

Discussion

Archaeological data have indicated that the Natufian populations of the Near East had a homogenous subsistence economy that relied on hunting wild animals and gathering wild plants (Bar-Yosef 1998; Henry 1989, 215). The results of the one-factor ANOVA indicate few significant differences between the microwear patterns of the populations at the two Natufian sites included in this study. The only variable shown to be significantly different is ST, which is not as informative for interpreting the dietary habits of a population as the density variables (Pérez-Pérez, Lalueza, and Turbon 1994). This may support the archaeological assumption that the Natufian populations, the last hunter-gatherers in the Near East, had a distinct homogeneous diet and dietary habits that relied mainly on the consumption of wild cereals. This would explain the high density of scratches observed in teeth from both sites. The difference between NH/VH indices seen in these two sites is discussed in more detail below.

The climatic conditions specific to any or a given region likely played an important role in determining the diet of ancient human populations. Drier conditions, for instance, might have forced ancient populations toward a higher consumption of meat (Pérez-Pérez et al. 2003). However, no differences in the density of striations were observed between the Natufian and the Pre-Pottery Neolithic (PPN) sites of the same geographical area (Near East), which suggest that the Neolithic transition did not impact the relative dependence of these two populations on abrasive foods such as wild or domesticated cereals (Alrousan 2009). Cultural practices in food preparation might also have played a role by affecting the quality and quantity of food ingested (Molleson and Jones 1991, 532; Lalueza et al. 1996; Romero et al. 2007; Alrousan and Pérez-Pérez 2008).

Lalueza et al. (1996, 381) have suggested that the NH/NV index may be used to distinguish dietary differences between hunter-gatherer groups. Figure 7.3 shows that hunter gatherers who relied more on meat and pastoralist populations tend to have low values of this index (smaller than 0.4) because they have more vertical than horizontal striations. In contrast, since mixed-diet hunter-gatherers have more horizontal than vertical striations, they tend to have higher values. In the present analysis, the Natufian site of El-Wad shows an index similar to the Bushmen, hunter-gatherers from arid environments, and the Andamanese, hunter-gatherers from tropical forests. However, individuals from El-Kebarah have a larger NH/NV index value, closer to that of the Tasmanians and Australian Aborigines (0.64), who practiced a more intensive hunting economy (Lauleza et al. 1996).

The two sites studied are located in the same ecological niche, and thus any differences in their diet should be indicative of cultural rather than dietary variation (Smith 1972, 272–273). Most of the results obtained in this study support this view, although the El-Wad teeth show severe dental attrition in comparison with the teeth from El-Kebarah. Smith (1972) suggested that this difference in wear was due to a higher consumption of vegetables and plants at El-Wad than at El-Kebarah. Teeth from El-Wad have dental wear rates similar to that of the early villages (PPN) of Çatal Huyuk and Tell Al-Judeiah, whose residents ingested cereals and grains as major components of their diet and used grinding tools to process the plant materials (ibid., 237). Grouping the amount of wear at El-Wad with the amount of wear seen at PPN sites of the Near East could indicate similarities in the subsistence economy and diet of these populations.

Yet comparing the NH/NV indices of the two sites to some PPN sites of the Near East suggests that the Natufian population of El-Wad could have more heavily relied on abrasive plant foods than people at the PPN sites. The PPN is a period characterized by domestication and cultivation of plants and cereals and the introduction of an agricultural economy (Twiss 2007). The introduction of cereals and grains into ancient diets generally results in higher rates of tooth attrition (Larsen 1995, 195) and the formation of distinctive microwear features on the occlusal tooth surfaces, such as pits and large striations (Mahoney 2006). The high NH/NV index of the people of El-Wad suggests that they tended to eat more plant foods, including cereals, than people at El-Kebarah. The presence of a permanent settlement and elaborate structures at El-Wad (Garrod 1931, 20) indicates this site contained a large population with long-term strategies that probably encouraged people to seek reliable and stable food resources by gathering cereals and grains. The people from El-Kebarah, on the other hand, would have consumed more meat foods than those at El-Wad, in addition to the plants they ate.

The results show that the Natufian people exploited various food resources, including those generally associated with agricultural societies. Despite maintaining a hunter-gatherer tradition, they consumed abrasive plant foods, including wild cereals. However, this was not homogeneous across the landscape, and the various Natufian populations could have exploited food resources in differing ways, even though they lived in similar environmental contexts. Differences in cultural practices, such as how food was prepared (using cooking, grinding, or drying techniques), might have greatly affected food chewing, causing differences in the buccal microwear patterns of these populations. In this regard, the Natufian time period might not have been as homogeneous in terms of diet as was initially hypothesized. Although analysis of buccal microwear patterns can provide information about how abrasive a people's diet was, it cannot discriminate among the food items ingested. Nevertheless, it is a valuable method in dietary reconstruction that can detect slight differences in the diet among a given set of populations. More samples from the Natufian period need to be analyzed to obtain a wider perspective of the dietary practices during this period. If cereals were included in the diet of the Natufian people, marked differences between their microwear patterns and those of the Neolithic populations, either Pre-Pottery Neolithic or Pottery Neolithic, should not exist, other than patterns showing an increase in the amount of cereal consumption with time in the agricultural groups. The evidence of this study shows that the dietary transition during the agricultural Neolithic revolution might have not so revolutionary as was initially theorized, but might have more closely resembled a transitional, gradual shift in subsistence strategy. Buccal microwear research can test such a hypothesis by including comparisons among the PPN populations from the Near East, which still constitute a mystery in human prehistory.

References Cited

Alrousan, Mohammad
2009   The Mesolithic-Neolithic Transition in the Near East: Biological Implications of the Shift in Subsistence Strategies Through the Analysis of Dental Morphology and Dietary Habits of Human Populations in the Mediterranean Area 12,000–5,000 P.B. PhD. dissertation, Department of Anthropology, University of Barcelona, Spain.
Alrousan, Mohammad, and Alejandro Pérez-Pérez
2008   Non-Occlusal Dental Microwear of the Last Hunter-Gatherers from Near East and Europe. In *Gene, ambiente y enfermedades en los poblaciones humanas,* edited by J. Nogués Amada and S. Pinilla, pp. 45–59. University of Zaragoza Press, Zaragoza, Spain.
Alrousan, Mohammad, Alejandro Pérez-Pérez, and Theya Molleson
2009   Dental Microwear Pattern as an Indicator of Dietary Behavior in a Human Neolithic Tooth Sample from Abu Hureyra. *American Journal of Physical Anthropology* Supplement 48:76.
Bar-Yosef, Ofer
1998   The Natufian Culture of the Levant, Threshold to the origin of Agriculture. *Evolutionary Anthropology* 6:159–177.
Bar-Yosef, O., and A. Sillen
1993   Implications of the New Accelerator Date of the Charred Skeletons from Kebara Cave (Mt. Carmel). *Paléorient* 19:205–208.
Buikstra, Jane E., and Douglas H. Ubelaker
1994   *Standards for Data Collection from Human Skeletal Remains.* Arkansas Archaeological Survey Research Series 44. Arkansas Archaeological Survey, Fayetteville, Ark.
El Zaatari, Sireen
2008   Occlusal Molar Microwear and the Diets of the Ipiutak and Tigara Populations (Point Hope) with Comparisons to the Aleut and Arikara. *Journal of Archaeological Science* 35:2517–2522.
Eshad, Vered, Avi Gopher, and Israel Herskovitz
2006   Tooth Wear and Dental Pathology at the Advance of Agriculture, New Evidence from the Levant. *American Journal of Physical Anthropology* 130:145–159.

Estebaranz, Ferran, Laura Martínez, Jordi Galbany, Daniel Turbón, and Alejandro Pérez-Pérez
2009   Testing Hypotheses of Dietary Reconstruction from Buccal Dental Microwear in *Australopithecus afarensis*. *Journal of Human Evolution* 57:739–750.
Galbany, Jordi, Ferran Estebaranz, Laura Martínez, Alejandro Romero, Joaquín De Juan, Daniel Turbón, and Alejandro Pérez-Pérez
2006   Comparative Analysis of Dental Enamel Polyvinylsiloxane Impression and Polyurethane Casting Methods for SEM Research. *Microscopy Research and Technique* 69:246–252.
Galbany, Jordi, Ferran Estebaranz, Laura Martinez, and Alejandro Pérez-Pérez
2009   Buccal Dental Microwear Variability in Extant African Hominoidea: Taxonomy Versus Ecology. *Primates* 50:221–230.
Galbany, Jordi, Laura Martínez, H. López-Amor, V. Espurz, O. Hiraldo, A. Romero, Joaquín De Juan, and Alejandro Pérez-Pérez
2005   Error Rates in Dental Buccal Microwear Quantification using Scanning Electron Microscopy. *Scanning* 27:23–29.
Galbany, Jordi, and Alejandro Pérez-Pérez
2004   Buccal Enamel Microwear Variability in Cercopithecoidea Primates as a Reflection of Dietary Habits in Forested and Open Savanna Environments. *Anthropologie* 42:13–19.
Garrod, D. A.
1932   A New Mesolithic Industry: The Natufian of Palestine. *Man* 32:19–20.
Grine, Frederick, Peter Ungar, and Mark Teaford
2002   Error Rates in Dental Microwear Quantification Using Scanning Electron Microscopy. *Scanning* 24:144–153.
Henry, D.
1989   *From Foraging to Agriculture: The Levant at the End of the Ice Age*. University of Pennsylvania Press, Philadelphia.
Hillman, G.
1996   Late Pleistocene Changes in Wild Plant Foods Available to Hunter-Gatherers of the Northern Fertile Crescent: Possible Preludes to Cereal Cultivation. In *The Origins and Spread of Agriculture and Pastoralism In Eurasia,* edited by D. R. Harris, pp. 159–203. UCL Press, London.
Lalueza, C., J. Juan, and A. Pérez-Pérez
1994   Dietary Information Through the Examination of Plant Phytoliths on the Enamel Surface of Human Dentition. *Journal of Archaeological Science* 21:29–34.
Lalueza, Carlos, Alejandro Pérez-Pérez, and Daniel Turbon
1996   Dietary Inferences Through Buccal Microwear Analysis of Middle and Upper Pleistocene Human Fossils. *American Journal of Physical Anthropology* 100:367–387.
Larsen, Clark Spencer
1995   Biological Changes in Human Populations with Agriculture. *Annual Review of Anthropology* 24:158–213.

Larsen, Clark Spencer, Mark C. Griffin, Dale L. Hutchinson, Vivian E. Noble, Lynette
    Norr, Robert F. Pastor, Christopher B. Ruff, Katherine F. Russell, Margaret J.
    Schoeninger, Michael Schultz, Scott W. Simpson, and Mark F. Teaford
2001   Frontiers of Contact: Bioarchaeology of Spanish Florida. *Journal of World Pre-
    history* 15:69–123.
Mahoney, Patrick
2006   Dental Microwear from the Natufian Hunter-Gatherers and Early Neolithic
    Farmers: Comparisons Within and Between Samples. *American Journal of
    Physical Anthropology* 130:308–319.
Martínez, Laura, and Alejandro Pérez-Pérez
2004   Post-Mortem Wear as Indicator of Taphonomic Processes Affecting Enamel
    Surfaces of Hominine Teeth from Laetoli and Olduvai (Tanzania): Implica-
    tions to Dietary Interpretations. *Anthropologie* 42:37–42.
Molleson, Theya, and Karen Jones
1991   Dental Evidence for Dietary Change at Abu Hureyra. *Journal of Archaeological
    Science* 18:525–539.
Molleson, Theya, Karen Jones, and Stephen Jones
1993   Dietary Changes and Effects of Food Preparation in Microwear Patterns in the
    Late Neolithic of Abu Hureyra, Northern Syria. *Journal of Human Evolution*
    24:455–468.
Munro, Natalie D., and Guy Bar-Oz
2005   Gazelle Bone Fat Processing in the Levantine Epipalaeolithic. *Journal of Ar-
    chaeological Science* 32:223–239.
Organ, Jason M., Mark F. Teaford, and Clark S. Larsen
2005   Dietary Inferences from Dental Occlusal Microwear at Mission San Luis de
    Apalachee. *American Journal of Physical Anthropology* 128:801–811.
Pérez-Pérez, Alejandro
2004   Why Buccal Microwear? *Anthropologie* 42:1–3.
Pérez-Pérez, Alejandro, Vanesa Espurz, José María De Castro, Marie-Antoinette De
    Lumley, and Daniel Turbón
2003   Non-Occlusal Dental Microwear Variability in a Sample of Middle and Late
    Pleistocene Human Populations from Europe and the Near East. *Journal of
    Human Evolution* 44:497–513.
Pérez-Pérez, Alejandro, Carlos Lalueza, and Daniel Turbon
1994   Intraindividual and Intragroup Variability of Buccal Tooth Striation Pattern.
    American Journal of Physical Anthropology 94:175–187.
Polo-Cerdá, M., A. Romero., J. Casabó, and J. De Juan
2007   The Bronze Age Burials from Cova Dels Blaus (Vall d'Uixó, Castelló, Spain):
    An Approach to Palaeodietary Reconstruction Through Dental Pathology, Oc-
    clusal Wear and Buccal Microwear Patterns. *Homo* 58:297–307.
Romero, A., and J. De Juan
2007   Intra- and Interpopulation Human Buccal Tooth Surface Microwear Analysis:
    Inferences About Diet and Formation Processes. *Anthropologie* 45:61–70.

Romero, A., J. Galbany, N. Martínez-Ruiz, and J. De Juan
2009   *In vivo* Turnover Rates in Human Buccal Dental Microwear. *American Journal of Physical Anthropology* Supplement 48:223–224.
Schmidt, Christopher W.
2001   Dental Microwear Evidence for a Dietary Shift Between Two Nonmaize-Reliant Prehistoric Populations from Indiana. *American Journal of Physical Anthropology* 114:139–145.
Smith, Patricia
1972   Diet and Attrition in the Natufians. *American Journal of Physical Anthropology* 37:233–238.
Teaford, Mark
1988   Scanning Electron Microscope Diagnosis of Wear Patterns and Artifacts on Fossil Teeth. *Scanning Microscope* 2:1167–1175.
Teaford, M., and O. Oyen
1989   In Vivo and In Vitro Turnover in Dental Microwear. *American Journal of Physical Anthropology* 80:447–460.
Turville-Petre, F.
1932a   Excavations at the Cave Mugharet-el-Kebarah, Near Zichron Jakob, Palestine. *Man* 32:20.
1932b   Excavations in the Mugharet El-Kebarah. *The Journal of the Royal Anthropological Institute of Great Britain and Ireland* 62:271–276.
Twiss, Katheryn C.
2007   The Neolithic of the Southern Levant. *Evolutionary Anthropology* 16:24–35.
Ungar, Petter, Fredrik Grine, Mark Teaford, and Sireen El Zaatari
2006   Dental Microwear and Diets of African Early *Homo*. *Journal of Human Evolution* 50:78–95.
Van Zeist, W., and S. Bottema
1977   Palynological Investigations in Western Iran. *Palaeohistoria* 19:19–85.
Weinstein-Evron, M.
1991   New Radiocarbon Dates for the Early Natufian of El-Wad Cave, Mt. Carmel, Israel. *Paléorient* 17:95–98.

8

Daily Activity and Lower Limb Modification at Bab edh-Dhra', Jordan, in the Early Bronze Age

JAIME M. ULLINGER, SUSAN G. SHERIDAN,
AND DONALD J. ORTNER

The purpose of this investigation is to document skeletal changes in the lower limb between the Early Bronze IA (EB IA; ca. 3150–2950 BC) and Early Bronze II–III (EB II–III; ca. 2800–2300 BC) at Bab edh-Dhra', a site located on the southeast plain of the Dead Sea in Jordan (Figure 8.1). Skeletal modifications from repetitive use, including squatting facets on tali, kneeling facets on metatarsals, degenerative joint disease of distal femora, and facets on the femoral neck, were examined to assess changes in daily activities between Early Bronze IA and Early Bronze II–III. This shift in time periods corresponded to the expansion of large, settled, fortified towns in the southern Levant. EB IA Bab edh-Dhra' is characterized by an expansive cemetery comprised of thousands of shaft tombs (Ortner and Frohlich 2007). The absence of settlement remains contrasts sharply with the extensive mortuary evidence, and it is unknown where the tomb occupants actually lived. Small, permanent structures were built on the site during Early Bronze IB (EB IB; ca. 2950–2800 BC). By EB II–III, a large town fortified with walls seven meters thick and multiple towers had been constructed near the cemetery (Rast and Schaub 2003). The current study hypothesizes that the construction and maintenance of a large walled town with extensive agricultural fields and orchards led to changes in the daily lives of the inhabitants of the town and that these changes are reflected in the skeletal evidence.

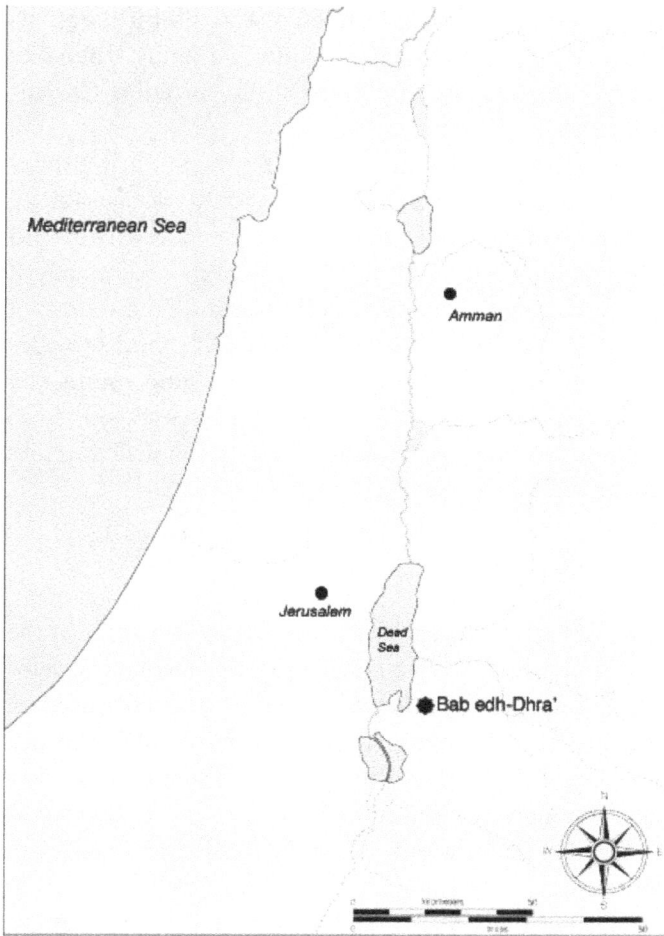

Figure 8.1. Map of the southern Levant.

Biocultural Context

The Early Bronze Age (EBA; 3150–2000 BC) in the southern Levant (an area that includes modern-day Jordan, Israel, and Palestine) was characterized by numerous innovations. These changes included the intensification of agriculture, including the widespread use of irrigation and the ox-drawn plow and increased cultivation of tree crops (Philip 2001); changes in social organization that included the expansion of corporate kinship groups (Chesson 2007; Philip 2003); new mortuary patterns (Philip 2003;

Paz 2005); the construction of walled, fortified towns (Philip 2003); increased trade (Mazar 1990); and a "higher standard of living" (Ben-Tor 1992). While some of these practices are noted in the preceding Chalcolithic, during the EBA these practices intensified.

Bab edh-Dhra' is one of the few thoroughly excavated Early Bronze Age cemeteries in the southern Levant and is one of only two sites (along with Jericho) where human skeletons have been recovered that date to EB II–III (Bloch-Smith 2003; Chesson 1999, 2001; Ilan 2002). Additionally, it is the only well-excavated site that contains burials from all subperiods of the EBA (Chesson 1999; Ilan 2002). Therefore, Bab edh-Dhra' provides a unique and important opportunity to examine emerging complexity throughout the EBA (Chesson 2003). This research used skeletons from EB IA and EB II–III. EB IB is represented by relatively few skeletons and therefore is not included in this study.

The Early Bronze IA at Bab edh-Dhra'

There is little evidence for permanent settlement by EB IA people in the area surrounding the cemetery of Bab edh-Dhra'. Archaeological remnants of temporary campsites from this time period, probably used by the tomb builders, exist near the tombs (Rast and Schaub 2003). The lack of settlement evidence precludes the identification of the group as either settled or nomadic, although Rast and Schaub tentatively refer to them as pastoralists who grazed in the area and seasonally visited the cemetery to inter group members.

There is evidence that the EB IA people had access to agricultural goods, although it is unknown whether these were locally cultivated or acquired through trade with settled populations. A juglet filled with grape pips was discovered in an EB IA shaft tomb (McCreery 1981), as were two peach pits (McCreery 2002), although the peach remains may have been intrusions (McCreery 2003). Just as there is no conclusive evidence regarding where the EB IA people at Bab edh-Dhra' lived, there is no evidence to identify their primary mode of subsistence.

Early Bronze II–III at Bab edh-Dhra'

Bab edh-Dhra' reached its zenith in EB II–III, around 2550 BC, at which point it covered approximately six hectares within a walled town site (Rast and Schaub 2003). During this period there is abundant evidence for incipient urbanism, including increased population density, the construction of municipal and administrative buildings and a fortified town wall, and the development of irrigation structures in the wadis. The size and morphology of plant remains (including wheat and barley) confirm that irrigation systems supported these crops (McCreery 1981, 2003). There is abundant paleobotanical evidence of plant use in EB II–III domestic contexts, particularly barley, wheat, fig, flax, lentils, chickpeas, and olives (McCreery 2002). These archaeological finds indicate that daily activities would have included tending to the agricultural fields and irrigation systems, producing ceramics and bricks, and mending walls.

The extensive mud-brick structures were subject to constant erosion and therefore would have necessitated a substantial, continuous workforce to produce new bricks for both domestic and communal structures. The massive town wall, which was constructed of mud brick on top of a stone and wood foundation and averaged about seven meters wide at the base (Rast and Schaub 2003), would have required a large amount of labor for initial construction and subsequent maintenance. Large above-ground communal burial structures (charnel houses) also were constructed of mud-brick superstructures. Rast (1995) noted that there was an abundance of rock in the nearby wadi, which would have been easier than mud brick to procure and then use for construction. He postulated that the rocks may have placed too much strain on the marl substrate, however, necessitating the use of lighter mud bricks (Rast 1995). Maintaining mud brick would have been an ongoing activity for EB II–III town inhabitants, while there is no archaeological evidence that EB IA people would have been engaged in this activity.

Further evidence of increasing specialization was found in a study of tempering types used in ceramics at Bab edh-Dhra' throughout the EBA (Benyon et al. 1986). Only one type of temper, wadi sand, is found in EB IA ceramics, while an additional three are found in the later EB II–III wares. Benyon and colleagues (1986) argue that this reflects increasing complexity in the construction of EB II–III ceramics. Some EBII–III tempering agents were larger (which correlated with larger vessels) and required more preparation. This, in turn, may mirror the increasing complexity and sedentism at the site. In addition, Schaub and Rast (2000) and Rast and Schaub (2003) note that there is increasing uniformity in the ceramics, suggesting that there may have been more formalized production in EB II–III. This may indicate that people were engaging in more specialized tasks. If this was the case, then we would expect to see evidence of varied types of skeletal modification in the archeological record.

Daily Activity Patterns in the Early Bronze Age

Numerous daily activities necessitate repetition that leads to skeletal modification. Archaeological remains provide a starting point for identifying potential stresses to the human body through repetitive work. The EB IA people of Bab edh-Dhra' were clearly involved in the construction of shaft tombs and unique ceramics, although they left little trace of other laborious tasks. The Early Bronze IA cemetery is comprised of hundreds of shaft tombs (Ortner and Frohlich 2008, 261). Each standard four-chamber shaft tomb would have required approximately 15 man-days to create (Ortner 1981). The estimated 225 average yearly deaths would have necessitated the construction of 19 new tombs each year (ibid.), which would have required 285 man-days of activity per year. In contrast, the construction of larger EB II–III tombs housing tens or hundreds of individuals may not have required the extensive human labor of EB IA shaft tombs. Therefore, digging tombs may have placed unique stresses on the bodies of EB IA individuals that would not be expected in the EB II–III sample.

Furthermore, during EB II–III, construction and maintenance of a large, fortified town wall and communal structures within that space would have required a significant labor force. The strenuous activities of constructing homes on the terrace next to the wadi and the irrigation systems within the wadi would also have required a number of people. Finally, planting and harvesting crops, including orchard crops, and processing food would have necessitated significant investment of human labor.

Daily activity can impact skeletal health and anatomy in a number of ways. Repetitive actions from construction, plant cultivation, food processing, and moving around the landscape are thought to be reflected in patterns of degenerative joint conditions and articular modifications in archaeological skeletal collections (Bridges 1991; Brunson 2000; Derevenski 2000; Peterson 2002). These patterns and frequencies have been studied to examine temporal differences in subsistence patterns (e.g., Peterson 2002) as well as gender differences in activity (Molleson 2007a). Four methods of quantifying the effects of activity on postcranial morphology

Table 8.1. Number of pubic symphyses in each stage using the Suchey-Brooks method of aging

	Suchey-Brooks Stage						Total
	1	2	3	4	5	6	
EB IA Right	3	1	4	6	2	2	18
EB IA Left	3	4	5	9	3	1	25
EB II-III Right	3	2	4	6	2	0	17
EB II-III Left	5	2	2	1	1	1	12

are observations of femoral neck alterations, degenerative joint disease, kneeling facets, and squatting facets.

Femoral neck alterations indicate modifications to the hip from habitual daily activity. These alterations include Allen's fossa, Poirier's facet, plaque extensions, and posterior imprints. The first three features occur on the anterior portion of the femoral neck, while posterior imprints manifest themselves on the posterior portion of the femur. Allen's fossa is identified as a depression or area of erosion (fossa) on the anterior femoral neck with exposed trabecular bone (Angel 1964; Brothwell 1981; Meyer 1924). Poirier's facet is a smooth extension of the femoral head onto the anterior portion of the femoral neck with a clearly defined inferior edge (Angel 1964; Brothwell 1981). This facet is formed when the femoral head makes consistent contact with the acetabular rim (Molleson 2007b). Plaque can occur with Allen's fossa or Poirier's facet and is identified as a bony scar or growth along the alteration (Angel 1964; Brothwell 1981). The posterior imprint resembles Poirier's facet, but is located on the posterior portion of the femoral neck (Kostick 1963). Allen's fossa and plaque are both associated with extreme extension of the hip joint (Angel 1964) and are not specific to squatting (Molleson 2007a).

Degenerative joint disease (DJD) is a disorder wherein the cartilage on joint surfaces breaks down, stimulating a reaction of the subchondral bone of the articular surface that includes eburnation and/or porosity. While DJD may be strongly affected by age (Jurmain 1977), here the commingled nature of the sample prevented the identification of age for most elements. Therefore, general age profiles were considered when interpreting results. Table 8.1 illustrates that there was no overall difference between the time periods when comparing pubic symphyses (either from the right or left), although the fragmentary nature of the remains prevented researchers from determining the age of many burials.[1] Finally, while it is widely accepted that specific activities cannot be identified on the basis of the distribution and severity of DJD (Jurmain 1999), changes in patterns between the groups may indicate changes in daily and repetitive activities.

Squatting facets are found on the distal end of the tibia and on the neck of the talus and result from hyperdorsiflexion of the ankle. They are identified on the tibia as an extension of the talar articular surface onto the anterior surface of the shaft. On the talus, these are identified as smooth, defined areas on the neck that are clearly different from extensions of the trochlear surface (Boulle 2001; Trinkaus 1975). Squatting facets are typically associated with a squatting posture, but are also caused by kneeling or sitting on one's feet (Dewar and Pfeiffer 2004), walking over rough terrain (Trinkaus 1975), or climbing (Capasso et al. 1999; Kennedy 1989). Baker and Papalexandrou (Chapter 6, this volume) note the presence of squatting facets, among other markers of occupational stress, in a skeleton of a woman identified as a tailor from medieval Polis, Cyprus. They surmise that she frequently sat or squatted while working.

Kneeling facets are located at the distal end of the dorsal surface of metatarsals and are described as "usually flat with sharply defined proximal borders" (Ubelaker 1979). It is argued that they form as the result of extreme hyperdorsiflexion at the metatarsophalangeal joint (Ubelaker 1979), often associated with postures related to grinding grains (Molleson 1989, 2000; Ubelaker 1979).

Based on the above discussion, it is hypothesized that there were differences in joint modification between the two time periods. As previously noted, archaeological evidence suggests that there may have been different daily activities in EB IA and EB II–III, which should be reflected in the bony joints. Moreover, it is hypothesized that the later townspeople were engaged in activities that were more repetitive and time-consuming than the potentially more mobile EB IA tomb builders. This would have created higher frequencies of modifications in the later group for many of the conditions recorded.

Materials

Early Bronze IA Cemetery

Early Bronze IA at Bab edh-Dhra' is represented by 578 individuals from 26 shaft tombs. The sample includes 268 individuals over the age of 12

(46.3 percent) in the shaft tombs (Ortner and Frohlich 2008). The MNI estimates were derived after reassembling individual skeletons from the commingled remains from each shaft tomb chamber, although many were fragmentary (ibid.). The Early Bronze IA shaft tombs were circular, approximately 1.20–1.30 meters in diameter, and 2.25 to 2.85 meters deep (Rast and Schaub 1980; Ortner and Frohlich 2008). The number of people interred in each chamber varied, as did the total number within each tomb. Each shaft tomb had one to five chambers and from one to 37 individuals (Ortner and Frohlich 2008). The disposition of the skeletons was repeated throughout the tombs: postcrania were in the center of the chamber and skulls were lined up to the left of this pile (Chesson 1999; Ortner and Frohlich 2008).

Early Bronze II–III Cemetery

The skeletal sample used in this study was from Charnel House A22, which measures 15.50 × 7.80 meters. It is the largest charnel house excavated (Rast and Schaub 1980). Mortuary practices changed at the beginning of EB II–III, when individuals began to be interred in above-ground rectangular mud-brick structures (Rast and Schaub 2003). These new structures were reminiscent of EB II broadrooms (Bloch-Smith 2003) and may have been a new way of expressing kinship systems (Chesson 1997). Or it may be that with this change the homes of the dead mirrored the homes of the living.

The Early Bronze II–III sample contained a minimum number of 194 individuals over the age of 12 (61.4 percent) and 122 under the age of 12. The MNI figures for EB II–III were derived from the mandible (Ullinger 2010). Extensive burning in the charnel house suggested that the tomb was destroyed by fire (Rast and Schaub 1980). As a result, the EB II–III bones investigated here were highly fragmented and commingled, making it impossible to associate bones with a specific burial.

Methods

Femoral Neck Alterations

Alterations on the femoral neck were scored as present or absent. Allen's fossa was identified as a depression or area of erosion (fossa) on the anterior femoral neck that contained exposed trabecular bone (Angel 1964;

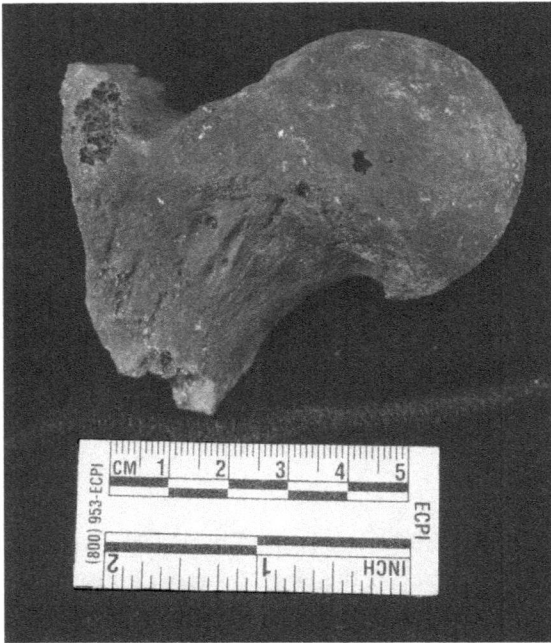

Figure 8.2. Poirer's facet with plaque identified on a right proximal femur (BD 1436.1001).

Brothwell 1981; Meyer 1924). Poirier's facet was scored as present upon observation of a smooth extension of the femoral head onto the anterior portion of the femoral neck (Angel 1964; Brothwell 1981). Plaque was identified as a bony scar or growth on the femoral neck near the head, often accompanying the edge of Poirier's facet or Allen's fossa (Angel 1964; Brothwell 1981; Figure 8.2). Posterior imprints were identified by examining the posterior femoral neck. They were recorded as present if a portion of the femoral head extended onto the neck, similar to Poirier's facet on the anterior neck (Kostick 1963). All of the femoral neck alterations were scored using visual observation under bright incandescent light and a 10X hand lens when necessary.

Degenerative Joint Disease

DJD of the distal condyles of the femur, indicating stress at the knee joint, was scored by examining four different factors on the joint surface: marginal bone lipping, osteophytosis, porosity, and eburnation. Each was

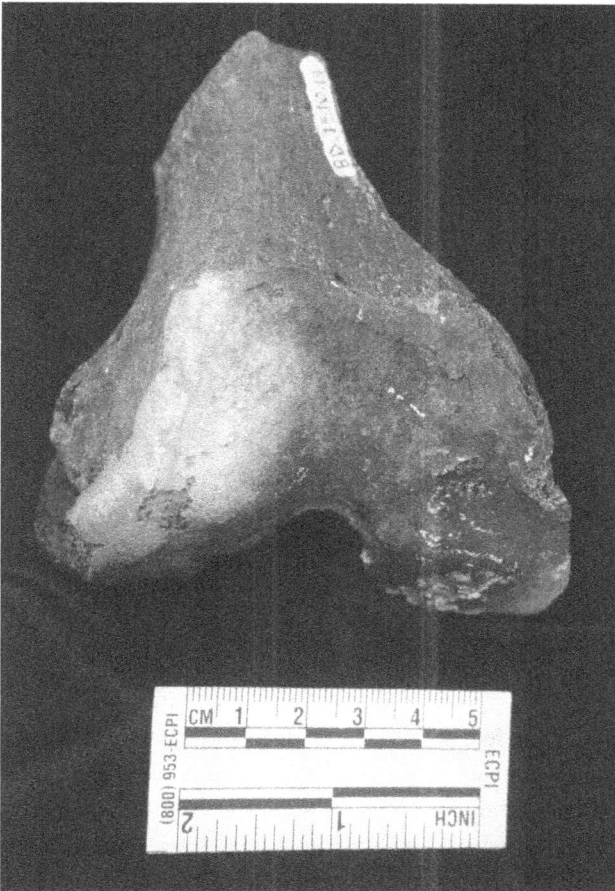

Figure 8.3. Degenerative joint disease (including severe lipping and eburnation) on a right distal femur (BD 1510.14).

scored by severity on individual bone surfaces according to Buikstra and Ubelaker (1994). While these four indicators of DJD are often examined from the perspective of the whole joint, that is not possible with fragmentary, commingled remains. This project used only those femora that had both lateral and medial condyles with more than 75 percent of the articular surface and articular margin preserved, upon which all of the criteria could be scored. A joint was considered to have degenerative joint disease if at least one of the four factors was scored as moderate or severe (Figure 8.3).

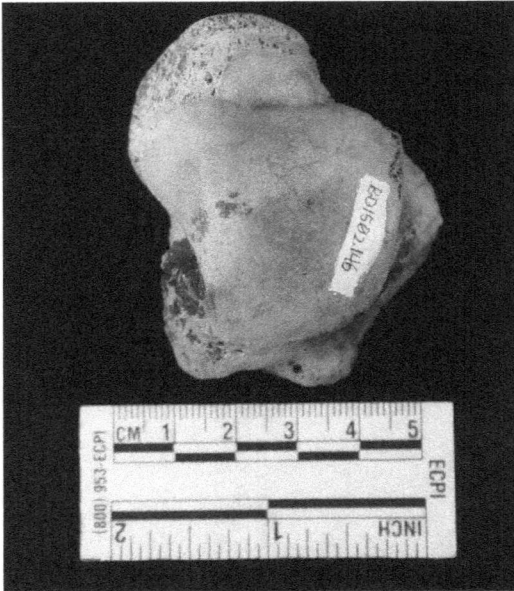

Figure 8.4. Large squatting facet on a right talus (BD 1502.146).

Squatting Facets

Squatting facets were recorded on tibiae and tali. On the tibiae, facets were noted as present upon observation of a smooth extension of the talar articular surface onto the anterior surface of the bone. They typically appear as half-moon facets on the distal anterior surface. We also noted if they were placed medially or laterally. Squatting facets on the talus were identified as smooth, defined areas on the talar neck (Figure 8.4). These were also recorded as medial, lateral, or extending across both surfaces.

Kneeling Facets

All right and left first through fifth metatarsals were examined for facets that would indicate kneeling. These were identified as flat, smooth areas on the distal portion of the metatarsals, just proximal to the head of the bone. They typically had a "sharply defined proximal border," as described by Ubelaker (1979). The presence or absence of facets was recorded for each bone.

Comparisons were analyzed using chi-square goodness-of-fit tests. Fisher's exact tests were used when sample sizes were too small (with expected frequencies less than five). Results were considered significant at $p < 0.05$.

Results

Overall, the results suggest a difference in lower limb activity between EB IA and EB II–III, particularly in the right ankle and foot. There was no difference in the knee or hip joints. There were no significant differences in femoral neck alterations between sides of the leg within either time period, nor was there a difference between the time periods (Table 8.2).

DJD in the distal femur was relatively low for both time periods: 50 percent of right and left knees in the EB IA sample and only 20–35 percent of joints in the EB II–III sample exhibited degradation (Table 8.3). No differences in DJD frequencies in the knee joint emerged when right and left sides were compared within each time period or between time periods. Exploring DJD by symptom indicated that significantly greater marginal lipping occurred in the distal right femoral joint in the EB IA sample (55 percent) than in the EB II–III (22.8 percent) sample. In contrast, no differences were observed between the two sites in marginal lipping of the left femoral knee joint, in osteophyte formation on joint surfaces, or in eburnation. Indeed, eburnation was notably scarce in both time periods, although the prevalence of eburnation actually may have been higher than indicated based on other skeletal evidence. Several femoral fragments that exhibited eburnation were excluded from the study, as they were not over 75 percent complete.

Lateral squatting facets in the tibia were more frequent in both samples, while few medial squatting facets were observed in either collection (Table 8.4). In both time periods, there was no significant side difference in the presence of medial or lateral squatting facets on the distal tibiae. There was also no significant difference between time periods in the prevalence of medial or lateral squatting facets on the left or right side (Table 8.3). In contrast, in EB IA, there was a significant side difference in talar lateral squatting facets (19 of 42, or 45.2 percent, occurred on the left side; 43 of 53, or 81.1 percent, occurred on the right side; $\chi^2 = 13.32$, df = 1, $p < 0.001$). But there was no significant side difference for medial facets, which were far fewer in number (0 of 39 were on the left side; 1 of 42, or 2.4 percent, were on the right side) (Table 8.4). There was no significant side difference for medial or lateral facets in EB II–III. More talar lateral

Table 8.2. Femoral neck alterations in Early Bronze IA and Early Bronze II–III Bab edh-Dhra'

		Poirier's Facet				Allen's Fossa				Plaque				Posterior Imprint		
		N	%	χ^2	p	N	%	χ^2	p	N	%	χ^2	p	N	%	p
Left	EB IA	27	18.5	0.03	0.86	31	19.4	0	1	29	51.7	2.93	0.087	38	0	1
	EB II–III	37	21.6			40	22.5			33	27.3			40	2.5	
Right	EB IA	34	17.6	1	0.32	34	14.7	0.1	0.75	35	48.6	0.09	0.76	30	0	0.53
	EB II–III	58	29.3			45	20			49	42.9			50	4	

Table 8.3. Prevalence of degenerative joint disease in the left and right sides of skeletons from Early Bronze IA and Early Bronze II–III Bab edh-Dhra'

		Degenerative Joint Disease		
		N	%	p
Left	EB IA	14	50	0.09
	EB II–III	27	22.2	
Right	EB IA	19	47.4	0.39
	EB II–III	32	34.4	

Table 8.4. Medial and lateral squatting facets in the tibia and talus in Early Bronze IA and Early Bronze II–III Bab edh-Dhra'

		Tibia						Talus						
		Medial Facet			Lateral Facet			Medial Facet			Lateral Facet			
		N	%	p	N	%	p	N	%	p	N	%	χ^2	p
EB IA	Left	25	12		33	93.9		39	0		42	45.2		
				0.33			1			1			13.32	< 0.001
	Right	28	3.6		33	97		42	2.4		53[a]	81.1		
EB II–III	Left	65	3.1		54	87		113	0.9		116	56.9		
				0.62			0.079			0.37			0.006	0.94
	Right	66	1.5		63	96.8		125	3.2		133	56.4		

Notes: a. Boldface numbers indicate a significant difference between EB IA and EB II–III in number of facets present on the right side of taluses ($p < 0.001$).

facets on the right side were found in EB IA ($\chi^2 = 10.00$, df = 1, $p = 0.0016$) than in EB II–III (Table 8.4).

There was no side difference in kneeling facets for any of the metatarsals within either time period. However, there were significant differences between the time periods. The EB IA group had more squatting facets on the right first metatarsals (16 of 46, or 34.8 percent, in EB IA; 10 of 96, or 10.4 percent, in EB II–III; Fisher's $p < 0.001$), right third metatarsals (5 of 21, or 23.8 percent, in EB IA; 0 of 32 in EB II–III; Fisher's $p = 0.0071$), and right fourth metatarsals (5 of 24, or 20.8 percent, in EB IA; 1 of 36, or 2.8 percent, in EB II–III; Fisher's $p = 0.033$) (Table 8.5). This difference was not seen in the left metatarsals, although it approaches significance for the first and fourth left metatarsals.

Table 8.5. Kneeling facets on metatarsals 1–5 in Early Bronze IA and Early Bronze II–III Bab edh-Dhra'

| | | Metatarsal 1 | | | Metatarsal 2 | | | Metatarsal 3 | | | Metatarsal 4 | | | Metatarsal 5 | | |
		N	%	p	N	%	p[a]	N	%	p	N	%	p	N	%	p
EB IA	Left	39	17.9		20	25		14	28.6		21	14.3		24	12.5	
				0.13			1			1			0.7			1
	Right	46[b]	**34.8**		24	20.8		21	**23.8**		24	**20.8**		19	10.5	
EB II–III	Left	80	6.3		18	11.1		26	7.7		29	0		41	14.6	
				0.48			1			0.2			1			0.29
	Right	**96**	**10.4**		26	7.7		**32**	**0**		**36**	**2.8**		49	6.1	

Notes: a. P values for metatarsals 2–5 were determined using Fisher's exact tests.
b. Boldface numbers indicate a significant difference between EB IA and EB II–III in number of facets present on the right side ($p < 0.05$).

Discussion

The lower limbs from Bab edh-Dhra' were examined for evidence of activity patterns through observing articular modifications from repetitive squatting or kneeling resulting in extra subjoint facets, degeneration of joint surfaces, and repetitive hip extension that can cause modifications around the femoral head and posterior surface of the femur. In general, there was no difference in the use of the hips between Early Bronze IA and Early Bronze II–III at Bab edh-Dhra'. The frequencies of articular modifications around the femoral head, including Allen's fossa, Poirier's facet, plaque, and posterior imprints, were comparable in EB IA and EB II–III.

Slight differences in the knee joint and numerous differences in the ankle and toes suggested a pattern of modification in the lower right limb, especially in the EB IA sample. There is a difference between time periods in lipping of the distal right femoral joint, and there is a significantly higher frequency of lateral squatting facets on the right talus than the left talus in EB IA. In addition, the frequency of lateral squatting facets in the right talus was substantially greater in the EB IA than the EB II–III period. In fact, the right and left tali in EB II–III have comparable frequencies of squatting facets to the EB IA left tali, suggesting that a unique activity was causing the high frequency of facets in the EB IA right tali. Kneeling facets observed in the metatarsals also were present in a higher frequency on the right side during the EB IA than during the EB II–III period. The first, third, and fourth right metatarsals from the EB IA had significantly more kneeling facets than those from EB II–III, although there was no difference between right and left metatarsals within the EB IA.

Although no differences in frequency of habitual hip extension existed by side or between time periods, a consistent pattern of modifications of the right side of individuals from the EB IA emerged through this analysis. This suite of modifications is related to habitual flexion of the knee, dorsiflexion of the ankle, and hyperdorsiflexion of the foot. One of the most likely explanations for this pattern is that a particular squatting or grinding posture in EB IA was placing stress on the right side. Metatarsal facets are most often associated with habitual kneeling that places stress on the toes (Ubelaker 1979), while tibial and talar facets have been interpreted as the result of squatting, which dorsiflexes the ankle (Trinkaus 1975; Boulle 2001). Squatting was a traditional means of rest for most of prehistory, as it is in many parts of the world today (Molleson 2007b). In

addition, squatting and kneeling are also associated with grinding postures (Ubelaker 1979; Molleson 1994). Molleson's (1994) reconstruction
of grinding positions at Abu Hureyra involved an individual kneeling on
the ground and bending over the quern, with legs crossed such that one
foot rested on top of the other. This resulted in the hyperdorsiflexion of
only one foot. It may be that the people of EB IA used a similar posture
while grinding grains. This may explain the side difference in frequency of
squatting facets in EB IA, although there was no significant difference in
metatarsal facets. The fact that it is not possible to match the tali or metatarsals to individuals in both time periods prohibits the identification of
side preference and, thus, specific grinding postures.

The decreased frequency of modifications in EB II–III suggests a shift
in habitual behaviors from the EB IA period, perhaps related to a change
in grinding postures. In addition, it is possible that fewer people were
involved in grinding grain, meaning that skeletal modifications would be
concentrated in a small group. If task/craft specialization was associated
with fortification, settlement, and population growth at Bab edh-Dhra',
then only a few individuals may have focused on food processing while
the rest had other, varied tasks. Researchers have noted that the ceramic
evidence implies that eating habits may have changed in EB II–III based
on an increase in wide, shallow bowls in the ceramic corpus (Rast and
Schaub 2003). Rast and Schaub suggest that meals produced by a few individuals may have been shared with a large number of people in the EB II–
III period. Furthermore, the ceramics became increasingly standardized
throughout the EBA (Schaub and Chesson 2007), supporting the idea that
increased craft specialization (and thus more centralized ceramic production) occurred in the EB II–III period.

Other scholars have suggested that the shift from pastoral-nomadic
mobility to sedentism would have resulted in a decrease in frequency of
squatting and kneeling facets (Robb 1994). Increased modifications also
would be seen in individuals who were involved in climbing and moving
over rough terrain (Trinkaus 1975). Perhaps the EB IA population had
more facets than the EB II–III group because they were more mobile and/
or dealt more with rough terrain. In our research sample, however, only
the right side exhibited significant differences between the time periods.
Thus, a change in the pattern of mobility or subsistence, which would be
reflected in changes on both sides of the body, cannot explain the decrease
in facet frequency observed in this case study. The best explanation for

the decrease in facets on the right side in EB II–III is a change in posture, most likely due to a change in activities that involve squatting or kneeling, such as grinding, although a variety of activities could have resulted in the change. Tasks such as knapping flints, producing ceramics, processing milk, or constructing buildings could have affected the lower limb.

Peterson (2002) also noted this bilateral pattern in upper limb bones from EB IA Bab edh-Dhra'. She examined musculoskeletal stress markers in the upper limb and found right-side asymmetry in shoulder-stabilizing ligaments but left-side asymmetry in brachialis and biceps brachii (flexors of the forearm) in the EB IA skeletons. She concluded that during the EB IA, some individuals may have been engaged in an activity where they were maintaining balance or placing weight on their right sides while using their left arms for repetitive flexing. This activity may be related to the side difference seen in this study, as stabilization of the right side of the body may have involved consistently placing weight upon the right leg. This may or may not be consistent with grinding postures, as grain processing is not typically done with one arm. Again, commingling and the inability to reconstruct complete skeletons has precluded the ability to determine if the people with lower limb alterations on the right side are the same as those with changes in the upper limb. However, this study illustrates that even in heavily fragmentary, commingled skeletal collections, changes in activity can be estimated. In sum, a consistent pattern was seen in the different use of the right lower limb in individuals from EB IA compared to individuals from EB II–III.

Conclusion

The evidence of DJD and other markers of activity in the lower limb suggests that there was a shift in daily activity from EB IA to EB II–III. No changes were noted in the hip, but the knee, ankle, and feet, particularly on the right side, exhibit less modification in EB II–III than in EB IA. Although specific activities for these bony changes could not be pinpointed, the asymmetrical change was most likely due to a habitual posture used during a specific, repetitive activity and not from a general decrease in mobility. Future research will focus on modifications of the upper limb using the same musculoskeletal stress markers as Peterson (2002) in order to more fully explore the relationship of these findings to changes in grinding postures. In addition, other techniques, such as cross-sectional geometry, will be employed to examine these changing stressors in more detail in both the arm and leg.

Acknowledgments

This research was funded by a Smithsonian Institution Predoctoral Fellowship, the National Science Foundation Research Experiences for Undergraduates (SES 0649088) Summer Research in Biocultural Anthropology at Notre Dame Program, the Sigma Xi Grants-in-Aid of Research program, and an Ohio State University Distinguished University fellowship.

Note

1. Pubic symphyses were scored for age following standard osteological methods (Buikstra and Ubelaker 1994).

References Cited

Angel, John Lawrence
1964   The Reaction Area of the Femoral Neck. *Clinical Orthopaedics* 32:130–142.
Ben-Tor, Amnon
1992   The Early Bronze Age. In *The Archaeology of Ancient Israel,* edited by Amnon Ben-Tor, pp. 81–125. Yale University Press, New Haven, Conn.
Benyon, Diane, Jack Donahue, R. Thomas Schaub, and Robert A. Johnston
1986   Tempering Types and Sources for Early Bronze Age Ceramics from Bab edh-Dhra' and Numeria, Jordan. *Journal of Field Archaeology* 13:297–305.
Bloch-Smith, Elizabeth
2003   Bronze and Iron Age Burials and Funerary Customs. In *Near Eastern Archaeology,* edited by Suzanne Richard, pp. 105–116. Eisenbrauns, Winona Lake, Ind.
Boulle, Eve-Line
2001   Osteological Features Associated with Ankle Hyperdorsiflexion. *International Journal of Osteoarchaeology* 11(5):345–349.
Bridges, Patricia
1991   Degenerative Joint Disease in Hunter-Gatherers and Agriculturalists from the Southeastern United States. *American Journal of Physical Anthropology* 85 (4):379–391.
Brothwell, Don R.
1981   *Digging Up Bones.* 3rd edition. Cornell University Press, Ithaca, N.Y.
Brunson, Emily
2000   Osteoarthritis, Mobility and Adaptive Diversity Among the Great Salt Lake Fremont. *Utah Archaeology* 13(1):1–14.

Buikstra, Jane, and Douglas Ubelaker
1994   Standards for Data Collection from Human Skeletal Remains. Arkansas Archaeological Survey, Fayetteville, Ark.
Chesson, Meredith S.
1997   "Urban Households in Early Bronze Age Communities of Syro-Palestine." Ph.D. dissertation, Harvard University, Cambridge, Mass.
1999   Libraries of the Dead: Early Bronze Age Charnel Houses and Social Identity at Urban Bab edh-Dhra', Jordan. *Journal of Anthropological Archaeology* 18(2):137–164.
2001   Embodied Memories of Place and People: Death and Society in an Early Urban Community. In *Social Memory, Identity, and Death: Anthropological Perspectives on Mortuary Rituals,* edited by Meredith Chesson, pp. 100–113. Archaeological Publications of the American Anthropological Association, Arlington, Va.
2003   Households, Houses, Neighborhoods and Corporate Villages: Modeling the Early Bronze Age as a House Society. *Journal of Mediterranean Archaeology* 16(1):79–102.
2007   House, Town, Field, and Wadi: Landscapes of the Early Bronze Age Southern Levant. In *Durable House: House Society Models in Archaeology,* edited by Robin A. Beck Jr., pp. 317–343. Center for Archaeological Investigations, Southern Illinois University, Carbondale.
Derevenski, Joanna R. Sofaer
2000   Sex Differences in Activity-Related Osseous Change in the Spine and the Gendered Division of Labor at Ensay and Wharram Percy, UK. *American Journal of Physical Anthropology* 111(3):333–354.
Dewar, Genevieve, and Susan Pfeiffer
2004   Postural Behaviour of Later Stone Age People in South Africa. *The South African Archaeological Bulletin* 59(180):52–58.
Ilan, David
2002   Mortuary Practices in Early Bronze Age Canaan. *Near Eastern Archaeology* 65(2):92–104.
Jurmain, Robert D.
1977   Stress and the Etiology of Osteoarthritis. *American Journal of Physical Anthropology* 46(2):353–365.
1999   *Stories from the Skeleton: Behavioral Reconstruction in Human Skeletons.* Gordon and Breach, Amsterdam.
Kennedy, Kenneth K. A. R.
1989   Skeletal Markers of Occupational Stress. In *Reconstructions of Life from the Skeleton,* edited by Mehmet Yasar Iscan and Kenneth K. A. R. Kennedy, pp. 129–160. Wiley-Liss, Inc., New York.
Kostick, E. L.
1963   Facets and Imprints on the Upper and Lower Extremities of Femora from a Western Nigerian Population. *Journal of Anatomy* 97(3):393–402.

Mazar, Amihai
1990   *Archaeology of the Land of the Bible: 10,000–586* BCE. Doubleday, New York.
McCreery, David W.
1981   Flotation of the Bab edh-Dhra' and Numeira Plant Remains. In *The Southeast-ern Dead Sea Plain Expedition: An Interim Report of the 1977 Season,* edited by Walter E. Rast and R. Thomas Schaub, pp. 165–169. American Schools of Oriental Research, Cambridge, Mass.
2002   Bronze Age Agriculture in the Dead Sea Basin: The Cases of Bab edh-Dhra', Numeira, and Tell Nimrin. In *"Imagining" Biblical Worlds: Studies in Spatial, Social and Historical Constructs in Honor of James W. Flanagan,* edited by David M. Gunn and Paula M. McNutt, pp. 250–263. Sheffield Academic Press, London.
2003   The Paleoethnobotany of Bab edh-Dhra'. In *Bab edh-Dhra': Excavations at the Town Site (1975–1981),* edited by Walter E. Rast and R. Thomas Schaub, pp. 449–463. Eisenbrauns, Winona Lake, Ind.
Meyer, A.W.
1924   The "Cervical Fossa" of Allen. *American Journal of Physical Anthropology* 7(2):257–269.
Molleson, Theya
1989   Seed Preparation in the Mesolithic: The Osteological Evidence. *Antiquity* 63(239):356–362.
1994   The Eloquent Bones of Abu Hureyra: The Daily Grind in an Early Near Eastern Agricultural Community Left Revealing Marks on the Skeletons of the Inhabitants. *Scientific American* 271(2):70–75.
2000   The People of Abu Hureyra. In *Village on the Euphrates,* edited by Andrew M. T. Moore, Gordon C. Hillman, and Anthony J. Legge, pp. 301–324. Oxford University Press, Oxford.
2007a   Bones of Work at the Origin of Labour. In *Archaeology and Women: Ancient and Modern Issues,* edited by Sue Hamilton, Ruth D. Whitehouse, Katherine I. Wright, pp. 185–198. Left Coast Press, Walnut Creek, Calif.
2007b   *A Method for the Study of Activity Related Skeletal Morphologies. Bioarchaeology of the Near East* 1:5–33.
Ortner, Donald J.
1981   A Preliminary Report on the Human Remains from the Bab edh-Dhra' Cemetery. In *The Southeastern Dead Sea Plain Expedition: An Interim Report of the 1977 Season,* edited by Walter E. Rast and R. Thomas Schaub, pp. 119–132. American Schools of Oriental Research, Cambridge, Mass.
Ortner, D., and Bruno Frohlich (editors)
2008   *The Early Bronze Age I Tombs and Burials of Bab edh-Dhra', Jordan.* Altamira Press, Lanham, Maryland.
Paz, Yitazkh
2005   The Megalithic Manifestation of the Urban Processes at the Golan during the Early Bronze Age. *Mediterranean Archaeology and Archaeometry* 5:5–14.

Peterson, Jane D.
2002   *Sexual Revolutions: Gender and Labor at the Dawn of Agriculture.* Altamira
        Press, Walnut Creek, Calif.
Philip, Graham
2001   The Early Bronze I–III Ages. In *The Archaeology of Jordan,* edited by Burton
        MacDonald, Russell Adams, and Piotr Bienkowski, pp. 163–232. Sheffield Aca-
        demic Press, Sheffield.
2003   The Early Bronze Age of the Southern Levant: A Landscape Approach. *Journal
        of Mediterranean Archaeology* 16(1):103–132.
Rast, Walter E.
1995   Building on Marl: The Case of Bab edh-Dhra'. *Studies in the History and Ar-
        chaeology of Jordan* 5:123–128.
Rast, Walter E., and R. Thomas Schaub
1980   Preliminary Report of the 1979 Expedition to the Dead Sea Plain, Jordan. *Bul-
        letin of the American Schools of Oriental Research* 240:21–61.
2003   *Bab edh-Dhra': Excavations at the Town Site (1975–1981).* Eisenbrauns, Winona
        Lake, Ind.
Schaub, R. Thomas, and Walter E. Rast
2000   The Early Bronze Age I Stratified Ceramic Sequences from Bab edh-Dhra'. In
        Ceramics and Change in the Early Bronze Age of the Southern Levant, edited by
        Graham Philip and Douglas Baird, pp. 73–90. Sheffield Academic Press, Shef-
        field.
Trinkaus, Erik
1975   Squatting Among the Neandertals: A Problem in the Behavioral Interpretation
        of Skeletal Morphology. *Journal of Archaeological Science* 2(4):327–351.
Ubelaker, Douglas H.
1979   Skeletal Evidence for Kneeling in Prehistoric Ecuador. *American Journal of
        Physical Anthropology* 51(4):679–686.
Ullinger, Jaime
2010   Skeletal Health Changes and Increasing Sedentism at Early Bronze Age Bab
        edh-Dhra', Jordan. Ph.D. dissertation, Department of Anthropology, Ohio
        State University, Columbus.

Contributors

Mohammad Alrousan is assistant professor of physical anthropology at Yarmouk University in Irbid, Jordan.

Brenda J. Baker is associate professor of anthropology in the Center for Bioarchaeological Research in Arizona State University's School of Human Evolution and Social Change. Her research concerns bioarchaeology, paleopathology, subadult osteology, and culture contact in the Nile Valley, Cyprus, and North America.

Jane Buikstra is director of the Center for Bioarchaeological Research and professor of bioarchaeology in the School of Human Evolution and Social Change at Arizona State University. She recently coedited *The Global History of Paleopathology: Pioneers and Prospects* with Charlotte Roberts and *Bioarchaeology: The Contextual Analysis of Human Remains* with Lane A. Beck. Dr. Buikstra is founding editor and editor-in-chief of the *International Journal of Paleopathology*.

Elizabeth Carter is professor of Near Eastern archaeology at the University of California, Los Angeles. She has been working in the Kahramanmarash region of Turkey since 1993. Her recent publications have appeared in *Paléorient* and an edited monograph entitled *Social Aspects of Human and Animal Sacrifice in the Ancient Near East*.

Drew S. Coleman is the Jaroslav Folda Distinguished Term Professor in the Department of Geological Sciences at the University of North Carolina at Chapel Hill. As director of UNC's Isotope Geochemistry Lab, he is interested in understanding the rates of geological processes as applied to geochronology, subvolcanic magma accumulation rates, and forensic geology.

David Dettman is a research scientist in the University of Arizona's Department of Geochemistry and manager of the Environmental Isotope Laboratory.

Sherry C. Fox is director of the Wiener Laboratory at the American School of Classical Studies in Athens.

Suellen C. Gauld is professor of anthropology at Santa Monica College, Santa Monica, California, and a research affiliate of the Cotsen Institute of Archaeology, University of California, Los Angeles. Her research is focused on skeletal anatomy, bioarchaeology, and paleoanthropology.

Lesley A. Gregoricka is a lecturer at The Ohio State University in Columbus. Her research focuses on stable isotope biogeochemistry and examines patterns of mobility, mortuary practices, and interregional trade in the Oman Peninsula during the Bronze Age.

Sarah Whitcher Kansa is executive director of the Alexandria Archive Institute, a San Francisco–based nonprofit organization dedicated to data sharing and publication in archaeology and related fields. She is a zooarchaeologist with a research focus on early complex societies of the Near East. Her recent co-authored publications have appeared in *Current Anthropology* and the *Journal of Archaeological Science*.

Ioanna Moutafi is a Ph.D. candidate at the University of Sheffield, UK. She studies the bioarchaeology and funerary archaeology of prehistoric Aegean, with a focus on reconstructing burial practices through holistic bioarchaeological approaches.

James S. Oliver is a research associate in anthropology and information technology at the Illinois State Museum. His research in zooarchaeology, taphonomy, and paleoanthropology is directed toward understanding carcass processing and hominin behavioral ecology.

Donald J. Ortner was a curator and research anthropologist in the Department of Anthropology, National Museum of Natural History, Smithsonian Institution. His publications have a major focus on human skeletal paleopathology. He is the co-author of *The EB I Tombs and Burials of Bâb edh-Dhrâ', Jordan*.

Amy Papalexandrou is an independent scholar and adjunct lecturer in the Department of Art History at the University of Texas at Austin.

Alejandro Peréz-Peréz is professor in the Department of Animal Biology (Anthropology Unit) at the University of Barcelona. He specializes in human evolution and human biology.

Megan A. Perry is professor of anthropology at East Carolina University. She is codirector of the Petra North Ridge Project and contributor to *The Global History of Paleopathology: Pioneers and Prospects* and *Colonized Bodies, Worlds Transformed: Toward a Global Bioarchaeology of Contact and Colonialism.*

William J. Pestle is assistant professor of anthropology at the University of Miami and a postdoctoral research associate in the College of Dentistry at the University of Illinois at Chicago. In addition to research on the Kish collection, he is conducting ongoing paleodietary studies in Puerto Rico and northern Chile. Some of his recent publications have appeared in the *Journal of Anthropological Archaeology* and the *Journal of Archaeological Science.*

Despo Pilides is with the Department of Antiquities of Cyprus in Nicosia.

Elena Anna Prevedorou is a Ph.D. student in the School of Human Evolution and Social Change at Arizona State University in Tempe, Arizona.

Susan G. Sheridan is professor of anthropology at University of Notre Dame in Notre Dame, Indiana.

Abdel Halim al-Shiyab is currently vice-dean and associate professor of physical anthropology in the Faculty of Archaeology and Anthropology at Yarmouk University in Irbid, Jordan. His research interests include archaeozoology, palaeoenvironment, paleopathology, and animal domestication in Jordan and the Near East.

Christina Torres-Rouff is assistant professor of anthropology at the University of California, Merced and curator of human osteology at the Instituto de Investigaciones Arqueológicas y Museo in San Pedro de Atacama, Chile. Some of her recent publications have appeared in *American Anthropologist* and the *American Journal of Physical Anthropology.*

Jaime M. Ullinger is assistant professor of anthropology at Quinnipiac University in Hamden, Connecticut. Her other publications have appeared in the *American Journal of Physical Anthropology* and *Dental Anthropology.*

Index

Note: Italicized page numbers indicate images and maps.

activity patterns: and dental wear, 104; and osteological analysis of Bab edh-Dhra' population, 195–97; and osteological analysis of Polis population, 109

aDNA analysis, 50, 68

age estimates: for Bab edh-Dhra' population, 185–86; for Cyprus populations, 63, 72–73, 77, 110; for Domuztepe population, 13–14; for Kish population, 42; for Khirbet Faynan population, 121; for Polis population, 82, 87; scholarly disagreement with methods of making, 50; for St. Stephen's population, 156

age-grades of infancy, 43, 51, 53

Aila, 126–27

Alassa-Ayia Mavri (AAM) site: burials at described, 71–72; described, 63–65; location of, 63; martyrion at, 72; population from time period of, 66. *See also* martyrion; tombs

Allen's fossa, 185, 187, 192

Angel, J. Lawrence, xi, 1–2

animal burials, 12–13, 19–20

artifacts in graves: at Alassa-Aia Mavri, 72; at the Hill of Agios Georgios, 73, 76. *See also* grave goods

Bab edh-Dhra' (Jordan) site: charnel houses at, 89, 183, 187–88; cultural practices at, 181–83, 195–96; described, 180; map of, *ii, 181*; joint degeneration in population of, 180, 184–85, 188–91, 193, 197; populations of described, 186–87. *See also* Allen's fossa; Early Bronze Age; femoral neck alterations; kneeling facets; Poirier's facet; posterior imprints on femur; shaft tombs; squatting facets

basilicas in Early Christian Cyprus: at Alassa-Ayia Mavri, 72; burials at or near, 66, 68–69, 77, 81, 83–93; described, 60, 62–63; at the Hill of Agios Georgios, 73; at Kalavasos-Kopetra, 66, 68–70, 74–75; at Maroni-Petrera, 70–71, 75; at Polis, 80–81, 83–84

beads, 12, 44, 47, 87

belt buckles, 89–90, 97

bioarchaeology: and analysis of burial customs, 61; defined, 41; methodology of, 42

blunt force trauma: and Domuztepe population, 16–18, 20–22; and Polis population, 106

bowls: and eating habits at Bab edh-Dhra', 196; as grave goods, 90, *92*, 94, 105; and infant jar burials, 15, *46*

breast-feeding: by biological mothers, 145; and stable isotope analysis, 142–43, 150, 152–53; by wet-nurses, 145, 157

buccal microwear analysis: and dietary abrasives, 166; results from El-Wad and El-Kebarah, 171–75; and specimen preparation, 168–70

Buck, Stacy, 82

burials in or near churches or temples: in Cyprus, 74–75; ; as an indicator of high status, 83–84; at Kish, 35, 48, 50–52; at Polis, 83–85

butchery, 22

208 · Index

Byzantine period. *See* Khirbet Faynan
(Jordan) site; St. Stephen's monastery site
(Jerusalem)

cannibalism: at Domuztepe, 8, 23–25,
27–28; mentioned, xii, 4. *See also* ritual
feasting
carbon isotope analysis: described, 138, 141;
of Khirbet Faynan population, 121; of St.
Stephen's population, 142–43, 147–48, 152,
154–57
ceramics: at Bab edh-Dhra', 183–84,
196–97; at Domuztepe, 11–12, 15–16; in
Early Christian Cyprus, 62, 68, 72, 74; at
Polis, 83, 93, 95. *See also* bowls; jar burials
charnel houses, 89, 183, 187–88
child sacrifice, 49, 52, 54n2
childhood: and archaeological record,
36–37; and cultural understandings of
personhood, 50; and death rate patterns,
19–20; and dental analysis, 101, 117–19,
125, 129; feeding practices during at St.
Stephen's, 138–40, 157; and infant burial
practices, 37; meaning of at Kish, 42–43,
47, 52–53; nutritional stress during, 109,
126; stable isotope analysis and, 128
children: as residents at Khirbet Faynan
mining site, 127, 129; as residents at St.
Stephen's monastery, 140, 143–44; mortuary practices for, 35–36, 68, 84, 94. *See
also* jar burials
Childs, William A. P., 80
cist graves: at Alassa-Ayia Mavri, 72; at
Maroni-Petrara, 71; mentioned, 74; at
Polis, 84–87, 91, 93–94, 99
cistern burials, 60, 62, 66, 68–70, 74, 97
Claudius Galen, 144
coffins, 60, 68, 76, 82, 92–95. *See also* iron
nails
coins, 84, 87, 90, 97, 105
cover slabs, 68, 84, 87, 90–91, 94
cribra orbitalia: in Khirbet Faynan population, 119–20, 126; in Kish population, 42;
in Polis population, 108
crosses, 73, 84–85
crypt burials, 64–66, 69–70, 74, 139
cut marks, 23

Death Pit: burial practices and, 15–16; and
butchery, 22; and catastrophic mortality,
20; described, 12; description of assemblage in, 19–20; and evidence of ritual
feasting, 23–28
defleshing, 13–14, 16, 18, 22
degenerative joint disease (DJD). *See* joint
degeneration
dental analysis: described, 121–22, 165–66;
of El-Wad and El-Kebarah populations,
166–76; of Polis population, 101–2. *See
also* buccal microwear; dental enamel
hypoplasia; diet; occlusal microwear
dental enamel hypoplasia, 119, 125–26
diet: and dental microwear patterns, 166;
at Khirbet Faynan, 119, 126; in Natufian
period, 166–67, 173–76; at Polis, 102,
109–10; at St. Stephen's, 146, 152–53,
155–57
Domuztepe (Turkey) site: location of, 9–11;
maps of, *ii, 10–11*; methods of analysis
of population, 13–14; population of
described, 12–13, 15–19. *See also* animal
burials; cannibalism; Death Pit; defleshing; Halaf culture; postmortem culinary
processing; ritual feasting

E.F2 excavation (Polis): cover slabs at,
93–94; described, 83–85; grave goods at,
94; image of, *85*; infant burial at, 94
E.G0 basilica (Polis): described, 87, 89;
image of, *88*; repositories for multiple
burials at, 89–91, 97–100
Early Bronze Age. *See* Bab edh-Dhra'
(Jordan) site
Early Christian burial practices, 61–62,
66–67, 74, 77, 81
Early Dynastic period. *See* Kish (Iraq) site
Elaiussa Sebaste, 100, 103, 106, 108–9
Eleutherna (Crete) site, 101, 103, 105, 108
El-Kebarah and El-Wad sites: dental analysis of populations of, 166–76; described,
167–68; diet of populations at, 166–67,
173–76; map of, *ii*; population described,
167. *See also* buccal microwear analysis;
hunter-gatherers
expanded diplöe, 108

family tombs, 97, 99–100
femoral neck alterations. *See* Allen's fossa; plaque extensions on femur; Poirier's facet; posterior imprints on femur
Field Museum of Natural History (Chicago), 41
Field, Henry, 50
fluoride analysis, 139
fractures: in Domuztepe population, 13–14, 16, 18, 20, *21*, 22–23, *24*; in Polis population, 105, *106*, 107–8

grave goods: at Kish, 47, 52; at Polis, 87, 89–90, 94–97, 105. *See also* beads; bowls; buckles; coins; jewelry; spear tips
grave markers, 12, 72, 85–86, 91. *See also* crosses

Halaf culture: burial practices of, 13, 15–16, 19; described, 8–9, 11; and ritual feasting, 25–26; and violent death, 20. *See also* Death Pit; Domuztepe (Turkey) site; postmortem culinary processing
Hill of Agios Georgios (HAG) site: basilica complex at described, 73; iron nails at, 73, 76; location of, 63, 73; population from described, 63–65; time period of, 66, 73
hunter-gatherers, 167, 172–75

Inanna. *See* Ishtar
infant burial: at Kish, 35, 37, 42, 45–53; at Maroni-Petrara, 71. *See also* jar burials
infanticide, 37, 49–50
iron nails: in Early Christian Cyprus, 60; at the Hill of Agios Georgios, 73, 76; at Kalavasos-Kopetra, 68, 70, 76; at Polis, 87, 93
iron-deficiency anemia: causes of, 119; in Khirbet Faynan population, 126, 129. *See also* sickle-cell anemia; thalassemia
Ishtar, 48, 51, 54n4

jar burials: at Kish, 46–53; in Mesopotamia, 15
jewelry, 72–73, 76, 87. *See also* beads
joint degeneration: in Bab edh-Dhra' population, 180, 184–85, 188–91, 193, 197; in Khirbet Faynan population, 118–19, 127, 129–30; in Polis population, 103, 105–6. *See also* osteoarthritis
Joint Oxford–Field Museum Expedition: described, 40; mentioned, 35; problems with data from, 37, 40; site report for, 41

Kalavasos-Kopetra (KK) site: basilicas at, 66; cistern burial at, 60, 62, 66, 68–70, 74, 97; importance of individuals buried in tombs at, 70; iron nails at, 68, 70, 76; location of, 63; mass burial at, 60, 62, 68, 70, 74; population from described, 63–66; sarcophagus burial at, 66, 69, 74–75; time period of, 66
Khirbet Faynan (Jordan) site: copper levels and, 122, 124–25, 128–29; history of, 115–16; joint degeneration in population of, 118–19, 127, 129–30; lead accumulation in population of, 118, 122, 124–25, 128–29; map of, *117*, *124*; mining at, 80, 115, 118–19, 127–29; population described, 116, 120–21, 127, 129; strontium isotope analysis of population, 116–18, 122, 124, 127–28
Kish Project, 41
Kish (Iraq) site: analysis of population at, 40–43; burial practices at, 45–46; described, 38; history of, 38; Joint Oxford–Field Museum Expedition to, 35, 40–41; maps of, *ii*, *39*; population at described, 42–47; temple to Ninlil at, 38, 40, 48, 51–53, 54n4. *See also* burials in or near churches and temples; childhood; grave goods; infanticide; jar burials; *ngíngar*
kneeling facets: in Bab edh-Dhra' population, 193–95; described, 185–86, *190*
Korytiani (Cyprus) site, 101–3, 107–8

Langdon, Stephen, 40
Langdon, Susan, 67

Mackay, Ernest, 40
Maroni-Petrera (MP) site: basilica at described, 71; location of, 63; population from described, 63–65; time period of, 66
martyrion, 72

mass burials: at Kalavasos-Kopetra, 60, 62, 68, 70, 74; mentioned, 18; at Polis, 96–98. *See also* cistern burials; Death Pit

Messene (Greece) site, 101, 103, 105, 108

Natufian period: described, 165–67; and diet, 166–67, 173–76

Natural History Museum (London), 41

Neo-Babylonian, 4, 35–54

Neolithic: and Mesopotamia, 8–10, 14–15, 18–19, 25, 27–28; and Syria and Turkey, 173–75

nigingar (cemetery for fetuses), 51

Ninlil, 48, 51, 54n4. *See* Ishtar

nitrogen isotope analysis: described, 142; St. Stephen's population and, 138, 147–48, 153–56

occlusal microwear: and dietary abrasives, 166; results from El-Wad and El-Kebarah, 171–75; and specimen preparation, 168–70

ossuaries, 72, 75–76, 97

osteoarthritis: in Khirbet Faynan population, 118–19, 126–27, 129–30; in Polis population, 103–4

osteological analysis: of Domuztepe population, 13; and evidence of infection, 100–101; of infant burials from Kish site, 35, 40–41, 43, 48; of Khirbet Faynan population, 118–19, 126–27, 129–30; of Polis population, 82, 100, 103–8

oxygen isotope analysis: of Khirbet Faynan population, 116–17, 121–22, 128; of Polis population, 96

Phaeno, Jordan. *See* Khirbet Faynan (Jordan) site

pit graves: at Domuztepe, 4, 8; at the Hill of Agios Georgios, 73–74; in London, 98; at Polis, 86, 91. *See also* Death Pit

plague, 68, 97–99, 143

plaque extensions on femur, 100, 185, 188, 192, 195

plaster burials, 67, 76

Poirier's facet: in Bab edh-Dhra' population, 192; described, 185, *187*

Polis (Cyprus) site: basilicas of, 81, 84–85; and blunt force trauma, 106; child burials at, 84, 94; cover slabs at, 68, 84, 87, 90–91, 94; diet at, 102, 109–10; evidence of changes in burial practices at, 95–96; fiber production at, 104; grave goods at, 87, 89–90, 94–97, 105; grave markers at, 85–86; history of, 83, 96–98; location of, 80; map of, *81*; mass burial at, 96–98; pit graves at, 86, 91; population from described, 60; previous excavations of basilicas at, 62; secondary burial at, 81, 89–91, 97–100. *See also* activity patterns; age-grades of infancy; age estimates; burials in or near churches or temples; cist graves; cist tombs; coffins; cribra orbitalia; dental analysis; E.F2 excavation; E.G0 basilica; expanded diplöe; iron nails; osteoarthritis; porotic hyperostosis; secondary burial

porotic hyperostosis: in Khirbet Faynan population, 119–20, 126; in Kish population, 42; in Polis population, 108

posterior imprints on femur: in Bab edh-Dhra' population, 192; described, 185–86

postmortem culinary processing, 22–25

radiocarbon dating, 9, 139

Rehovot-in-the-Negev site, 126–27

ritual feasting, 8, 25–28. *See also* cannibalism

sarcophagus burials: at Alassa-Aia Mavri, 74; at Kalavasos-Kopetra, 66, 69, 74–75

secondary burial: in Early Christian Cyprus, 60–62, 72, 75–76; mentioned, 13, 24, 68, 71, 76; at Polis, 81, 89–91, 97–100

sex determination: of Early Christian populations at Cyprus, 64; ; of infants, 50of Khirbet Faynan population, 120; of Polis population, 82

shaft tombs, 180, 182, 184, 186–87
sickle-cell anemia, 107, 119. *See also* iron-
deficiency anemia; thalassemia
Soranus of Ephesus, 144
Sourtara Galanious Kozanis (Cyprus) site,
101–3, 105, 108
spear tips, 97
squatting facets: in Bab edh-Dhra' population, 191, 193, 195; described, 185–86, *190*;
in Polis population, 104
stable isotope analysis: at Corinth, 96;
and dating of weaning process, 142–43,
157; described, 141–42; and diet, 138;
mentioned, xii. *See also* carbon isotope
analysis; oxygen isotope analysis; nitrogen isotope analysis; strontium isotope
analysis
*Standards for Data Collection from Human
Remains,* 42, 63
stillborn children: significance of in Neo-
Babylonian society, 51; and thalassemia,
107
stone supports in graves, 93–95
strontium isotope analysis, 116–18, 122, 124,
127–28
St. Stephen's monastery site (Jerusalem):
data from described, 138–39; described, 139; maps of, *139–40*; population described, 140, 146–47. *See also*

breast-feeding; diet; weaning process;
wet nurses

taphonomic analysis, 13, 18
Tepe Gawra (Iraq) site, 18–19
thalassemia: in Khirbet Faynan population,
126, 129; mentioned, 119; in Polis population, 107–8. *See also* iron-deficiency
anemia; sickle-cell anemia
tile graves, 60, 62, 73–74, 93
tombs: at Bab edh-Dhra', 186, 188; in Early
Christian Cyprus, 60, 62, 64, 66–77, 81–
82, 84–87, 91, 93; reuse of at St. Stephen's,
139, 146, 157; scholarly neglect of, 2–3. *See
also* cist graves; family tombs; shaft tombs
trauma: and Domuztepe population,
16–18, 20–21, 26; and Kalavasos-Kopetra
population, 69; and Polis population, 101,
104–7, 109
vertebral degeneration, 118–19, 125–27

Watelin, Louis Charles, 40
weaning process: influence of Roman physicians on practices at St. Stephens, 144–45,
157–58; and stable isotope analysis, 138,
142–43, 150, 152, 154–55, 157
wet nurses, 145, 157

Yümük Tepe (Turkey) site, 14, 18–19

Bioarchaeological Interpretations of the Human Past: Local, Regional, and Global Perspectives
Edited by Clark Spencer Larsen

Ancient Health: Skeletal Indicators of Agricultural and Economic Intensification, edited by Mark Nathan Cohen and Gillian M. M. Crane-Kramer (2007; first paperback edition, 2012)

Bioarchaeology and Identity in the Americas, edited by Kelly J. Knudson and Christopher M. Stojanowski (2009; first paperback edition, 2010)

Island Shores, Distant Pasts: Archaeological and Biological Approaches to the Pre-Columbian Settlement of the Caribbean, edited by Scott M. Fitzpatrick and Ann H. Ross (2010; first paperback edition, 2017)

The Bioarchaeology of the Human Head: Decapitation, Decoration, and Deformation, edited by Michelle Bonogofsky (2011; first paperback edition, 2015)

Bioarchaeology and Climate Change: A View from South Asian Prehistory, by Gwen Robbins Schug (2011; first paperback edition, 2017)

Violence, Ritual, and the Wari Empire: A Social Bioarchaeology of Imperialism in the Ancient Andes, by Tiffiny A. Tung (2012; first paperback edition, 2013)

The Bioarchaeology of Individuals, edited by Ann L. W. Stodder and Ann M. Palkovich (2012; first paperback edition, 2014)

The Bioarchaeology of Violence, edited by Debra L. Martin, Ryan P. Harrod, and Ventura R. Pérez (2012; first paperback edition, 2013)

Bioarchaeology and Behavior: The People of the Ancient Near East, edited by Megan A. Perry (2012; first paperback edition, 2018)

Paleopathology at the Origins of Agriculture, edited by Mark Nathan Cohen and George J. Armelagos (2013)

Bioarchaeology of East Asia: Movement, Contact, Health, edited by Kate Pechenkina and Marc Oxenham (2013)

Mission Cemeteries, Mission Peoples: Historical and Evolutionary Dimensions of Intracemetery Bioarchaeology in Spanish Florida, by Christopher M. Stojanowski (2013)

Tracing Childhood: Bioarchaeological Investigations of Early Lives in Antiquity, edited by Jennifer L. Thompson, Marta P. Alfonso-Durruty, and John J. Crandall (2014)

The Bioarchaeology of Classical Kamarina: Life and Death in Greek Sicily, by Carrie L. Sulosky Weaver (2015)

Victims of Ireland's Great Famine: The Bioarchaeology of Mass Burials at Kilkenny Union Workhouse, by Jonny Geber (2015; first paperback edition, 2018)

Colonized Bodies, Worlds Transformed: Toward a Global Bioarchaeology of Contact and Colonialism, edited by Melissa S. Murphy and Haagen D. Klaus (2017)

Bones of Complexity: Bioarchaeological Case Studies of Social Organization and Skeletal Biology, edited by Haagen D. Klaus, Amanda R. Harvey, and Mark N. Cohen (2017)

A World View of Bioculturally Modified Teeth, edited by Scott E. Burnett and Joel D. Irish (2017)

Children and Childhood in Bioarchaeology, edited by Patrick Beauchesne and Sabrina C. Agarwal (2018)

Bioarchaeology of Pre-Columbian Mesoamerica: An Interdisciplinary Approach, edited by Cathy Willermet and Andrea Cucina (2018)

.